W9-CQZ-933

WILD SPAIN

BY

FREDERIC V. GRUNFELD

WITH TERESA FARINO

SIERRA CLUB BOOKS

SAN FRANCISCO

Published in the United States by Sierra Club Books,
San Francisco, 1994

Designed and produced by
Sheldrake Press,
188 Cavendish Road,
London SW12 0DA

Grunfeld, Frederic V.
  Wild Spain / by Frederic V. Grunfeld. — 2nd ed.
  224p. 21.0 x 14.9cm.
  Includes bibliographical references and index.
  ISBN 0-87156-477-7
  1. Natural history—Spain—Guidebooks.
  2. Natural areas—Spain—Guidebooks.
  3. Spain—Guidebooks.   I. Title.
  QH171.G78   1994
  508.46—dc20   93-28700
                                               CIP

Printed in Spain by Imago

EDITOR: SIMON RIGGE
Art Direction and Book Design: Bob Hook, Ivor
Claydon
Assistant Editors: Sarah Bevan, Lisa Cussans
Researcher: Dolors Udina
Picture Researcher: Kate Duffy
Editorial Assistants: Linda Aitken, Fenella Dick, Joan
Lee, Sophia Ollard, Gail Reitano, Sally Weatherill
Production Manager: Hugh Allan
Production Assistant: Helen Seccombe
Artwork: Maggie Raynor
Maps: Oxford Cartographers
Captions: David Black, Ferdie McDonald

Managing Editor (second edition):
Malcolm Day

THE AUTHOR

FREDERIC V. GRUNFELD, who died
shortly after completing this book, lived in
Mallorca for more than 25 years and travelled
extensively in mainland Spain. He wrote for
Time-Life on Germany, France, Spain, Italy
and Scandinavia as well as on places beyond
Europe. Among his books are *Berlin* in the
Time-Life Great Cities series, *Prophets
Without Honour,* a history of German-Jewish
thinkers and artists, *The Art and Times of the
Guitar, Wayfarers of the Thai Forest* and,
most recently, a biography of Auguste Rodin.

THE GENERAL EDITOR

Douglas Botting has travelled to Brazil, South
Yemen, the Sahara, Arctic Siberia, and to
many European wild places including the reed
marshes of the Danube Delta and the primeval
Forest of Bialowieza in Poland. His travel
books include *One Chilly Siberian Morning,
Wilderness Europe* and *Rio de Janeiro.*

CONTRIBUTORS

TERESA FARINO is an ecologist, writer and
broadcaster who researched and wrote the
chapter on Northern Spain as well as the
exploration zones for Monfragüe and
Aiguamolls de l'Emporda. She also

contributed greatly to the ecological and
geological material which appears in the text.
Ms Farino is still involved in the struggle for
the preservation of the Picos de Europa.

PHILIPPA FRASER, who researched and
wrote sections on the Canary Islands' national
parks, is a freelance journalist fluent in five
languages, including Spanish and Chinese.
She has travelled extensively in both Europe
and China.

DOLORS UDINA, who made extensive
contributions to this book, is a freelance
Catalan writer whose literary essays appear
in *El Pais* and *La Vanguardia.* She has
translated into Spanish numerous works of
British and American writers.

CONSULTANTS

DAVID BLACK is a writer and editor who
has worked on many nature books including
Gerald and Lee Durrell's *Practical Guide for
the Amateur Naturalist.*

ALLAN MARLES is a map consultant with
many years' experience with the Ordnance
Survey.

For a full list of credits and acknowledgements
see page 222.

CONTENTS

ABOUT THE SERIES

What would the world be, once bereft
Of wet and of wilderness? Let them be
  left,
O let them be left, wildness and wet;
Long live the weeds and the wilderness
  yet.
Gerard Manley Hopkins: Inversnaid

These books are about those embattled
refuges of wildness and wet: the wild
places of Europe. But where, in this most
densely populated sub-continent, do we
find a truly wild place?

Ever since our Cro-Magnon ancestors
began their forays into the virgin forests of
Europe 40,000 years ago, the land and its
creatures have been in retreat before
Homo sapiens. Forests have been cleared,
marshes drained and rivers straightened:
even some of those landscapes that appear
primordial are in fact the result of human
activity. Heather-covered moorland in
North Yorkshire and parched Andalucian
desert have this in common: both were
once covered by great forests which
ancient settlers knocked flat.

What then remains that can be called
wild? There are still a few areas in Europe
that are untouched by man – places
generally so unwelcoming either in terrain
or in climate that man has not wanted to
touch them at all. These are indisputably
wild.

For some people, wildness suggests
conflict with nature: a wild place is a part
of the planet so savage and desolate that
you risk your life whenever you venture
into it. This is in part true but would limit
the eligible places to the most
impenetrable bog or highest mountain
tops in the worst winter weather – a rather
restricted view. Another much broader
definition considers a wild place to be a
part of the planet where living things can
find a natural refuge from the influence of
modern industrial society. By this
definition a wild place is for wild life as
well as that portmanteau figure referred to
in these pages as the wild traveller: the hill
walker, backpacker, birdwatcher, nature

lover, explorer, nomad, loner, mystic,
masochist, afficionado of the great
outdoors, or permutations of all these
things.

This is the definition we have observed
in selecting the wild places described in
these books. Choosing them has not been
easy. Even so, we hope the criterion has
proved rigid enough to exclude purely
pretty (though popular) countryside, and
flexible enough to include the greener,
gentler wild places, of great natural
historical interest perhaps, as well as the
starker, more savage ones where the wild
explorers come into their own.

These are not guide books in the
conventional sense, for to describe every
neck of the woods and twist of the trail
throughout Europe would require a
library of volumes. Nor are these books
addressed to the technical specialist – the
caver, diver, rock climber or cross-country
skier, the orchid-hunter, lepidopterist or
beetlemaniac – for such experts will have
reference data of their own. They are
books intended for the general outdoor
traveller – including the expert outside his
field of expertise (the orchid-hunter in a
cave, the diver on a mountain top) – who
wishes to scrutinize the range of wild
places on offer in Europe, to learn a little
more about them and to set about
exploring them off the beaten track.

One of the great consolations in the
preparation of these books has been to
find that after 40,000 years of hunting,
clearing, draining and ploughing, Cro-
Magnon and their descendants have left so
much of Europe that can still be defined
as wild.

Douglas Botting

WILD SPAIN – AN INTRODUCTION

'Among European countries Spain stands unique in the range of her natural and physical features. In no other land can there be found, within a similar area, such extremes of scene and climate as characterize the 400 by 400 miles [640 by 640 kilometres] of the Iberian peninsula. Switzerland has alpine regions loftier and more imposing, Russia vaster steppes and Norway more arctic scenery; but nowhere else in Europe do arctic and tropic so nearly meet as in Spain. Contrast, for example, the stern grandeur of the Sierra Nevada, wrapped in eternal snow, with the almost tropical luxuriance of the Mediterranean shores which lie at its feet.'

These words are as true today as when they were first published a century ago in the opening paragraph of a pioneering book about hunting, natural history and exploration in Spain. Its authors were Abel Chapman and Walter J. Bucks; its title: *Wild Spain*, alias *España Agreste*.

In many respects I have followed in their footsteps when writing and photographing my own report on the Wild Spain of the 1980s. Spain is still the 'wildest' country in Europe; not far from any of the big cities you can always find areas that are light-years removed from modernity. Half an hour from Madrid begins the Sierra de Guadarrama, with its towering cliffs and bizarre rock formations, its ancient footpaths winding through forests of beeches, poplar and pine. Behind Barcelona looms the massif of Montserrat; behind Gerona the extinct volcanoes of Olot; behind Oviedo the mountains of the Cantabrian range; behind Málaga the Serranía de Ronda. Take a bus to the outskirts of almost any city and you can walk from the last stop to a wild place in as little as an hour or two.

The *Wild Spain* of today is for people who want to walk quietly through some of the world's most splendid countryside, breathing some of the last unpolluted air of Western Europe. It is designed to help hikers, wanderers and explorers who want to get away from it all. I have tried to think of their needs both in choosing the areas to be covered and in selecting the factual information to be annexed to each entry. I myself have been a hiker-wanderer in Spain for many years, and in writing this book have renewed acquaintance with many areas of the country that I first got to know 15 or 20 years ago.

Some of *Wild Spain's* exploration zones require strenuous activity: climbing, pitching a tent, backpacking and so on. But I should like to stress that we have confined our entries mainly to those areas that have been officially reserved for such purposes – national and regional parks, and the like. Indeed, I have had to make a selection of what I regard as the finest of these, for there are far more forest reserves and state lands than you could cover even in fragmentary fashion, and thus the line had to be drawn somewhere to keep the guide from having as many entries as the telephone directory. The *Inventario Nacional de Paisejes Sobresalientes*, an exhaustive list published by ICONA (the National Institute for the Conservation of Nature), comprises two volumes, both of more than 500 pages, and yet each of the 'outstanding landscapes' of Spain receives only one picture and a few lines of description.

Spain is indescribably rich in rugged landscapes, and I could easily fill a second volume with other wild places. No matter where you might happen to be in Spain you will have no difficulty finding remote areas of your own to explore. 'Our Spain begins where byways end,' declared Chapman and Buck. 'We write of her pathless solitudes, of desolate steppe and prairie, of marsh and mountain-land – of her majestic sierras, some well-nigh inaccessible, and, in many an instance, untrodden by British foot save our own. Lonely scenes these, yet glorified by primeval beauty and wealth of wildlife. As naturalists – that is, merely as born lovers of all that is wild, and big, and pristine – we thank the guiding destiny that early

5

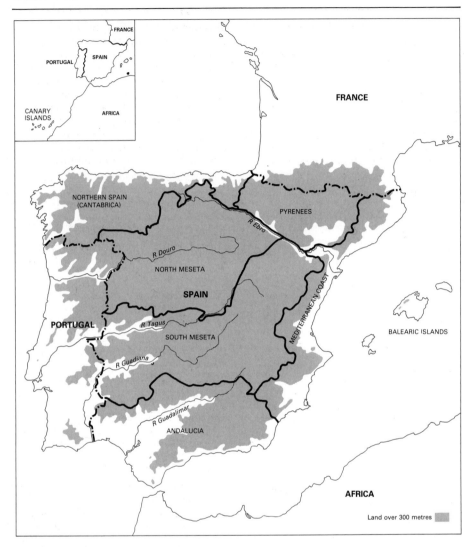

directed our steps towards a land that is probably the wildest and certainly the least known of all in Europe – a land worthy of better cicerones than ourselves.'

These are precisely the feelings with which I approached the writing of this book. Yet like my predecessors I did not mean to disparage the other, cultured Spain. Indeed *Wild Spain* usually co-exists in close proximity with the Spain of the castles, ancient villages and medieval churches. At the end of a walk through

the Pyrenees you will come to a village of thousand-year-old fieldstone houses, clustered around a church containing a masterpiece of Romanesque mural painting or a crucifix that might otherwise adorn The Cloisters of the Metropolitan Museum. If you wander through Las Hurdes of Extremadura (an area where Luis Buñuel shot a famous documentary) you will come upon churches that have a human skull placed in a niche on an outside wall, to remind church-goers of the souls of their departed ancestors. Nature and people have here worked hand-in-glove for two thousand years or more, and as a result the ruins augment the effect of the landscape: 'to come on San Pere de Roda looming shattered on its Catalonian mountain,' writes Rose Macaulay, 'San Miguel de Cullera, the Cartujas near Jerez and at Porta Coeli, so lovely in their desolation, as much utterly one with their background as ancient mouldering trees, has a breath-taking excitement that the carefully ordered trimness of our own Tintern or Fountains or Glastonbury cannot give.' If you travel along these worn paths you will find, as she did – and as do so many other visitors – that there is nothing more fascinating than wandering through Spain: 'it seems still, to each fresh and eager tourist, to have a wild virgin quality, as if oneself were its first ravisher for centuries.'

THE KEY TO SPAIN'S WILD PLACES

THE SHAPE OF THE WILD

One reason why there are so many more wild places in Spain than in the rest of Europe is that Spain has the highest mean altitude of any country in Europe, barring Switzerland. Spain is basically a highland plateau, 'a huge table-mountain', as Chapman and Buck call it, framed and intersected by ranges of still loftier mountains, but with hardly any lowlands except along some of the major rivers, such as the Ebro Valley, and in thin alluvial strips along the coasts.

About 40 per cent of peninsular Spain is taken up by the windblown, largely treeless Meseta, with its torrid summers and freezing winters. Much of the rest consists of mountains: the Pyrenees, the Picos de Europa, the Sierra de Gredos, the Sierra Morena, the Sierra Nevada and so on, which serve to hem in this great inland plateau. Few natural routes traverse these ranges, and the alluvial plains of the coast are sharply cut off from the interior. As a result, Spain incorporates as many different kinds of landscape as it does ethnic groups. The rest of the world usually thinks of Spain in terms of white-washed Andalucian patios and lace mantillas, but there is so much more to it than that. Along the Bay of Biscay Chapman and Buck found a region 'absolutely Scandinavian in type', with its abrupt peaks and deep valleys and rivers abounding in salmon.

On the Mediterranean shore lies Almería, with Europe's only true desert. At the other extreme are the inundated rice-fields of the Ebro delta and La Albufera de Valencia: when you see the local farmers working ankle-deep in their rice paddies you could easily imagine yourself to be in South-east Asia. And then there are the Spanish island groups; by virtue of their climate and geography the Balearics and the Canaries have both become favourite seaside playgrounds, to which endless flights of airplanes bring millions of tourists every year. Yet they have managed to hold their own against this influx: Mallorca, with its most Mediterranean of mountain landscapes to offset the overcrowding of its sandy beaches, and the Canaries, which counterbalance their tourist invasions by setting aside their most dramatic landscapes as national parks.

WILD HABITATS

The huge range of habitats in Spain – the result of ancient geological processes and the effects of climate – make it difficult to divide them neatly into a handful of categories. Here I have attempted to describe them briefly under the four greatest landscape divisions present, between which some overlap is inevitable.

Mountains: more than 35 per cent of Spain exceeds 800 metres (2,600 feet) in height; peripheral areas lifted above the central plateau are rucked into a series of mountain ranges. North has two great east-west ridges – *Pyrenees* and *Cordillera Cantábrica*. Flora ranges from Mediterranean to Atlantic, from pines to beechwoods, with high numbers of endemic species – fritillaries, gentians, jonquils and pasque-flowers – especially in traditional haymeadows, and in the alpine zone (2,500 – 3,000 metres/8,200 – 9,850 feet). Fauna is exceptional: large mammals include wolves, bears, wild boar, chamois; smaller beasts of note are salamanders and asps, and these mountains are last stronghold of the Pyrenean desman. Raptors in large numbers, especially vultures, owls and eagles, with two outstanding birds of region being capercaillie and wallcreeper; butterflies boast many endemic races, some confined to a single valley in the Pyrenees. Extreme south of Spain is dominated by *Sierra Nevada*, running parallel to the coast and containing southernmost glacier in Europe. Slope vegetation highly Mediterranean, with typical 'hedgehog' zone of spiny, drought-resistent shrubs, but peaks have snow-tolerant flora showing level of indigenousness almost unrivalled in Western Europe – glacier toadflax, Nevada saxifrage, daffodils, buttercups and crocuses. Nevada blue butterfly found only in these mountains. Further north is *Sierra de Cazorla*, with endemic violets, butterworts and columbines, but more famous as headquarters of Spanish ibex. Central Spanish mountains – *Sierras de Gredos, Francia & Guadarrama* – are less imposing, oak and pine-clad in the lower reaches, with brooms, cistuses and heathers above, and few alpine zones; hawks, eagles and kites abound, with warblers, wheatears and shrikes in the valleys, and ibex in the Gredos peaks.

Plains: make up much of central plateau and least 'wild' of Spain's habitats in that man has almost inevitably had some influence – many outstanding landscapes and wildlife features associated with *subterranean water supply* (e.g. Tablas de Daimiel, now drying out; Laguna de Gallocanta – famed for European crane and red-crested pochard; Laguna de Fuente de Piedra – more than 3,000 breeding pairs of flamingo; Laguna de Zónar – white-headed duck and purple gallinule). Arid, barren-looking *steppe* habitat, half-cultivated, also very interesting, however, especially for birds – home of great and little bustard, pin-tailed sandgrouse, red-necked nightjar, Andalucían hemipode, stone curlew, quail, white storks, many lark species and harriers – as well as for a rapidly diminishing group of plants in Europe: arable weeds. Feature of south-western plains is *dehesa* – evergreen oak 'parklands' over rich pastures – supreme habitat for small birds in Spain: golden oriole, woodchat shrike, roller, azure-winged magpie, bee-eater. Also famed as breeding grounds for threatened Spanish imperial eagle and black-winged kite (e.g. Monfragüe, Extremadura – also has black storks and black vultures on barren cliffs).

Coastal features: *dunes* – rich flora that varies with position on Cantabrian-Atlantic, Mediterranean or South Atlantic coasts – many rare and endemic plants (*Corema album, Romulea clusiana, Linaria arenaria*), sea daffodils, sea holly, with marram grass

stabilising dunes – threatened by popularity of Spain's beaches as holiday resorts. *Coastal marshes* – halophytic vegetation including glassworts, sea lavenders, sea plantains, but birds of greater importance, e.g. Aiguamolls de L'Empordà – migrating egrets, herons and bitterns, breeding black-winged stilts, and inland lesser grey shrikes; Coto Doñana – superlative aquatic avifauna includes marbled teal, crested coot, ruddy shelduck, ferruginous duck and glossy ibis. *Cliffs* important for specialist flora and for birds: on northern Atlantic coast, shags and guillemots breed; on Gibraltar – peregrines, blue rock thrushes and famed Barbary partridge.

Islands: may combine elements of other three categories. *Canaries* – (seven islands) part volcanic, highly influenced by both oceanic and Saharan climates; highest mountain in Spain – El Teide – on Tenerife; almost 600 endemic plant taxa, e.g. Canary laurels, Canary pine, Teide violet, many spurge and viper's bugloss species; milkweed butterflies. *Balearics* – (15 islands) flora less rich than Canaries but equally unique; Ibiza/Formentera pine-clad with oleanders. Fauna more diverse – cliff-nesting Cory's shearwater and Eleonora's falcon; Hermann's tortoise, Mallorcan mid-wife toad, Lilford's wall lizard are all highly localised and endangered species.

PROTECTED WILD PLACES

Spain has a long history of protecting its wildest and most beautiful countryside by law; indeed some of the foremost national parks in Europe were declared in the mountains of Northern Spain in 1918 – Covadonga in the Cordillera Cantábrica and Ordesa in the Pyrenees. Today there are nine Spanish national parks, covering over 120,000 hectares (300,000 acres); four of these are in the Canary Islands.

ICONA, the state institution for nature conservation, is responsible for the national parks, and until recently was also in charge of the *reservas nacionales de caza* (natural hunting reserves). Following the promulgation of the 1978 constitution, however, when the 17 Spanish autonomies were established, the management and protection of these hunting reserves has devolved to the newly formed regional governments. They cover a vast area of Spain. Over one and a half million hectares (3.7 million acres), mostly in mountainous zones, are covered by this designation; the largest is Saja, in Cantabria, which alone is considerably larger than all nine national parks put together. Although formerly such rare – now fortunately protected – beasts as bears, capercaillie, chamois and roe deer were considered fair game, hunting today is limited to wild boar, and the occasional red deer where numbers permit.

A fairly recent initiative in habitat conservation is the natural park, differing from the state-controlled national park in that the regional autonomy is empowered to declare and manage such an area for nature conservation. This is an exercise which is rapidly gaining momentum as interest in the environment and awareness of the beauty of Spain's wild heritage increases. The majority of these *parques naturales* lie in Cataluña, Galicia and Andalucía, although a further notable example is Monfragüe, in Extremadura. In 1985 an area over three times that covered by the nine national parks had already been declared as natural parks by the regional governments, a figure which has been increasing steadily ever since.

Another legal designation is that of *reserva integral*, although this is usually only employed where a national or natural park is already in force, and usually takes the form of an inner sanctum. This status is reserved for areas of exceptional wildlife interest, such as the marshes of Coto Doñana National Park, or the imperial eagle breeding grounds within Monfragüe.

The Spanish ecological movement has not endeavoured to acquire land in order to protect it, but rather has attempted to increase the awareness of the population as a whole. Where political pressure has been applied in the past, this has often been accompanied by eloquent and moving statements in both the national and local press. The relative youth and enthusiasm of the conservation movement in Spain can only bode well for the future preservation of this, the wildest and most unspoiled country in Western Europe.

TO THE READER

Eagle symbols: the eagle symbols used at the head of entries in this book indicate the wildness of the place to which they refer. This is based on a number of factors, including remoteness, ruggedness, spaciousness, uniqueness, wildlife interest and the author's subjective reactions. Three eagles is the highest rating, no eagles the lowest.

Updating: while everything possible has been done to ensure the accuracy of the facts in this book information does gradually become outdated. For this reason we would welcome readers' updates, corrections and comments for incorporation in subsequent revised editions. Please write to The Editor, The Traveller's and Naturalist's Handbook Series, Sheldrake Press, 188 Cavendish Road, London SW12 0DA.

Non-liability: both author and publishers have gone to great pains to point out the hazards that may confront the traveller in certain places described in WILD SPAIN. We cannot under any circumstances accept any liability for mishap, loss or injury sustained by any person venturing into any of the wild places listed in this book.

Spanish place names: there are a number of spelling variations for place names throughout Spain, including Castilian, Catalan and various local spellings. In this book we have used Castilian spellings throughout (followed by the Catalan or local version in parenthesis the first time a word appears in each chapter), except for some smaller towns and villages where we have opted for one of the local spellings. Names commonly used in English have been spelled in English throughout.

The Pyrenees

The Pyrenees have been my favourite mountains for at least 25 years, ever since I first hiked and climbed in the parks of Ordesa and Aigüestortes during the 1960s, and started skiing in the Valle de Aran (Vall d'Aran). Altogether these peaks form a belt of natural wonders that stretches from the Bay of Biscay to the Mediterranean, and for the most part the main crest of the range constitutes the Franco-Hispanic frontier.

The Alps may be higher and more theatrical, what with the Jungfrau, Matterhorn, Mont Blanc and so on, but the Pyrenees are more isolated and forbidding, which has served to keep them wilder and far less touristed. They form, moreover, a truly formidable barrier to cross-mountain traffic. The Alps, by contrast, have a great many convenient passes that lead across the great chain of mountains at far lower levels than those of the flanking peaks. Not so the Pyrenees. The two main routes from France to Spain lie at the western and eastern extremities of the range; in the centre, until modern times, there were only two passes that could, with great difficulty, be used by wheeled traffic – the Col de la Perche, between the valleys of the Tet and the Segre, and the Col de Somport, on the old Roman road between Oloron and Jaca. The age of tunnels and superhighways has made things a lot easier for vehicles, yet the Pyrenees remain remote and wild.

With few exceptions, the valleys of the Spanish Pyrenees all run more or less at right angles to the east-west

Snow-capped peaks dominate the Valle de Pineta, a typically rugged Pyrenean valley carved by glaciers and now covered with scree and scrub

thrust of the principal chain. As a result there is no easy way to get from the Catalan Pyrenees to the Basque Pyrenees unless you descend to the lowlands of the Ebro valley. East-west travel in the mountains involves a complicated series of twisting, narrow roads that lead from one cross-compartment to another.

I am always grateful for these impediments to travel, since they have served to protect vast areas from exploitation and development. Tucked away in inaccessible valleys are innumerable quiet corners that are surprisingly untouched by the fell hand of the late twentieth century. For alpinists and expert skiers there are the high mountains; for hikers and back-packers, lush meadows and magnificent forests; for families with small children, village inns on the banks of shallow mountain streams where toddlers can splash and float toy boats. Sadly, many Pyrenean mountain villages have been abandoned by their inhabitants and now stand in ruins. But where the villages are still inhabited, the conjunction of peasant architecture and mountain scenery is often nonpareil.

Here are fieldstone houses and Romanesque churches that seem to grow out of their hilltop sites like so many stone mushrooms. Except for telephone and electric lines you could easily imagine yourself back in the Middle Ages. Virtually the entire region makes good rambling country, and, indeed, some of the most enjoyable areas for walks and explorations are not among the loftiest peaks but further down, in gentler valleys like that of the Río Isábena, which is flanked by peaks in the 1,500–2,000 metre (4,900–6,500 foot) range. Here there is even a whole cathedral in miniature, one of the most astonishing

Romanesque buildings in existence, which looks out across fields and meadows. I had never heard of the cathedral of Roda de Isábena until someone described to me this amazing edifice in the middle of nowhere. It was built a thousand years ago when a local count attained a certain regional autonomy, and his brother became the first bishop of this newly independent countship, notwithstanding that the entire see could not have numbered more than two or three thousand inhabitants. Atop the count's tiny hillside 'capital' they built a perfect little tenth-century cathedral, complete in every way, although it takes up only about as much space as the average parish church. When I first came across it some years ago, I found that this architectural jewel was being looked after very well by an aristocratic priest who spent most of his time in overalls, restoring medieval stonework and repairing the ancient carvings: it was clear that here, in this forgotten valley, he had found his life's vocation looking after this sleeping beauty of an abandoned cathedral.

Throughout the Pyrenees you're apt to make discoveries of this kind: crystal-clear mountain lakes and glacier-fed waterfalls; remnants of ancient castles and monasteries; alpine meadows smothered in wild flowers and populated with chamois; monumental remains of Bronze Age inhabitants about whom nothing is known except that somehow they managed to survive in this inhospitable terrain. On the whole, wildlife is abundant and well cared for in the major national parks of the Pyrenees – Ordesa and Aigüestortes – which harbour sizeable populations of such fauna as roe deer and wild boar, eagles, vultures and falcons, as well as fox and ermine. In addition to these wholly protected zones there are *reservas nacionales de caza* (hunting reserves), of which there are eight in the Pyrenees: Alto Pallars-Aran, Cadí, Cerdaña, Los Circos, Freser and Setcases, Los Valles Visaurin, Benasque and Viñamala.

Topographically, the Pyrenees are usually divided into three regions – the Navarran, Aragonese and Catalan regions. The mountains of Navarre are gentler and less rugged than the rest of the Pyrenees, and the villages look correspondingly more prosperous: it is a lot easier to farm the lush, gradual slopes at the western end of the range. Above the passes of Belaqua and Ibañeta loom the highest peaks in the region, the Pico de Anie, Ory and Mesa de los Tres Reyes, the point where the kingdom of Navarre adjoined its neighbouring kingdoms of Aragón and Bearn.

The Aragonese Pyrenees, at the centre of the chain, extend eastward from this meeting place and include the highest summits of the range: Aneto in the Maladeta ridge, Posets and Monte Perdido. This central nucleus also contains the wildest scenery, with deep gorges, immense rock walls, and natural amphitheatres such as that of Piedrafita. Yet nestled among the loftiest mountains is the famous spa of Panticosa, a sort of high-altitude Baden-Baden, with a small casino and a little park for summer visitors who come to take the waters in the world's most improbable hydrotherapy centre. The road running north-south through the Barrosa valley used to be a dead-end street, but there is now a convenient tunnel that connects it to France at an altitude of 2,465 metres (8,090 feet). Benasque, still farther east, is the steepest-walled valley of the central Pyrenees and the jumping-off point for excursions to both Pico de Aneto and Posets.

On the eastern slope of the towering Pico de Aneto begins the Valle de Aran, and with it the Catalan Pyrenees. Here the frontier with France curves northward before dipping south again to make way for the independent principality of Andorra, one of the world's most interesting mountain states. Andorra was once the Bhutan of Europe, but in recent years the prosperity of its tax-free shops and a flourishing tourist industry have ended its erstwhile isolation. Yet its form of government has hardly changed in 500 years. In the Middle Ages it was jointly ruled by the bishops of Urgel and the counts of Foix; now its co-princes are the bishop of Urgel and the president of France, on whom have devolved the feudal rights formerly exercised by the counts of Foix.

East of Andorra, just north of the border town of Puigcerda, lies another feudal anomaly, the small Spanish township of Llivia, which is entirely surrounded by French territory. But mountains are no respecters of boundary lines. They continue to present a barrier to north-south traffic almost to the Mediterranean shore, maintaining their elevation with remarkable uniformity, through the provinces of Lérida (Lleida) and Gerona (Girona), until at last a sudden dip occurs in that part of the range called the Montes Alberes, which allows the Perpignan-Gerona superhighway to cross the mountains without difficulty. The last outrunners of the Pyrenees form a small peninsula in the Mediterranean that culminates in the Cabo de Creus, just north of the teeming bird habitats of the Golfo de Rosas.

The Catalan Pyrenees contain some of the finest nature reserves in the

13

whole of Spain. The national park of Aigüestortes in the province of Lérida is certainly the best known, but all the surrounding region – especially the valleys drained by the Río Noguera Ribagorzana – are ideally suited to long hikes and to rambling nature-cum-Romanesque-village explorations. Another important valley, that of the Río Segre, is dominated by the ancient citadel of the bishops of Urgel – the town of Seo de Urgel (La Seu de Urgell) which provides a convenient base from which to explore the eastern Pyrenees. (My favourite European work of art is the great book of the *Apocalypse Commentary* of Beatus de Liébana, in the episcopal museum of Seo de Urgel.)

Although the Catalan Pyrenees be-

come more densely populated as you move eastwards, Gerona province offers some splendid mountain terrain in the Ripoll, Garrotxa and Alto Ampurdan regions. La Garrotxa is something very special – a region of steep cliffs and small hidden valleys, punctuated by the craters of scores of extinct volcanoes, an extraordinary intrusion in this part of Spain.

A word about the terminology of these mountains: the peaks are called *puigs* in Cataluña, *pueyos* or *puertos* in Aragón, *poyos* in Navarra, and *puys* in France – all are thought to derive from *podium*, the Latin for an elevation. Depressions at the heads of valleys or the necks of ridges are called *colls* in Catalan and *collados* in Castilian Spanish; the passes that lead over them are *puertos* – gates, doorways – or *portillos* (in other words, small doors).

There are about 70 or 80 passes in

The Valle de Aran, cut off from the rest of Spain on the north side of the Pyrenees, shelters meadows filled with orchids

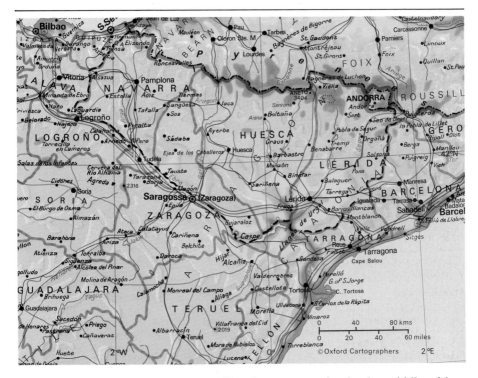

© Oxford Cartographers

all, and the great majority are still negotiable only on foot, impassable during the snowed-in months and dangerous in the summer.

Indeed, the most significant change that the twentieth century has wrought is that people are now coming to the Pyrenees for pleasure rather than just as smugglers, hunters or shepherds. Thus what Richard Ford wrote about these mountains in the middle of last century, is still demonstrably true – that Nature 'here wantons in her loneliest, wildest forms. The scenery, sporting, geology and botany, are Alpine, and will repay those who can "rough it" considerably, [those] who love Nature with their heart, strength and soul, who worship her alike in her shyest retreats, in her wildest forms.'

GETTING THERE

By air: the main airports are at Bilbao and Barcelona. In addition, there are international flights to Gerona (often charters) and to Pamplona, San Sebastián, Santander and Zaragoza via Madrid or Barcelona. All these airports are also served by internal airlines. When open, the airport at Seo de Urgel offers a very convenient means of getting to the heart of the Pyrenees.

By sea: Barcelona is the nearest major port for access to the eastern Pyrenees, San Sebastián the nearest for the western end.

By car: from France, you can approach the Pyrenees from either the east or west, on the superhighways running along the coast, or via one of the mountain pass roads, which include the Toulouse–Ripoll–Barcelona road.

The roads connecting the different regions of the Pyrenees are mainly secondary and tertiary grades.

By rail: from Madrid, there are frequent trains to Barcelona, Bilbao, Zaragoza, Vitoria and San Sebastián; and 1 or 2 a day to Pamplona, Lérida, Gerona, Huesca, Jaca and Canfranc.

15

From Barcelona, there are 1 or 2 trains a day to Pamplona, Vitoria, San Sebastián, Irún, Logroño and Bilbao. There are also 3 express trains a day to Barcelona from Madrid, via Lérida.

For information, call RENFE in Madrid, open 9am–9pm daily, T: (91) 429 82 28.

By bus: to San Sebastián from major European cities such as London and Paris by bus is a feasible enough though lengthy means of travel to the Pyrenees. There are good regional bus services between all major towns and most mountain villages; for information, call Barcelona (93) 302 65 45.

WHERE TO STAY
The best towns and villages in which to find accommodation are listed in the entries for individual exploration zones. For detailed lists, contact the tourist offices in Madrid or Barcelona, or any of the regional offices listed below.

ACTIVITIES
Walking/climbing: in summer, walking in the Pyrenees is generally fairly easy; it is only in the most mountainous parts, such as in Huesca, that the going gets tough. In winter you will need crampons and some experience.
Mountaineering clubs:
Federación Aragonesa de Montañismo, Albareda 7, Zaragoza, T: (976) 22 79 71; Federació d'Entitats Excursionistes de Catalunya, Ramble 61–1°, Barcelona 2, T: (93) 302 64 16; and Federación Vasco-Navarra de Montañismo, Avda Navarra 25, Hotel Urteaga, Beasain (Guipúzcoa), T: (943) 88 08 50.
Guided walks/adventure holidays: contact Club de Viatjers, Ronda de Sant Pere
16

11–6°, 3ª Barcelona 10, T: (93) 302 50 81.
Fishing: there is good trout fishing all through the Pyrenees, notably in the headwaters of such rivers as Segre, Garona, Cinca, Aragón and Gállego. Salmon fishing is confined to the western Pyrenees, notably in La Bidasoa, Navarre. Fishing licences are issued by ICONA; the fishing season is normally open from the 3rd Sun in Mar–31 Aug.
Skiing: the major ski resorts of the Spanish Pyrenees are: Gerona province – La Molina and Nuria; Lérida province – Baqueira-Veret (Valle de Aran), Cerler, El Formigal, Llesuy (Pallars) and Super Espot; Huesca province – Astún, Benasque, Candanchú and Panticosa; and Navarra province – Burguete and Ibañeta.

FURTHER INFORMATION
Barcelona (93): tourist office, Ajuntament Bldg, Pl. de Sant Jaume, T: 318 25 25. Red Cross, T: 300 21 12. Highway information, Doctor Roux 80, T: 205 13 13.
Gerona (972): tourist offices, C. Cuidadanos 12, T: 21 06 94; and C. Juan Margall 35, T: 20 17 24. Red Cross, T: 20 04 15. Highway information, Gran Vía Jaume I 41, T: 20 92 58.
Huesca (974): tourist office, C. Coso Alto 23, T: 22 57 78. Red Cross, T: 22 11 86. Highway information, General Lasheras 6, T: 22 09 00.
Lérida (973): tourist offices, Arc del Pont, T: 24 81 20; and Avda Blondel 1, T: 26 74 25. Red Cross, T: 22 66 40. Highway information, Avda Alcalde R. Roure 21, T: 23 28 75.
Pamplona (948): tourist offices, C. del Duque de Ahumada 3, T: 22 07 41; and C. Beloso Alto, T: 24 93 93.
San Sebastián (943): tourist

office, C. Andia 13, T: 42 17 74.
Zaragoza (976): tourist offices, Torreón de la Zuda, Glorieta Pío XII, T: 23 00 27; and C. Alfonso I 6, T: 22 26 73 and 22 25 79. Red Cross, T: 44 07 49. Highway information, Pl. de Santa Cruz 19.

Weather information can be obtained by calling the Centro de Análisis y Predicción (Cuidad Universitaria), T: (91) 244 35 00.

FURTHER READING
C. Lana, *Ruta del Pirineo Español* (Madrid, 1933); Henry Myhill, *The Spanish Pyrenees* (London, 1966); Kev Reynolds, *Walks and Climbs in the Pyrenees* (Milnthorpe, 1983); C. Sarthou, *A la Découverte du Haut Aragon* (Paris, 1973); A. W. Taylor, *Wild Flowers of the Pyrenees* (London); Georges Véron, *Haute Randonnée Pyrénéene; traversée des Pyrénées d'est en ouest* (La Flèche, 1973); and Ramón Violant y Simorra, *El Pirineo Español* (Madrid, 1949).

La Garrotxa

Ancient volcanic landscape contrasted with trees, shrubs and farmland

La Garrotxa, with its astonishing parade of volcanic cones amid neatly terraced fields, is a fascinating aberration. Volcanic action is virtually unknown in the Iberian peninsula, and in many ways the topography of La Garrotxa (literally, 'torn earth') resembles that of some beached South Sea island, forming a 'fantastic and inaccessible natural fortress', as the Catalan writer José Pla describes it.

As if in response to this challenge, the people of La Garrotxa have, over the centuries, endowed the valley with a series of equally fascinating and dramatic structures, so that the balance between the natural and the manufactured is beautifully maintained. Here is the town Castellfullit de la Roca ('the Mad Castle of the Rock'), poised on the edge of a basalt abyss overlooking the Río Fluvià; the town of Besalú, with its Roman bridge and medieval towers at the confluence of the Fluvià and the Río Capellades; and villages such as Santa Pau, in the centre of the volcanic plain, with massive fieldstone houses and arcaded streets. This last must be one of the oldest inhabited places in Cataluña for there is a megalithic menhir on the Pla de Reixac. Out of the same volcanic soil grows the famous beech forest known as La Fageda d'En Jordà.

The volcanic eruptions that shook this region took place no less than 17,000 years ago – long enough to have covered the basalt with a heavy layer of topsoil that has produced splendid meadows and rich farmland. Time has lined the craters with a carpet of trees and shrubs, but their outlines are still visible: the crater of Santa Margarida, for example, is nearly 350m (1,150ft) in diameter, and there are a dozen other notable extinct volcanoes, such as Montolivet, Treiter, Garrinada and Croscat.

BEFORE YOU GO

First step *Maps:* SGE 1:50,000 No. 257; Carta geológica de la regió volcànica d'Olot 1:20,000 (Ajuntament d'Olot); Mapa de la vegetació de Catalunya 1:50,000 No. 33 (Generalitat de Catalunya); and Mapa topográfic, La Garrotxa 1:40,000.
Guidebooks: La vegetació de la regió volcànica d'Olot by Miquel Riera i Tussell (Olot, 1981), and *Els volcans olotins i el sue paisatge* by J. M. Mallarach and M. Riera (Barcelona, 1982).

Getting there *By car:* from Gerona, take the C150 highway to the volcanic region just west of Bañolas (Banyoles). The southern road between Bañolas and Olot is the shortest distance between these 2 points. The northern route is more picturesque; it follows the Río Fluvià and touches on both Besalú and Castellfullit de la Roca, 2 of the most interesting towns in La Garrotxa.
By bus: there is a regular service from Gerona to Olot; for information phone (972) 57 00 53 or 26 01 96. Olot also has bus connections to Barcelona and to Figueras; the same telephone numbers apply.

Where to stay: La Garrotxa is only 54km (30 miles) from Gerona, which has a range of good accommodation. In Olot there are 7 hotels, including Montsacopa, T: (972) 26 07 62, and the hostel Europa, T: (972) 26 02 95. Besalú has Pensión Siques, Pl. Major 6.
Outdoor living: the campsite near Olot, Les Tries, T: (972) 26 24 05, is open from 1 Apr–30 Sep. South of Olot, in San Felio de Pallerols, La Vall d'Hostoles, T: (972) 44 40 31, open 15 Jun–30 Sep with space for 180.

Activities *Walking:* from Olot to the Volcà de Santa Margarida, the largest crater, via the beech forest, La Fageda d'En Jordà. Or follow the Río Fluvià down the Vall d'En Bas, which will take you through a series of pretty villages.
Viewpoints: there are a number of good viewpoints over the volcanoes – notably, overlooking the Serra de Finestres, near the *château* at Santa María de Finestres; by Puigsacalm; and north at Santa Bárbara de Prüneres.
Further information *Tourist information:* Mulleres, Pl. del Mercat, Olot, T: (972) 26 01 41; Pl. de la Libertat 1, Besalú, T: (972) 59 02 25; and Pl. del Vi 1, Gerona, T: (972) 20 20 79. ICONA, Avda San Francisco 29, Gerona, T: (972) 20 09 87.

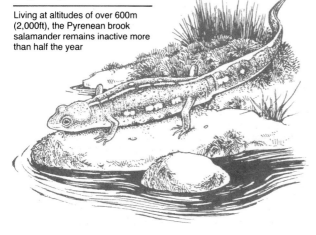

Living at altitudes of over 600m (2,000ft), the Pyrenean brook salamander remains inactive more than half the year

Cadí-Moixeró

A parque natural near Puigcerdà in the eastern Pyrenees

The astonishingly varied and beautiful Pyrenean countryside of Cadí-Moixeró provides a wonderful setting for lone rambles and quiet strolls. It comprises mountain ranges and several other massifs, together with all their valleys, villages, meadows and forests. More than two dozen villages and hamlets set against a superb backdrop of mountains that are snow-capped for half the year.

These mountains are lower, gentler and on the whole more user-friendly than, for example, the high peaks of the Montes Malditos. The chains of Cadí and of Moixeró, which are the park's dominant physical features, together extend for about 30 kilometres (20 miles) from east to west and are linked by the Pas de Tancalaporta (the 'close-the-door' pass). There is more than enough scope for serious mountain-climbing here. Altitudes range from the 900-metre (2,950-foot) valley floors to the 2,647-metre (8,685-foot) Puig de la Canal Baridana (also called Puig Vulturó), the highest peak in the Cadí range, and Pedraforca. The most common starting-points for assaults on the Pedraforca are the villages of Gósol and Gisclareny. Both can also be enjoyed as bases for walks through adjoining valleys.

As you explore the area, it will become apparent that the ecosystems are alpine rather than Mediterranean: dense forests and fertile meadows contrasting with the rugged contours of limestone massifs. Low temperatures and high humidity support species not usually associated with Spain. Above 2,000 metres (7,000 feet) there are typically alpine meadows on the lower slopes, forests of mountain pine with juniper and rhododendron. There are large stands of silver fir and beech trees; oaks, maple and aspen occur in sizeable numbers, as well as Scots pine and box.

The only mountain pass in this range is the 1,800-metre (5,900-foot) Collada de Toses, which has the richest alpine flora in the whole of the eastern Pyrenees. The screes abound with parnassus-leaved buttercups (*Ranunculus parnassifolius*), a thickset perennial with shining green leaves and pink-tinged flowers, growing with one of the more attractive yellow crucifers – decumbent treacle-mustard (*Erysimum decumbens*); both are limestone-loving plants. Another handsome species is the diminutive Rhaetian poppy (*Papaver rhaeticum*), which flowers in July and August; it replaces the springtime Pyrenean pheasant's-eye (*Adonis pyrenaica*). The very beautiful *Ramonda myconi* is found in these mountains too.

The park's animals are also alpine in character. The Pyrenean chamois lives on the highest peaks during the summer; in winter the herds move downhill to the southern slopes. Red and roe deer are common and golden eagles, buzzards and capercaillies may be seen too.

BEFORE YOU GO
Maps: SGE 1:50,000 Nos. 215, 216, 217, 253, 254 and 255; and IGN 1:200,000 Mapa provincial of Gerona and Barcelona.
Guidebooks: Agusti Jolis and M. Antònia Simò: *Cerdanya* (Barcelona, 1986) and *Pedraforca* (Barcelona, 1969).

GETTING THERE
By air: small airport at Seo de

Urgel has flights to Cadí-Moixeró. Sometimes closed for rebuilding, and in bad weather.
By car: there are 4 main routes to the park. Highway N152 from Barcelona to Puigcerdà via Vich and Ripoll brings you to the Collada de Toses, at the eastern end of the park. Highway C1411 branching off N-11 from Barcelona towards Berga and

Bellver de Cerdaña follows the Río Llobregat, then crosses the Cadí tunnel; the same road, branching off towards the west some distance before Guardiola de Berguedà, runs through the southern part of the park. The C1313 from Puigcerdà to Seo de Urgel skirts the northern limits of the park.
By rail: a regular service runs from Barcelona to Puigcerdà

by way of La Molina and Alp. **By bus:** there is a service from Barcelona to La Seu d'Urgell, and from La Seu to Puigcerdà; for information, call (93) 302 65 45 and (973) 27 14 70.

WHERE TO STAY
Wide choice in an around the park. Try San Francisco, a 2-star hostel in Gósol, T: (973) 37 00 75; the 2-star Hotel María Antonieta, T: (973) 51 01 25, in Bellver; and the Pensión Arderiu, T: (93) 224 02 31, in Guardiola de Berguedà. **Outdoor living:** Solana del Segre in Bellver de Cerdaña, T: (973) 51 03 10, open all year. **Refuges:** inside the park, there are a number of well-tended shelters, most open summer only. The Refugi de Gréixer, north of the village of Gréixer, is open all year and the only one to accept reservations, T: (93) 824 42 40. The Refugi Cèsar A. Torras can be reached by a 1.5-km (1-mile) forest path from Martinet via Montellà. The Refugi de l'Ingla and Refugi del Pla de les Esposes are both near Bellver de Cerdaña; in winter, the keys are obtainable from the Agent Forestal del Medi Natural in Bellver de Cerdaña. The Refugi Cortgal d'en Vidal, 8km (5 miles) from Urús, is often blocked by snow during the winter. The Refugi de Rebost stands within the boundaries of Bagà; keys are available from the Unió Excursionista de Catalunya in Bagà.

The Refugi d'Erols de Baix is on the road from La Pobla de Lillet. The Refugi de Sant Jordi, near Bagà, is accessible only on foot.

ACTIVITIES
Walking: extensive and well-marked trails throughout the park. About 9hrs are required for the north-south excursion from Martinet to Gósol through the Coll de l'Homme Mort ('dead man's pass') and the Pas dels Gosolans. **Guides:** for the Servei de Guies de Natura (nature-guide service) consult the town halls of Bellver de Cerdaña and Seo de Urgel. For long mountain walks, contact the experienced guide Joan Cassola, Escoles d'Olià, Bellver de Cerdaña, T: (973) 51 01 90.

Parc Nacional d'Aigüestortes & Llac de Sant Maurici

A magnificent national park of mountains, lakes and meadows, just west of Andorra

The deep, unruffled waters of the Estany Negre de Peguera lie trapped in one of the glacial depressions of Aigüestortes

This is, without question, the jewel of the Catalan Pyrenees, and except for Ordesa to the west, there is not a more pristine and breathtaking area in the entire Pyrenees region. Indeed, it has some of the finest mountain scenery in the whole of Europe, a magnificent conjunction of meadows, peaks, lakes, streams and forests. Aigüestortes means 'twisted waters' in Catalan, in the sense of 'rough' or 'uneven'; now that the park falls under the jurisdiction of the Generalitat de Catalunya, its entire name is officially designated in Catalan even in the Generalitat's Spanish-language publications. (Privately, though, published books in Castilian still refer to it as the Parque Nacional de

Aigües Tortes y Lago San Mauricio.)

The park covers an area of 10,230 hectares (25,280 acres) and is divided into two nearly equal halves: the Aigüestortes zone in the west, near the Boí valley, and the Lake of Sant Maurici zone in the east. A crest of high mountains, including the Pala Alta de Serrader (2,982 metres/9,783 feet), the Pic de Contraig (2,966 metres/9,730 feet) and the Gran Tuc de Colomers (2,932 metres/9,619 feet), marks the park's boundary on the north and underlines its inaccessibility. Until the end of the last century this was one of the most isolated regions in the whole of Europe, and no one except shepherds and big game hunters ever came this way. There were no roads leading into the area, and no bridges spanning the dizzying precipices that have to be crossed. But with the age of hydro-electric power, the utility companies moved in, building roads, bridges, dams and generating stations. These signs of a now rather antiquated modernity are kept largely out of sight, however, and do little to detract from the mountain splendours of what has justly been called a 'Pyrenean paradise'. The only thing that might diminish enjoyment of this paradise is the weather: it rains a great deal,

and snows even more. In Sant Maurici, during the average year there are 50 days of rain and 100 of snowfall.

The rounded valleys and rough-cut mountaintops – imposing masses of granite and slate – were formed during the Primary era some 200 million years ago; were upthrust and folded by plate-collision pressures during the Tertiary; and finally were carved, ground and polished by glacial action during the early phases of the Quaternary era, which gave the mountains their present distinctive shape and scooped out the hollows for 140 or so lakes. Some of these lakes are nearly 50 metres (165 feet) in depth, thanks to the implacable abrasive energy of the Pyrenean glaciers. These lakes are the special glory of Aigüestortes: most are of a spectacular clarity and brilliance, and some are fed by waterfalls.

The vegetation follows much the same pattern as that of Ordesa, with fir, beech and silver birch forests in areas up to 2,000 metres (6,600 feet). The Pyrenean chamois flourishes in the high meadows, and golden eagles build their nests in caves on sheltered buttresses. There are otters in the lakes and grouse and capercaillie in generous numbers inhabit the woods.

BEFORE YOU GO
Maps: SGE 1:50,000 Nos. 181 and 182; Parc Nacional d'Aigüestortes i Llac de Sant Maurici, 1:30,000; Sant Maurici 1:25,000; and Montardo, 1:25,000.
Guidebooks: *Sant Maurici* by N. Llopis Lladó, and *Montardo*

by Rosendo Vila Blanch.

GETTING THERE
By car: there are 2 main access routes to the park. For the western entrance – the Aigüestortes sector – take the N230 from Lérida to Viella via Alfarrás and Benabarre. Just

past Pont de Suert, turn east on L500 towards Caldas de Bohí (Caldes de Boí). Or from Lérida take the C1313 to Balaguer, the C147 to La Pobla de Segur and thence C144 to Pont de Suert.

Access to the eastern side and Lago de San Mauricio (Estany de Sant Maurici) is provided by the C147 from Balaguer to Esterri d'Aneu via La Pobla de Segur; 6km (4 miles) before Esterri d'Aneu turn west on LV5004 toward Espot.
By rail: at least 2 trains a day (more during summer) run from Barcelona to La Pobla de Segur by way of Lérida and Tarragona.
By bus: there is a regular service from Lérida and La Pobla de Segur to Pont de

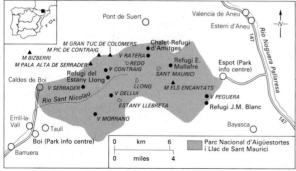

Suert and from there to Caldes de Boí (the bus stop is about 1km/½ mile from the village centre). There are daily buses from Barcelona and Lérida to Esterri d'Aneu and Viella, which stop at the crossroad leading to Espot (7km/4½ miles from the village).

WHERE TO STAY
Four villages near the western sector of the park – Barruera, Boí, Caldes de Boí and Errill-la-Vall – and the town of Espot on the east offer a range of accommodation. Try in Barruera, the 4-star Manantial, T: (973) 69 01 91; in Errill-la-Vall, the 2-star Hostal Noray, T: (973) 69 60 50; and in Espot, the 2-star Saurat, T: (973) 63 50 63.
Outdoor living: Boneta, T: (973) 69 60 29, is open from Easter; it also has all-year apartments for rent. Two sites in Espot are open during the summer: La Mola, T: (973) 63 50 24; and Sol i Nev, T: (973) 63 50 01.
Refuges: 2 are open all year – Refugi E. Mallafré, at the foot of Els Encantats near Lake

Sant Maurici, and the Refugi del Estany Llong, in Sant Nicolau Valley, between the meadows of Aiguadassí and Estany Llong. The Refugi J. M. Blanc, beside the Estany Tort de Peguera in the Peguera valley, and the Chalet Refugi d'Amitges, near the Estany d'Amitges in the Ratera valley, are open during the summer only.

ACTIVITIES
Walking: approaching from the west, the normal route is to follow the course of the Río Sant Nicolau, along whose banks runs a road that can barely be negotiated by Landrovers; it leads uphill past the lake known as the Estany Llebreta ('of the small hare') to the plain of Aigüestortes. Here are the trail-heads for most of the footpaths leading into the surrounding mountains.
Climbing: many of the ascents are simple climbs even for beginners; few are more than 1-day excursions. For detailed information, see *Walks and Climbs in the Pyrenees* by Kev Reynolds (Milnthorpe, 1983).

Pyrenean snake's head (*Fritillaria pyrenaica*) has large, nodding bell-shaped flowers of a brownish-purple colour with green markings

FURTHER INFORMATION
Tourist information: Arc del Pont and Avda de Blondel 1, Lérida, T: (973) 27 20 85. In summer, information offices are open in Espot and Boí. The park administration office is at Camp de Mart 35, Lérida, T: (973) 24 66 50.

Valle de Aran

A botanical treasure-house in an isolated corner of the high Pyrenees, on the border with France

In Spanish eyes the Valle de Aran is the valley of all valleys (the word *aran* means 'valley'). It is a green and fertile oasis of forests and meadows, enclosed by jagged mountain summits. In spring, the valley comes alive with meadows of horned pansy (*Viola cornuta*), alpine pasque-flower (*Pulsatilla alpina*) and four species of daffodil – the pale Lent lily (*Narcissus palli-*

The ptarmigan, a mainly arctic and alpine bird, nests on the stony mountainside of the Pyrenees, its most southerly outpost

diflorus) and the pheasant's-eye narcissus (*N. poeticus*) as well as *N. abscissus* and *N. bicolor* – all in great swathes of purple, white and yellow. Autumn heralds the arrival of merendera (*Merendera montana*) and a purple-flowered crocus (*Crocus nudiflorus*), which sprout from the cut meadows.

The crystalline rocks in the tributary valley of the Río Iñola support three of the more spectacular geranium species: bloody cranesbill (*Geranium sanguineum*) with its crimson flowers grows alongside dusky cranesbill (*G. phaeum*), its blackish-purple petals turned back like fragile cyclamen, while the shadier sites beneath overhanging rocks are home to the Pyrenean cranesbill (*G. pyrenaicum*). In late May, it is easy to overlook the graceful arches formed by the purple-and-green chequered bells of the Pyrenean fritillary (*Fritillaria pyrenaica*) hidden among the heathers and brooms on these acid slopes. And the woods and meadows are full of herbs and wild flowers useful to witches or practitioners of alternative medicine, such as arnica, liquorice and several varieties of what the Aranese call 'mountain tea'.

The Valle de Aran used to be cut off from the rest of Spain as soon as the first snows blocked the mountain passes leading to the south and east. Not until 1948, and the completion of the tunnel to Viella (Vielha), was the area accessible from Spain all 12 months of the year. Even then there were days when, in the words of the old joke, you couldn't get there from here. Now snow-proof approaches are being built at both ends of the tunnel, the Valle de Aran need never be cut off from the mother country.

The abundance of snow here in the high Pyrenees has proved to be a great boon to the economy of this once-pastoral district. The ski resorts of Vaqueira-Beret and La Tuca are among the finest in the country, in terms of both the terrain and snow conditions. But the valley's ski boom has also brought with it the usual aesthetic disfigurements of ski-resort architecture. Viella, once a beautiful half-medieval town, now resembles a French *station de ski*, and some of the ancient villages further up the valley have acquired a sudden modernism that has practically extinguished their original fieldstone and slate-roof architecture.

Still, the Valle de Aran has the potential makings of a great national park, although it hasn't yet been turned into one. There are marvellous walks through the forests and the valleys of the Río Garona, numerous cross-country ski trails and plenty of scope for climbing: the surrounding peaks include Maubermé (2,880 metres/9,450 feet), on the French border, the Besiberri Nord (3,014 metres/9,885 feet) on the valley's southern flank, and the Tuc de Mulleres ('the women's peak'; 3,010 metres/9,873 feet) toward the south west.

BEFORE YOU GO
Maps: SGE 1:50,000 Nos. 148, 149 and 181; IGN 1:200,000 Mapa provincial of Lérida; and Mapa Topográfica Excursionista, 1:40,000 Vall d'Aran.
Guidebooks: *La Vall d'Aran turistica y documental* by Ramon de Semir i de Arquer (Granollers, 1984); *Pallars-Aran* by A. Jolis and M. A. Simo (Barcelona, 1971).

The profusion of wild flowers in the meadows of the Valle de Benasque provides a summer paradise for butterflies

GETTING THERE

By car: highway C230 from Lérida leads to Viella through the Túnel de Viella. Highway C142 runs from Esterri d'Aneu to Port de la Bonaigua, the south-eastern pass into the Valle de Aran.

From France, highway N618 joins the C230 in Pont de Rei; or, from the north west, N125 joins the Spanish C141 at the Portillo de Bossòst.

By bus: there is a regular service from Barcelona and Lérida to Viella and Saqueira. For further information, call (93) 302 65 45, (973) 27 14 70, (973) 26 85 00 or (974) 22 70 11.

At 1,000–2,000m the woods of the Valle de Aran are made up of beech and birch interspersed with conifers such as black pine and fir

BUTTERFLIES IN THE VALLE DE ARAN

Aran is such a special valley botanically that it is hardly surprising that it holds a number of rather scarce butterflies as well. These include the alpine grizzled skipper (*Pyrgus andromedae*) and the chequered skipper (*Carterocephalus palaemon*). The clouded apollo (*Parnassius mnemosyne*), a beautiful creamy-white butterfly with charcoal and yellow circular markings and some 7.5cm (3in) in wingspan, is not a rare species internationally, but this is one of the few localities in Spain where there is an endemic sub-species – *republicanus*. The larvae feed off various plants of the poppy family, such as fumitories, and also from stonecrops. As expected, it is a mountain species, flying between 1,200–2,000m (3,900–6,500ft) during Jun–Jul, often in damp meadow areas.

Also localized around the Aran area is the silvery argus (*Pseudaricia nicias*), a species found only where there is an abundance of meadow and wood cranesbills (*Geranium pratense* and *G. sylvaticum*), between 1,200–1,700m (3,940–5,580ft). This butterfly is found only in the Pyrenees, the south-west Alps, Finland and Russia; the Aran population is described as a separate race (*judithi*).

WHERE TO STAY
There is no lack of accommodation in the Vall d'Arán: there are 23 hotels in Viella, Salardú has 7, and Bossòst 6. Try the Aran, T: (973) 64 00 50, a 2-star hotel in Viella; or the Tuc Blanc, T: (973) 64 51 50, a 3-star hotel in Salardú. For a full list, contact the tourist office at Viella or Lérida.
Outdoor living: there are 2 official campsites – El Prado Verde, T: (973) 64 82 86 and Artigane, T: (973) 64 01 89 – but you can camp in any of the mountain areas *de utilidad pública*; contact the tourist offices for details.

ACTIVITIES
Walking: there are numerous scenic routes, for example, the simple walk to the Circo de Saboredo, at the south-eastern end of the valley; the trail begins at the end of a forest road that starts at Salardú and hugs the western bank of the Río Garuda de Rudo as far as the Font de Campo ('spring of the meadow'), from where a 1hr ascent brings you to the Estany Major of Circo de Saboredo, a superb high-mountain region with 35 lakes and tarns of all sizes, which is ideal for camping or fishing.
Climbing: the Pic de Maubermé and Mont Valier

offer several strenuous but not too difficult climbs as well as rock climbing. For detailed information, see *Pyrenees Andorra and Cerdagne* by Arthur Battagel (Reading, 1980).
Fishing: there are some 200 lakes, or *estanys*, full of trout, and many of these are truly spectacular. Enquire at the tourist office in Viella (see below).

FURTHER INFORMATION
Tourist information: Sarriulera 9, Viella, T: (973) 64 09 79; and Arc del Pont and Avda de Blondel 1, Lérida, T: (973) 27 20 85.

Valle de Benasque

The highest mountains of the Pyrenees, which are rich in wildlife and provide plenty of scope for climbers

The Valle de Benasque runs like a green-and-blue ribbon between the two glacier-capped massifs of the Pico de Posets and the Macizo de la Maladeta. At 3,404 metres (11,165 feet) the Maladeta's Pico de Aneto is the highest mountain in the Pyrenees; the Pico de Posets is second, at 3,375 metres (11,070 feet).

In summer the whole valley becomes one irresistible field of wild flowers, rampant with buttercups and gentians, irises and forget-me-nots.

All the villages are concentrated in the southern half of the valley: Sahún, Eriste, Anciles, Cerler and Benasque. Going higher and farther north means getting into really harsh weather, with scarcely a ray of sunshine during the winter months. Even in summer the weather is tricky, as elsewhere in the Pyrenees. The streams and rivers are at their fullest then. June and August, incidentally, are the stormiest months, and the storms here in the past have sometimes

proved fatal to climbers and hikers.

Quaternary glacial action was the sculptor of the Pyrenees. It gradually reduced the upthrust mountains, cracking them and sanding them down. Igneous rock acquired needle-sharp profiles, peaks and crests. Limestone and slate were split into small pieces and took on rounded forms, producing underlays for the gently curving meadows.

The higher reaches of the valley are so rich in wildlife, the area really should be turned into a national park. The Picos de Eriste and Valhiverna (alias Vallibierna) are inhabited by hundreds of Pyrenean chamois. There are weasels, sable, hares and marmots; the last-named are said to make the trip from France, in groups, to the high meadows of the Esera, there to hibernate in deep burrows during the winter. The capercaillie lives here in the most inaccessible parts of the forest: it is such a remarkable bird that a simple word like 'grouse' will not do – the Spanish call it *urogallo*. It flies very swiftly for such a heavy bird, and has splendid black-blue plumage, a small beard and red circles around the eyes.

Dozens of lakes and tarns occur in the Posets massif, most of them above 2,500 metres (8,200 feet). The largest is the Lliterola, at 2,730 metres (8,955 feet). One of the glaciers, indeed, is actually lower than that, at 2,570 metres (8,430 feet) – the

Coma de la Paul. The northern part of the Benasque valley is wilder and less hospitable to climbers and hikers. There are other small valleys to the east and west.

Following the Río Esera toward the north east, the slopes become steeper and the landscape still more rugged. At the Plan del Hospital begins the twisting trail to the pass known as the Portillón de Benasque (2,445 metres/8,020 feet); this is the old route to France, hewn during the Middle Ages.

The rocky outcrops of the Montes Malditos support a jumble of matted globularia (*Globularia coridifolia* ssp *nana*) clinging to the bedrock like moss, together with the irregular pink flowers of fairy foxglove (*Erinus alpinus*) and the yellow Pyrenean toadflax (*Linaria supina*) which grows outwards from a central point, the flower-stems radiating like the spokes of a bicycle.

In the Puerto de Benasque alpine mouse-ear (*Cerastium alpinum*) and the tiny pink-and-green cushions of moss campion (*Silene acaulis*) hug the stony ground, while the screes are held together by the trailing stems of Pyrenean vetch (*Vicia pyrenaica*).

The alpine grizzled skipper butterfly (*Pyrgus andromedae*) is an endemic species to Europe, its Spanish population being restricted to just three localities in the Pyrenees, including Aran and Benasque. It flies in open mountainous regions above 2,000 metres (6,560 feet) in June and July, always keeping near to watercourses. Apart from this little is known of its life-cycle, and the larval food plants are still unidentified.

BEFORE YOU GO
Maps: SGE 1:50,000 Nos. 148, 149, 180 and 181; IGN 1:200,000 Mapa provincial de Huesca; Posets, 1:25,000 (Ramón de Semir de Arquer); Mapa Turístico-Montañero (Editorial Alpina); Maladeta-Aneto, 1:25,000 (Ramón de Semir de Arquer); and Mapa Topográfico Excursionista (Editorial Alpina).
Guidebooks: *Posets, Perdiguero, Valle de Benasque* (Editorial Alpina, 1985); *Maladeta, Aneto* (Editorial Alpina, 1984); and *El Valle de Benasque* by Santiago Broto Aparicio (Editorial Everest, 1981).

GETTING THERE
By car: whether you start from Lérida, Huesca or Zaragoza, the gateway to Benasque is the village of Graus, on highway N230 from Lérida; N240 from Huesca. From Graus, highway C139 leads north to Benasque and all the villages of the valley.
By bus: there is a daily bus from Lérida to Graus and another from Huesca to Graus and points north, which stop at all the villages in the valley.

WHERE TO STAY
Benasque has several 1- and 2-star hotels, including the 2-star Aneto, T: (974) 55 10 61, and the 2-star Hostal El Puente, T: (974) 55 12 79.
Outdoor living: for official sites, Aneto, in Benasque, is open all year round with a 130-person capacity, T: (974) 55 11 41; and Ixeia, north of

An alpine marmot adopts an alert posture, ready to issue a short sharp whistle if danger threatens

Benasque, open all year round with a capacity for 255 people. The Plan d'Están, at the end of the Pista de Vallivierna, and Llanos del Hospital in the Esera valley are good areas for pitching a tent.
Refuges: several refuges are open all year – Angel Orus, T: (974) 55 30 03 in the Valle de Eriste; and Refugio de Estós, T: (974) 55 30 03 in the Valle de Estós.

ACTIVITIES
Walking/climbing: The ruined Cabañas de Sallent near the turbulent stream known as the Aigueta de Eriste at 2,080m (6,820ft), marks the starting point for the standard excursion to the Pico de Posets, which takes 4hrs of steady climbing through the gorges and Llardaneta.

Plan del Hospital is the start of the twisting trail to the pass known as Portillon de Benasque (2,445m/8,020ft).

FURTHER INFORMATION
Tourist information: Coso Alto 23, Huesca, T: (974) 22 57 78. ICONA, General Las Heras 8, Huesca, T: (974) 22 11 80.

Parque Nacional de Ordesa

The isolated Ordesa canyon and the great Monte Perdido dominate this dramatic national park on the Franco-Hispanic border

Ordesa is full of geological curiosities like these natural limestone buttresses

Ordesa is magnificent enough when the sun is shining but absolutely awe-inspiring during a thunderstorm. I remember one particularly violent down-pour when it seemed that we were being treated to a replay of Noah's flood: it was early July, but the skies opened up, water descended in sheets and hailstones rico-chetted from my hat. All of this was pleas-ant enough at the end of a hot day, but then a mist began moving up the valley and as the rain continued to fall, great cascades of dirty yellow water came pouring off the rock walls, dislodging a shower of small stones that bounced and splashed their way into the valley. It made me think of the medieval Aragonese mountain-dwellers, fighting off invading armies of lowlanders by pelting them with rocks and boulders.

The next day was clear and beautiful. We proceeded up the valley past caves and waterfalls, following the path of the Río Arazas. When we finally caught sight of our destination, the superb Circo Soasa, a young Catalan woman turned to me. 'I've never been to Canada,' she said, 'but this is what I imagine it to be like – this sense of space, a crystal stream, majestic moun-tains, this uncluttered landscape.'

The Valle de Ordesa has always been considered something quite special and extraordinary by people with eyes to see. Of course, the local shepherds had always known about this isolated canyon, but Louis Ramond de Charbonnières, a French alpinist, is regarded as its modern 'discov-erer'. One day at the turn of the century, while looking down from the summit of Monte Perdido, he decided to go down and investigate the great sickle-shaped depres-sion, which had been scooped out of the calcareous bedrock by Quaternary glacia-tion. He published a description of what he found in his *Voyages au Mont-Perdu* (1901).

Three of the national park's constituent valleys – Ordesa, Añisclo and Pineta – form the legs of a kind of tripod supporting the

26

great massif of Monte Perdido ('lost mountain'), whose 3,355-metre (11,000-foot) summit lies just south of the Franco-Hispanic frontier, and whose northern slope includes the famous French gorge known as the Cirque de Gavarnie. The fourth valley, Las Gargantas de Escuaín, carries its mountain waters down towards the south east and the village of Tella: it is the least known of the park's valleys but far from the least interesting, with its great flanking walls of rock, some of them reaching a height of 300 metres (984 feet), and the mysterious dolmen that stands in a meadow above Tella.

Monte Perdido is the highest of the three high mountains known as Las Tres Sorores ('the three sisters') that dominate the park; the other two are El Cilindro de Marbore (3,328 metres/10,915 feet) and El Sum de

27

Ramond (3,262 metres/10,700 feet). The mountain chain was formed by cataclysmic pressure at the beginning of the Tertiary period. Then the glaciers began their slow work: in the Quaternary a frozen sea covered Las Tres Sorores and there were rivers of ice in the canyons that have become the Ordesa, Añisclo and Pineta valleys. What makes Ordesa geologically unusual is that it runs parallel to the main spine of the Pyrenees, unlike most of the other valleys, which are perpendicular to it.

The Ordesa valley is a tongue of green vegetation running for 15 kilometres (9½ miles) between two imposing walls of bleached, calcareous rock. Looming above the beech trees, the pines and dark green firs, are the dramatic rock cornices known as *fajas* – balconies of stone formed by erosion – which afford magnificent views of the canyon and its many waterfalls.

Pyrenean chamois, currently multiplying at a furious rate, are fond of the vertiginous terraces of the valley. Ordesa has one of Europe's largest populations of chamois, but the ibex, or *cabra montés*, which the park was intended to protect, has not done nearly as well: there are said to be no more than 15 ibex in the park these days.

The lammergeier has one of its major European strongholds in these mountains and is found elsewhere in Spain only at one non-Pyrenean site. Formerly, it was easy to see at Ordesa, but sightings have been more irregular in recent years and you would be well advised to search somewhere else: the area of Santa Cruz, west of Jaca, has this grand bird as do the towering pinnacles above the monastery of Riglos to the south. With a wingspan of 2.5 metres (eight feet) and a long, wedge-shaped tail, they are easily recognized, especially the adults which have golden-hued underparts and a habit of dropping bones to break them prior to extracting the marrow. The sheer cliff faces of Ordesa are also home to the elusive wallcreeper, a grey moth-like rock-climber that continually flicks its wings to show bright scarlet feathers. Higher up are snow finches on the bare screes and, lower, citril finches are found where the trees and bare ground meet.

Apart from these endangered species, Ordesa constitutes a favourable habitat for 171 species of birds, 32 mammals, eight species of reptiles and five amphibia. Wild boar are a fairly common sight, and there are otters and foxes in the valleys. There is one species of poisonous snake, the asp (*Vipera aspis*). The Ordesa valley is also home to a specific race of the Spanish argus butterfly (*Aricia morronensis ordesiae*), found nowhere else in the world.

In the valleys the predominant trees are firs and beeches that grow strong and tall up to altitudes of about 1,700 metres (5,600 feet); above 2,300 metres (7,550 feet) the only tree hardy enough to survive is the dwarf mountain pine whose short, contorted trunk reflects its struggle against the elements. Above the treeline there are only bushes and meadows where the chamois love to browse. The park's wild flowers include the edelweiss – in Spanish, *el pie de león* ('lion's foot') or *flor de nieve* ('snow flower') – gentians, orchids and anemones. The alpine rose (*Rhododenderon ferrugineum*) likes to live in the shade of the pine, while violets and belladonna prefer the protection of the fir tree.

The lammergeier (or bearded vulture), with only 40 pairs in all Spain, has its main breeding stronghold in the Pyrenees

BEFORE YOU GO
Maps: SGE 1:50,000 Nos 146 and 178; IGN 1:200,000 Mapa provincial of Huesca Valle de Ordesa; and Mapa Topográfico Excursionista (Editorial Alpina).

GETTING THERE
By car: the simplest access to the Valle de Ordesa is via highway C136, Huesca–Biescas, followed by C140, Biescas–Broto via the Cotefablo Pass, then north to Torla, from where you can drive into the park.

Access to the Añisclo, Escuaín and Pineta valleys involves highway C138, Aínsa–Bielsa, and side roads that branch off toward the valleys; all are paved except the one to Escuaín, which is an ICONA logging road.

From Oct–Apr weather conditions, particularly snow levels, should be checked because often the park is inaccessible by car during these months.
By rail: from Madrid there is a

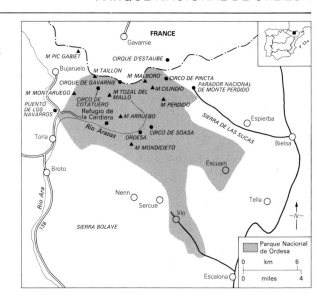

service to Sabiñánigo (on the Zaragoza–Canfranc line).
By bus: from Sabiñánigo there is a daily bus to Torla, a 1½-hr journey. There is no bus from Torla to the Puente de los Navarros, 3km (1¾ miles) farther north along the Río Ara, where the park begins.

WHERE TO STAY
Torla has several hotels within striking distance of the park, including the 2-star Ordesa, T: (974) 48 61 25, and there are also hotels at Broto and Bielsa; the 3-star Parador Nacional de Monte Perdido, T: (974) 50 10 11, is in Biesla. The Hotel Circo de Gavarnie, located on the Circo, is an excellent starting point for climbing the mountain wall.
Outdoor living: not permitted inside the park, but you can bivouac using a tent just for the night – provided you strike it the next morning – in the Ordesa valley above 2,200m (7,200ft), in the Añisclo valley above 1,400m (4,600ft), in the Escuaín valley above 1,500m (4,100ft) and in the Pineta

Ramonda myconi has a purple flower and dark-green crinkly leaves

The flowers of *Geranium cinereum* may be lilac, white and strongly veined, or a deep reddish-purple

valley above 2,500m (8,200ft).
Refuges: there are many in the park, on both the Spanish and French sides. In the Circo de Goriz, there is the Refugio Delgado Obeda, open all year. The Brecha is the site of a Franco-Hispanic *refugio,*

29

Turracoya, currently in need of an overhaul. North west of the Vignemale glacier is the Refugio Oulettes de Gaube, one of the most modern in the Pyrenees. The Refugio Baysselance nearby is open Jul–Sep; the Refugio Brecha de Rolando is open in summer but has an outbuilding open all year. South east of Gavarnie is the Refugio Paílla, open Sep–Easter.

There are some rough shelters in Duascaro, Celcilaruego, Rivereta, Cadiera, Carriata, Cotatuero, Frachinal and Loaso.

ACTIVITIES
Walking/climbing: from the Parador Nacional de Monte Perdido, a short walk takes you to the spectacular Circo de Pineta. The Añisclo valley also has its own access route: the regional road that

Medieval monks enjoyed the tranquil isolation of San Juan de la Peña

branches off the Aínsa–Bielsa highway toward Nerin.

The normal starting point for Ordesa is the village of Torla, on the road leading north from Aínsa along the Ara valley. Most of the trailheads for the main excursion routes are located near the visitors' information centre here. There are dozens of possible trails, though for good reasons the hike to the Circo Soasa – about 5–7hrs of easy walking – remains the most popular.

An easy ascent to the *fajas* of the Ordesa valley is provided by a series of *clavijas* – iron rods driven into the stone to provide footholds in some of the more slippery places: the first of these were installed years ago by a Torla blacksmith at the behest of an English hunter. One set of 13 *clavijas* leads to the Circo de Cotatuero, which rivals the Circo Soasa as a natural amphitheatre. The latter marks the eastern terminus of

the Ordesa valley, but a trail leads further up into the massif, to the Refugio de Goriz, which serves as base-camp for more strenuous assaults on the higher reaches of Monte Perdido.

The trail to Cotatuero, on the other hand, leads on to the Refugio de la Cardiera and to the famous Brecha de Rolando, the mythical breach in the rock hewn by the mighty Roland with his great sword, Durandal. The Brecha is on the French frontier: walking due north will bring you to the Cirque de Gavarnie and finally down to Gavarnie itself, the first village in France. Following the ridge toward the north west will take you to Vignemale, one of the last glaciers in the Pyrenees and still an imposing sight though it has been gradually melting away for many years. Behind it rises the Petit Vignemale (3,032m/ 9,950ft), a very popular mountain with experienced climbers because it offers almost every conceivable kind of technical challenge.

From the Refugio de Goriz it takes about 2½hrs to reach the Lago Helado ('frozen lake'), which has not, however, been living up to its name in recent years. Another ½hr brings you to the summit of Monte Perdido, highest of the three sisters, Las Tres Sorores. Expert climbers are also fond of the Añisclo valley as it offers some of the park's most demanding ascents.
Mule rides: available around the Ordesa valley. Ask for details at the information centre.

FURTHER INFORMATION
Tourist information: Coso Alto 23, Huesca, T: (974) 22 57 78. ICONA, General Las Heras 8, Huesca, T: (974) 22 11 80.

The mists of legend turned Basques of the forest of Roncesvalles into the Saracens of the Chanson de Roland

A visitors' information centre is located at the entrance to the park close to Torla.

Detailed information about the park is found in a small booklet available locally, written in Spanish but easily comprehensible with finely detailed maps: *Cartographic Guide to Ordesa, Vignemale and Monte Perdido*.

Note: sturdy tramping boots are recommended for all walks in this rugged area; a pair of thick socks will no doubt be very much appreciated on the day as well!.

San Juan de la Peña & Canfranc

Mountain fastness south of the French border; and nature valley harbouring rare birdlife

I've always thought that San Juan de la Peña (Saint John of the Crag), south west of Jaca, is one of the world's great hiding places. This monastery in the mountains has long ago lost its monks and has become a romantic destination for nature-lovers. Tucked away under the brow of an enormous cliff, it overlooks an isolated valley in one of the outer ranges of the Pyrenees. To the north the view is bounded by the snow-capped peaks on the French border. The surrounding forests are ideal for pleasant rambles as far as the nearby town of Jaca.

Here, according to tradition, the C11th king, Ramiro I, entrusted 'the sacred chalice of the Last Supper' – the Holy Grail, in other words – to the monks of San Juan for safekeeping. Its presence in this castle-like community of friars could well have given rise to the legend recounted in the C12th French grail sagas, which speak of the distant castle of Munsalvaesche – the wild mountain, *monte salvaje* – where the grail is piously guarded by a company of knights. It is an elusive and inaccessible place, not unlike San Juan de la Peña: 'Those who seek it find it not. It is

31

only found unsought. Munsalvaesche its name.' The monks of San Juan de la Peña did, in fact, possess an elaborate jewelled chalice, which is now under lock and key in the treasury of the cathedral at Valencia.

The Río Aragón which flows past Jaca is the main artery of another important nature valley, Canfranc. It also includes the 2 tributary valleys of the Ríos Lubierne and Estarrún. Canfranc extends all the way to the French border and is bounded on the east by the Tena valley with its Río Gallego and a line of high peaks; on the west by another range of mountains and the Valle de los Angeles; and on the south by the Peña Oroel (1,769m/5,800ft). The northern portion of the valley includes the ski resorts of

The round-leaved sundew, *Drosera rotundifolia*, is threatened by the disappearance of its moorland habitat

Astún and Candanchú, on the slopes of the Tuca Blanca (2,323m/7,620ft).

The flora and fauna of these 2 valleys are famous for their variety and abundance. About a thousand species of flowers grow in the fields and meadows adjoining forests of fir and beech that also include maple and hawthorn. Herbalists come here for the spectacular *Adenostyles pyrenaica*, with its 2-m (6½-ft) stem and large silvery leaves.

The isolation of San Juan de la Peña makes it ideal for bird-watching. Although the Spanish imperial eagle and black vulture are mentioned as occurring here, it must have been a long time ago. Today the cliffs and buttresses that line the valley are a noted haunt of griffon and Egyptian vultures, while short-toed and Bonelli's eagles are both regularly seen. Here, too, are the sadly declining lesser kestrels, summer visitors that nest gregariously in church towers and old buildings, as well as more naturally in cliff holes. Other species include the delightful black-eared wheatear, cirl and rock buntings and the piping blue rock thrush.

Before you go *Maps:* SGE 1:50,000 Nos. 143, 144, 175 and 176; IGN 1:200,000 Mapa provincial of Huesca and Guia Cartográfica: Ordesa, Vignemale y Monte Perdido. *Guidebooks: Jaca-Canfranc, 'Cuadernos de Aragon'* (Zaragoza).

Getting there *By car:* from Pamplona take highway N240 to Puente la Reina de Jaca, then C134 to Jaca. From Huesca, Zaragoza and Cataluña, highway N330 leads directly to Jaca, the gateway to Canfranc and to the monastery of San Juan de la Peña and the surrounding Sierra de la Peña. N330

continues from Jaca north to the French border and Candanchú. Highway C125 south from Jaca, then HU230 to the west, brings you to San Juan de la Peña by way of a little-used and highly scenic route. The shorter, more prosaic route, is to take C134 west from Jaca for about 21km (13 miles), then turn south on HU230; the distance between Jaca and the monastery is about 30km (19 miles). *By rail:* 4 trains daily from Zaragoza via Huesca to Jaca and Canfranc. The journey from France through the mountains to Jaca via Canfranc is spectacular.

Further information *Tourist information:* Pl. de Calvo Sotelo, Jaca, T: (974) 36 00 98; it has excellent leaflets on hikes in the area as well as bus and train schedules serving the region. ICONA, Vázquez de Mella, Zaragoza, T: (976) 35 39 00.

Where to stay: there is hotel accommodation available in Candanchú, Canfranc and Jaca; for example, in Candanchú, the Tobaza, T: (974) 37 31 25, a 2-star hotel; in Canfranc, the 2-star Villa Anayet, T: (974) 37 31 46; and in Jaca, the 2-star Pensión Aboira, T: (974) 36 01 00. The 'new' monastery of San Juan de la Peña has a hostel with 10 rooms; it has no phone and is often full.

Roncesvalles

Historic battlefield descending to deep ravine, on the French border

In this celebrated valley, in the year AD778, the rearguard of Charlemagne's army, lead by the legendary Roland, were massacred by infuriated Basques as they tried to slip back into France. Near the battlefield at Roncesvalles there is one of the great oak forests of Europe, the wood of Garralda, where you can obtain at least an inkling of what these Navarran Pyrenees must have looked like in Charlemagne's day. And if you descend from Roncesvalles into the deep ravine called Valcarlos, the old trees seem to leap out at you through the mist and the clouds like the ghosts of Roland's warriors.

This part of northern Navarre has a whole series of fertile valleys that, for the most part, run perpendicular to the main thrust of the Pyrenees – notably the valleys of Aezcoa, Salazar and Roncal with their respective rivers, the Irati, Salazar and Esca. The encircling mountains are rarely higher than 1,500m (4,900ft), although the higher peaks afford some splendid panoramic views: Mount Ory, on the French border, allows you to enjoy a truly international view from a towering 2,021m (6,630ft).

The Coto Nacional de Quinto Real, the westernmost nature reserve in the Pyrenees, is centred on Monte Adi (1,459m/4,785ft), just west of Roncesvalles. It comprises 5,982ha (14,800 acres) of mountain woodlands just south of the frontier with France.

Modern life has made some inroads into this ancient landscape. Orzanzurieta peak (1,570m/5,150ft) is a tremendously impressive spot on which to be whipped by hurricane winds that hurl dense clouds across the sky. Unfortunately, a television booster antenna rather blots out these heights.

Before you go *Maps:* SGE 1:50,000 Nos. 90 and 91 (bis), 116 and 117; IGN 1:200,000 Mapa provincial of Navarra; and Mapa Topográfico Excursionista 1:40,000 Roncesvalles.
Getting there *By car:* the line of retreat taken by Charlemagne is still the main north-south route through this part of the Pyrenees. Highway C135 runs from Saint Jean Pied-de-Port in France to the border post at Arneguy and then south-west to Pamplona via Roncesvalles and Burguete.

The main east-west highway is the so-called Ruta Alpina, a secondary road that runs parallel to the Pyrenees, from C135 just south of Burguete to Escároz, located in the Salazar valley.
By bus: 1 bus a day runs

Black woodpeckers tend to nest in beech or pine

Mon–Sat from Pamplona La Montañesa to Burguete, from which there is a 2.5km (1½-mile) walk through the forest to Roncesvalles.
Where to stay: Roncesvalles itself has 2 pensions – the 2-star La Posadea, T: (948) 76 02 25, and the Casa Sabina, T: (948) 76 00 12. There are others in the nearby towns of Burguete, Valcarlos, Ochagavia and Isaba.
Outdoor living: there are campsites at Urrobi, in the Urrobi valley, T: (948) 76 02 00, and at Isaba, Asolaza, T: (948) 89 31 68.
Activities *Walking:* much of this area is ideal for hiking and camping or simply driving from village to village, stopping to take strolls through the most inviting forests and meadows – in the Coto Nacional de Quinto Real, for instance.

A cross-country trail leads from Orzanzurieta to the vast oak forest that fills much of the area in the Garralda–Garayoa–Olaldea triangle. Another notable excursion begins just to the north of this forest, at the village of Orbaiceta, where a path follows the Río Irati into the Aezcoa valley. If the weather holds, you can work your way from valley to valley until you reach the banks of the Río Esca.
Further information *Tourist information:* Leyre 13, Pamplona, T: (948) 24 81 40; Mercado 2, Sangüesa, T: (948) 87 03 29, and Yesa (on the N240), T: (948) 88 40 40.

The Federación Vasco-Navarra de Montañismo, Avda Navarra 25, Hotel Urteaga, Beasain, T: (943) 88 08 50, provides information on climbing, mountaineering, cave exploration and walks in general, and has links with some 150 related clubs and organizations.

33

CHAPTER 2

Northern Spain

Some of my most vivid memories of the mountains of northern Spain are of night creatures rarely seen during the day: a hare zig-zagging frantically in the headlights; a pair of wild cats skulking in the bushes, staring at me arrogantly with luminous eyes; a badger ambling about sleepily; a chestnut-coated mink, not the fur-farmed American beast, but the native and truly scarce European one.

I doubt if anyone can claim to know these mountains of the Cordillera Cantábrica well. Far off the beaten tourist track, the Cordillera is one of the largest areas of wild terrain remaining in Europe. South of the Costa Verde, from the shores of Galicia eastwards to Bilbao and inland to the foothills of the Meseta, lie wave after wave of mountain ranges covering some 3.5 million hectares (over 8½ million acres). Like the Pyrenees, they form an almost impenetrable barrier. The Cordillera Cantábrica has insulated these northern lands from the mainstream of Spanish events, and from effective domination from Madrid. It is hardly surprising that the traditions and culture are somewhat different.

The Cordillera is a national stronghold for the lithe and agile chamois, and somewhat appropriately the curve of these mountains resembles the horn of this creature. From the borders of the Basque country – where the mountains subside into wooded hillocks before soaring upwards again into the Pyrenees – the mountains run westwards on a course more or less parallel with the sea, before curling southwards

The Picos de Europa are the highest point in the Cordillera Cantábrica, the 500-km (300-mile) mountain chain that spans northern Spain

to meet the Portuguese border at Sanabria. The tip of the horn, fittingly, is represented by the Sierra de la Cabrera ('goatherd'), which effectively divorces Galicia from central Spain, and extends to within 30 kilometres (19 miles) of Zamora.

The rocks of the Cordillera Cantábrica vary considerably in age and composition, but most of the oldest massifs lie in the west, with the younger strata to the east. Throughout these mountains, but especially along the coast, you can see the varying effects of erosion that has followed their birth. The durable quartzites and granites have emerged as prominent peaks and headlands, and the softer slates and sandstones have been carved by river and sea into gentle valleys and sandy coves. Elsewhere, especially along the eastern shores, the limestones have been eroded to form a typical karstian relief featuring spectacular siphons and blowholes, which throw up foaming spouts of seawater at high tide. Inland, these karstian formations are best developed in the Picos de Europa, the highest point of the Cantábria chain.

The tilt of the mountains is by no means constant throughout northern Spain; Galicia slopes northwards or westwards towards the Atlantic Ocean, and to the east Cantábria has a pronounced list towards Castille and the Meseta. In between is the province of Asturias with its central longitudinal depression, bordered by the Cordillera Cantábria to the south, and the Sierra de Cuera to the north. The pattern is further complicated by the chasms of great rivers: most cut northwards to discharge into the Atlantic, but others wend their way southwards. The great Ebro, for example, originates in the mountains of western Cantabria; it is a mountain stream in the upper reaches

before carving a bed across the north-east corner of Spain in a series of leisurely meanders, to form a huge delta on the Mediterranean coast. Similary, the Río Esla flows across the north-western Meseta before joining the Duero on the Portuguese borders and heading towards Porto.

Many of the rivers which cut through the Cordillera coincide with ancient crossing points from the Meseta to the sea: the principal western passes are El Puerto de Pajares, between Oviedo and León, and Piedrafita, in the mountains of El Bierzo on the pilgrims' route from León to Santiago de Compostela. In the east, the Pas valley from Burgos and the Río Besaya from Palencia have provided access to Santander since the eleventh century. These highways were undoubtedly a hive of activity for mule trains carrying the wool of the *merino* sheep of the Mesta for export to Flanders.

The Cordillera Cantábrica is thought to be one of the earliest areas of Europe to be settled by palaeolithic peoples in the early stages of the last Ice Age, and evidence of their existence can be found along the length and breadth of these mountains. There are megaliths and dolmens at Peña Tú, for instance, located to the south east of Llanes on the Asturian coast, and cave paintings such as those at Altamira, thought to be between 10,000 and 25,000 years old. There are various theories that these people were the ancestors of the Basques, whose language, Euskadi, is one of the oldest in the world and has no affinity with any existing tongue. In their heyday, the Basques were superlative sailors and fishermen, venturing as far afield as Labrador and Newfoundland.

Bronze and Iron Age settlements abound throughout the Cordillera, as the nomadic peoples settled down to a pastoral, and later arable, existence. These little fortified villages, known as *castros*, are mostly located in the mountains, although Castro de Coaña is one example that lies rather closer to the coast, in western Asturias, on the Río Navia. Each wave of Romans or Moors saw the natives retreat to their mountain fortresses, although no invader had any degree of success in taming these mountains; a ten-year bloody battle between the legions of Augustus Caesar and the native Asturians has been well-documented, as have the celebrated battles of Covadonga and Liébana in the eighth century, which saw off the Arab invaders. In times of peace, the native peoples decamped to the more friendly coastal lands, and into the fertile basins of the Duero and Ebro valleys. As a result, for almost ten centuries the mountains have been like a deserted outpost, with a fragmented population and an antiquated agricultural system. But that isolation hasn't kept them completely from the modern world.

Sadly, the splendid, floristically rich hay meadows are gradually being converted to weedy pastures and what little woodland remains is being cleared to make way for extensive grazing lands. The native *lacha* breed of sheep is being replaced by other varieties, and the indigenous races of cattle are almost extinct. It is rare now to encounter the small, sweet-faced *casina* cow in the mountains of Asturias, or the wide-horned, grey *tudanca* of Cantábrica, except in isolated settlements, confined to the most inhospitable terrain.

But for the most part northern Spain presents the same face to the world as it did in medieval times. Along the coast there are craggy, inhospitable cliffs that stretch for miles, with settlements confined to sheltered river mouths, or *rías*, where fishing, timber exportation and hazelnuts are the prime economic activities. In Galicia, the *palloza gallega*, a small oval house with a thatched roof, is still the dominant type of dwelling in mountain villages, and in Asturias, the *hórreo* – a square, stilted barn, used to store maize and potatoes and completely rodent-proof – is a common feature throughout.

Few fragments of the original forests persist today, having been largely replaced by secondary grassland and heathland communities. Beech woods are the most characteristic and natural vegetation type, especially high up on north-facing slopes. One of the largest areas stretches from the pass of Pandetrave to Panderruedas, separating the towering Picos de Europa from the main bulk of the Cordillera Cantábrica. The southern slopes of the Cordillera are covered in Pyrenean oak, and the Mediterranean enclaves of the Liébana and Ebro valleys are dominated by evergreen species such as holm, cork and holly oaks. South of Oviedo there are extensive groves of the introduced sweet chestnut, but rather more worrisome are the monotonous, sterile plantations of non-native eucalypts and pines – a situation likely to be exacerbated by the recent entry of Spain to the European Community, with its attending forestry incentives that could be disastrous to the wildlife of these mountains.

But the general absence of intensive farming methods and the lack of artificial fertilizers and pesticides here have preserved some of the most botanically diverse Atlantic grasslands in the world. Even the roadsides are veritable treasure troves: here a lizard orchid, there a patch of sky-blue speedwell, or perhaps pink-purple sainfoin.

In the upper realms of the mountains there lurks a wealth of sub-alpine and alpine plants which are endemic to the Cordillera Cantábrica. Amid dwarf juniper and blazing masses of broom and gorses, heathers and greenweeds, you can find delicate saxifrages and columbines that bloom nowhere else in the world. On the limestone crags flower blue-leaved petrocoptis (*Petrocoptis glaucifolia*), Cantabrian bell-flowers (*Campanula cantabrica*), Asturian daffodils (*Narcissus asturiensis*), snow tormentil (*Potentilla nivalis* ssp *asturias*), chamois-cress and Cantabrian moon-carrot (*Seseli cantabricum*). The coastal zone is no less botanically rich, boasting blue-purple sheets of sea lavenders in the tidal salt marshes, together with glassworts, sea purslane and sea asters. The inaccessible rocky cliffs shelter rock samphire, sea spleenwort and golden samphire, and the dune systems support such denizens as sea holly, saltwort, and a wealth of clovers.

Northern Spain has been described as one of the few surviving regions of Europe where the original post-glacial mammalian fauna remains virtually intact. Wolves and bears still roam the forests, both so isolated from the populations of central Europe that they have evolved into separate Spanish races. There are only five or six hundred wolves left in Iberia today; of these, most are in Galicia, and a good number can be found in the Cordillera Cantábria, especially to the west.

Other large mammals include the chamois, which in the middle of the last century was threatened with extinction here, but today, after careful conservation measures, numbers some 3,000 in the Picos de Europa national hunting reserve alone. The *asturcón* wild horse,

however, has not been so fortunate, with only a handful of pure-bred animals surviving, mostly in the *reserva nacional* of Sueve. Of the three species of deer that live in these mountains, only the roe deer is truly indigenous; the native red deer population died out at the beginning of the century and has since been re-introduced, while the fallow deer requires frequent infusions of new blood to maintain numbers.

All manner of birds frequent northern Spain, but the most characteristic is the capercaillie. Again, so isolated from the other European populations that it has evolved into a separate race, this cumbersome bird here lives in deciduous beech woods rather than coniferous forests. Birds of prey abound here, too: golden, Bonelli's, booted and short-toed eagles circle in the warm updraughts of the valleys, and griffon and Egyptian vultures scour the upland pastures for carrion. The vultures are most frequently seen from the major north-south roads where southward-flowing rivers have cut deep gorges as they descend to the Meseta. The diversity and abundance of small birds is not great, but the species involved are typically montane and seldom found elsewhere in Spain. The coastal salt marshes provide wintering grounds for a variety of waterfowl and waders, as well as welcome feeding areas for those on migration.

The rivers of the Cordillera and Galicia teem with fish, especially those bound for the Atlantic, which are the spawning grounds for salmon. There are sea trout and brown trout in abundance in the rivers of western Asturias, while the smaller streams and marshlands provide a home for a wealth of amphibian creatures.

GETTING THERE

By air: the 2 main airports are Bilbao (Sondika), T: (942) 453 13 50, and Santiago de Compostela, T: (981) 59 74 00. There is an airport at Santander for internal flights.

By sea: there are ferry services to Santander from Plymouth in England. For information, contact Brittany Ferries, Estación Marítima, Santander, T: (942) 21 45 00.

By car: from France, the main route is the Autoroute Côte Basque, which runs along the Golfo de Vizcaya to San Sebastián, and turns into the Autopista del Cantábrico on its way to Bilbao.

From Madrid, the N-I takes you to Burgos; at this crossroads, you can follow the road on to Bilbao, take the faster E3, or branch off on the N623 to Santander. To Galicia from Madrid, the N-VI goes to Lugo in the heart of the region and on to La Corunna (Coruña) on the western coast. Highway N634 winds along the northern coast connecting the cities of Asturias and Cantabria with those of Galicia.

By rail: there are regular services connecting northern Spain with France and a network of lines running through the region, including the narrow-gauge FEVE line. Regular RENFE services also run on the Madrid–Palencia–Valladolid line to Santander, Barcelona to Bilbao, Madrid, via Valladolid and Zamora to the Galician coast, and Madrid via Palencia to León and Gijón.

By bus: there are regular services run by a number of private bus companies connecting the towns and cities of northern Spain, and in some cases they provide the only means of public transport to the wild areas.

WHEN TO GO

Between Oct–Apr most of the high passes are completely snowbound. Jul and Aug are the hottest and driest months, but daytime temperatures rarely exceed 25°C (76°F). The closer to the coast, the less extreme the temperature variations are: on the southern side of the mountains the nights can be bitterly cold, even in May.

WHERE TO STAY

Out of the normal tourist areas – the coastal resorts – the accommodation is not as abundant as in other parts of the country. Ask at tourist offices for detailed lists and suggestions. Most smaller villages have a *fonda*, or you may be able to find a room by asking at the local bar.

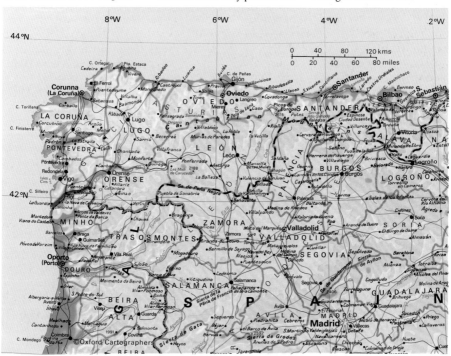

ACTIVITIES

Mountaineering clubs:
Federación Asturiana de Montañismo, Melquíades Alvarez 16, Oviedo, T: (985) 21 10 99; Federación Gallega de Montañismo, Colón 9, Vigo, T: (986) 22 42 92; Federación Leonesa de Montañismo, Alcázar de Toledo 16, León, T: (987) 22 73 00; Federación Palentina de Montañismo, Onésimo Redondo 6, Palencia, T: (988) 71 18 97; Federación Vasco-Navarra de Montañismo, Avda Navarra 25, Hotel Urteaga, Beasain, T: (945) 88 08 50; and Federación Cantabra de Montaña, Pablo Carnica 4, Torrelavega, T: (942) 89 06 90.

Caves: at Altamira, near Santillana del Mar; Castillo and Pasiega at Puente Visgo, south of Santander; and Pindal, to the west of San Vicente de la Barquera. Also the extensive galleries of Tito Bustillo at Ribadasella, still not completely excavated, but one of the world's 3 most important cave systems for prehistoric paintings.

Skiing: the major ski resorts of northern Spain are: Asturias province – Valgrande Pajares (Puerto de Pajares); León province – San Isidro (Puebla de Lillo), and Esla 2002; Cantabria province – Camaleño (Picos de Europa), and Alto Campóo; Burgos province – La Lunada; and Orense province – Manzaneda.

FURTHER INFORMATION

Bilbao (94): tourist office, Alameda Mazarredo, T: 423 64 30.

Burgos (947): tourist office, Paseo de Espolón 1, T: 20 18 46, and Pl. Alonso Martínez 7 bajo, T: 20 31 25. Red Cross, T: 21 23 11. Highway information, Avda del Cid 522–24, T: 22 45 00.

León (987): tourist office, Pl. de Regla 4, T: 23 70 82. Red Cross, T: 25 25 35. Highway information, Ordoño II 27, T: 25 02 12.

Lugo (982): tourist office, Pl. de la Soledad 15, T: 23 13 61 and Pl. de España 27, T: 21 13 61. Red Cross, T: 21 22 99. Highway information, General Primo de Rivera, T: 21 31 41.

Orense (988): tourist office, Amos Enríquez 1, Edificio 'Torre', T: 23 47 17. Red Cross, T: 22 14 62. Highway information, Antonio Sáenz Díaz 43, T: 21 65 40.

Oviedo (985): tourist office, Cabo Noval 5, T: 21 33 85. Red Cross, T: 21 54 47. Highway information, Pl. de España sn, T: 23 62 00.

Palencia (988): tourist office, C. Mayor 153, T: 72 07 77, and C. Mayor 105 bajo, T: 74 00 68. Red Cross, T: 74 41 40. Highway information, Avda de Castilla 23, T: 75 45 00.

Santander (942): tourist office, Pl. de Velarde 1, T: 21 14 17 and 22 73 81/2/3. Highway information, Juan de Herrera 14.

FURTHER READING

Juan Alvarez-Riera et al, *Flores de Asturias* (Oviedo, 1979); Frank Barnett and Chris Gill, *Spain's Hidden Country – a traveller's guide to northern Spain* (London, 1987); Carlos Carvasco Múroz de Vera, *Cornisa Cantábrica* (Editorial Everest 1984); Antonio Cendrero Uceda et al *Guía de la Naturaleza de Cantabria* (Santander, 1986); Nina Epton, *Grapes and Granite* (1960); *Cordillera Cantábrica: Colección Naturaleza y Turismo* (Secretaria General de Turismo, 1986); Matías Mayor y Tomás E. Díaz *La Flora Asturiana* (Ayalga Ediciones, 1977); Alfredo Noval, *La Fauna Salvaje Asturiana* (Ayalga Ediciones, 1976); Kate O'Brien, *Farewell Spain* (London, 1937); Cedric Salter, *Northern Spain* (London, 1979).

Orduña & Sierra Salvada

Varied landscape of forested slopes and pastureland south of Bilbao

Approaching from the south you reach the 900-m (2,950-ft) Puerto de Orduña without any real sense of height: the surrounding countryside is gently undulating pastureland dotted with young pine plantations. The Mediterranean feel of the flora gives no hint of the closeness of the Bay of Biscay and the Atlantic Ocean.

I rounded an insignificant bend and felt the earth drop away beneath the wheels of the car. The road down to the C8th town of Orduña switchbacks alarmingly, each new bend providing a slightly different vista: the dense beechwoods growing on the steep north-facing slopes, the monument to the Virgen de la Antigua on the distant Cumbre de Txarlazo to the west.

Two interesting butterflies are found here. The woodland brown (*Lopinga achine*), a large, golden-brown creature with a row of ocellated markings along the outer edge of each wing, is confined to just 3 small localities in the Iberian peninsula. The Spanish race is that of *murciegoi*, and flies between 600–1,200m (1,950–3,900ft) in shady places. The second butterfly is the chequered

skipper (*Carterocephalus palaemon*), a species characteristic of light woodland; the larval food plants are grasses of the genus *Bromus*.
Before you go *Maps:* SGE 1:50,000, Nos. 86 (21–6) and 111 (21–7).
Guidebook: José R. de Madaria, *La Ciudad de Orduña* (1981).
Getting there *By car:* from Bilbao, take the N625 south to Orduña. From Burgos or Vitoria-Gastiez, take the N-I, turning north on to the N625 leads; as the road winds down from the pass you get a

panoramic view of the town of Orduña.
By rail: Orduña lies on the tortuous Logroño–Miranda de Ebro–Bilbao line, which follows the Nervión valley, and does a complete anti-clockwise circuit around Orduña town itself.
By bus: there are regular services to Vitoria-Gastiez; details available from the bus terminus at C. Calvo Sotelo, Vitoria.
Where to stay: there is a good selection of hotels, hostels and pensions in Orduña; it is a charming town with narrow streets and several good

restaurants – the nearest campsites are at Ameyugo on the N-I Burgos–Vitoria road just before the turning of the N625 to Orduña, and El Desfiladero at nearby Pancorvo.
Activities *Walking:* Orduña is within 10km (6¼ miles) of 1 of the highest mountains in the Basque country: Peña Gorbea (1,475m/4,840ft), near the village of Inoso on the A68.
Further information *Tourist information:* Alameda Mazarredo 3, Bilbao, T: (947) 20 18 46; and Dato 16, Vitoria, T: (947) 23 25 79.

Las Marismas de Santoña

Coastal wetlands in the shelter of Monte Buciero which attract migratory birds and a diversity of marine life

The sparkling rivers that stream down from the heights of the Cordillera Cantábrica and the lesser mountains of Galicia eventually wend their way to the Atlantic coast, where they form numerous estuaries, or *rías*, amid marshes and flood-plains. Despite the ever-increasing flow of

The shelduck, more familiar on North Sea coasts, is also a breeding bird of the Santoña marshes

waste products and pollutants into the once-crystalline waters of the mountain streams and ocean, there remain some *rías* which are of immense importance to wildlife.

From the highest point of Monte Buciero, Alto de Peña Ganzo, some 400 metres (1,300 feet) above the sea, you can look across the whole of the *marismas*, or marshes, of the bay of Santoña. Winding through the maze of narrow creeks and salt marshes is the Río Asón, the main river feeding this coastal wetland, which starts life as a spectacular waterfall in the Puerto del Asón, some 25 kilometres (15 miles) south west of the bay. Sheltered from the often violent Atlantic storms by the huge limestone bulk of Monte Buciero at the harbour mouth, the river attracts sun-seekers during the summer and flocks of migratory wildfowl and waders in winter.

Among the birds of special significance are spoonbills, which frequently break their long migration here to feed and recuperate; the only other Spanish locality with appreciable numbers is the southern wetland of Doñana. In recent years, Santoña has found favour with shelduck, another bird which was formerly regarded as a Doñana speciality. Other species whose presence make Santoña the principal site for wintering birds on the north coast are avocet, grey plover, greenshank, curlew and dunlin among the marshes, and puffins, razorbills and guillemots on the open sea and around the cliffs of Monte Buciero.

This mountain exhibits typical Cantabrian evergreen oak scrub and forests, along with many Mediterranean species, such as Spanish laurel and the strawberry tree. The higher parts of the mountain are completely devoid of vegetation. Most of the native fauna at Monte Buciero has disappeared, due to loss of habitat, hunting and general persecution. Today, the most frequent large bird is the raven, although peregrines have started to re-establish themselves in the area as the natural balance of the woodland is slowly regained.

BEFORE YOU GO
Maps: SGE 1:50,000 Nos. 35 and 36; and Mapa Topográfico Nacional de España; Castro-Urdiales No. 36 1:50,000; Santoña No. 36 – I 1:25,000; and Laredo No. 36 – III 1:25,000.
Guidebook: Jose Luis Gutierrez Bicarregui, *Datos Culturales, Turísticos, Históricos y Otros Aspectos*, (Santoña, 1983).

GETTING THERE
By sea: ferry service runs between Santoña and Laredo; half-hourly in summer but infrequently in winter.
By car: Santoña is situated on a small coastal peninsula which can be reached by several turnings off the E50 Bilbao–Santander highway.
By bus: about 5 coastal buses per day run from Santander; they depart from Bar Machichaco on C. Calderón de la Barca and take 1½–2hrs. There are also bus connections with the Santander–Bilbao FEVE train line; from Cicero station or from Gama.

WHEN TO GO
The best time to visit las Marismas de Santoña is between Sep–May, as the site is particularly important for migratory birds. Autumn is

better as the weather is very unreliable along this Atlantic coast in the spring. When the tide is coming in, the birds are forced on to the higher ground within the marshes, and are thus more easily visible amongst the web of creeks and islands; it is best to time your visit so it coincides with high tide. Stormy weather will drive the birds into the shelter of the bay to feed and roost, and you will be amply rewarded if you brave the elements at these times. Wellington boots are more or less essential. A leaflet showing the recommended observation points is available at the tourist office.

WHERE TO STAY
There is no shortage of hotels, hostels and *fondas*, both in Santoña itself and in the nearby towns of Laredo and Colindres; they do tend to be pretty full during the summer months so book ahead. In Santoña, the 2-star Castilla, T: (942) 66 22 61, and Juan de la Cosa, T: (942) 66 01 00. In Laredo, the 3-star Cosmopol, T: (942) 60 54 00. In Colindres, the 1-star Hostal Residencía Montecarlo, T: (942) 65 01 63.
Outdoor living: there are almost a dozen camp sites in the vicinity, including that on

the renowned Playa de Berria, the beach lying just to the west of the Santoña estuary itself; open from 1 Jun–15 Sep with space for 270, T: (942) 66 22 48, and a small site at Islares: ask at tourist office (see below) for details.

ACTIVITIES
Ruins: at the southernmost tip of the Santoña peninsula, opposite Laredo, you can still see the remains of a massive fort constructed by the French during the Peninsula War. Such was the strategic importance of this site that Santoña was known as the 'Gibraltar of the North'. Another feature of the area is the penitentiary of El Dueso, magnificently located between Monte Buciero and Playa de Berria.
Viewpoint: Faro del Caballo, on the seaward face of Monte Buciero is reached by means of some 684 steps hewn into the limestone.

FURTHER INFORMATION
Tourist information:
C. Santander, Santoña, T: (942) 66 00 66; Laredo, T: (942) 60 54 92; and in Santander at Jardines de Pereda, T: (942) 21 61 20 and Pl. de Velarde, T: (942) 21 14 17. ICONA, Rodriguez 5, Santander, T: (942) 21 25 00.

Las Sierras Palentinas & Alto Campóo

The quiet, untouched sierras of the eastern Cordillera Cantábrica include some of the highest mountains in the region

Stretching from the Ebro dam south of Santander, to the León–Palencia borders south of the Picos de Europa, this eastern section of the Cordillera Cantábrica has a rich and varied landscape, vegetation and wildlife. The western part of the area comprises the Reserva Nacional de Fuentes Carrionas: 47,755 hectares (112,000 acres) of palencian mountain ridges, culminating in the peak of Curavacas (2,525 metres/ 8,282 feet).

The massif of Fuentes Carrionas, the

most westerly, is almost unmarked by roads, except for shepherds' tracks and forest trails. The main crossing point between Picos de Europa and the Meseta, the Puerto de Piedrasluengas, at the head of the Liébana valley, is a complex jumble of calcereous limestones and silicious materials. In springtime the montane pastures in the col are covered with Lent lilies (*Narcissus pseudonarcissus*), meadow saxifrages (*Saxifraga granulata*), cowslips and Pyrenean horned pansies (*Viola cornuta*). From the top of the pass you can see the towering pinnacles of Picos de Europa to the north, the southern plateau, and the square-topped outline of Pico de Tres Mares to the east. If you head north east from Piedrasluengas, you reach the gorge of the Río Nansa, now almost devoid of water due to the construction of a hydro-electric station, but nevertheless stunningly beautiful.

Further east is the more densely populated valley of Campóo, at the head of which lies Pico de Tres Mares (literally, 'three seas'). The mountain marks the point where five rivers are born and then head towards the three seas of the Iberian

High in the Picos de Europa, summer brings out many wild flowers, including these long-stemmed leopard's bane in the foreground

peninsula: Ríos Nansa and Saja flow northwards to the Cantabrian sea; Ríos Areños and Pisuerga join the Duero, and meet the Atlantic coast at Lisbon (Lisboa); and the Río Híjar runs into the Ebro, and then on to the Mediterranean.

The endangered almond-eyed ringlet butterfly (*Erebia alberganus barcoi*) has been recorded on the slopes of Pico de Tres Mares and the area around Reinosa. This is the only colony in Spain, and is considered to be a different race from the rest of the European populations: it flies in only one brood per year, in late June/July, over grasslands between 1,000–1,200 metres (3,280–3,940 feet), and the larvae feed off various mountain grasses.

The great Ebro river is born at the tiny village of Fontibre (literally, 'Fuente Ebro') just to the west of Reinosa, and encounters a dam some 10 kilometres (6¼ miles) to the east. The resulting reservoir is 20 kilometres (12½ miles) long, the largest area of fresh water in Cantabria; no less than 12 flooded villages lie beneath it. The Ebro reservoir is too high to attract large numbers of breeding birds, but has great crested grebe and is a useful stopover for variable numbers of migrant birdlife.

The Campóo valley proper is a gentle landscape spliced between the Sierra de Peña Labra to the south and the Sierras del Cordel and Híjar to the north. It is rather unusual for a valley in the Cordillera Cantábrica in that it is orientated east-west rather than north-south, and consequently is subjected to the full force of the continental climate of the Spanish interior. The hay meadows are few and far between, needing irrigation in the dry season. For the most part, the valley consists of montane pastures, grazed by Swiss cattle and horses.

What woodland there is in Campóo is either Pyrenean oak (*Quercus pyrenaica*) or the highly Mediterranean species, the Lusitanian oak (*Q. faginea*), both providing shelter for bears and wolves. Griffon vultures are common here too, and an occasional booted eagle can be seen circling overhead.

From Espinilla it is now possible to take a new road to the south over an old Roman route. The banks along the roadsides contain soil of all shades from ochre to crimson, salmon pink to that shade of rose that decorates old ladies' faces.

BEFORE YOU GO

Maps: SGE 1:50,000 Nos. 81, 82, 83, 107 and 108.

Guidebooks: Federación Palentina de Montañismo, *Fuentes Carrionas* (Palencia, 1973); and *Guía del Macizo del Alto Carrión* (Palencia, 1978).

GETTING THERE

By car: take the N611 Santander–Palencia road to Reinosa, then the C625 to Espinilla followed by the C628 which ends near Alto Campóo. Alternatively, the area can be approached via the C627, Potes–Cervera road heading over the Pass of Piedrasluengas, or via the S224 through the Río Nansa valley.

By rail: the Santander–Palencia train stops at Reinosa, Puerto de Pozaza and Aguilar de Campóo.

WHERE TO STAY

Reinosa is the best choice, offering a range of hotels and hostels, such as Vejo, T: (942) 75 17 00, and the 3-star La Corza Blanca, T: (942) 75 10 99. In the town of Aguilar de Campóo is the 3-star Valentin, T: (942) 12 21 25 and Pensión Centro, T: (942) 12 28 96.

Refuges: there are a number of refuges in the Campóo valley; ask at the tourist office in Santander (see below) for details.

Outdoor living: you can camp almost anywhere as long as you are discreet about it. There is an official camping ground at Aguilar de Campóo, the Monte Royal, which is open from 1 Jun–30 Sep.

ACTIVITES

Walking: from the village of Fontibre there are several signposted paths leading to the source of the Río Ebro. Many pleasant walks follow the banks of the streams near Fontibre and traverse the woods of birch, oak and beech.

FURTHER INFORMATION

Tourist information: Pl. de Velarde 1, Santander, T: (942) 21 14 17.

The Federación Cantabra de Montaña at Pablo Carnica 4, Torrelavega, Santander, T: (942) 89 06 90, and Federación Palentina de Montañismo, Onésimo Redondo 6, Palencia, T: (988) 71 18 97, both offer information on mountaineering, climbing, etc.

Picos de Europa

A mountain range comprising 3 towering massifs divided by deep gorges and including the Parque Nacional de la Montaña de Covadonga

L ike the backbone of some great supine beast, the Cordillera Cantábrica runs along the north coast of Spain, from the Pyrenees to the Portuguese border. Continuing the analogy, the Picos de Europa is like a slipped disc, displaced to the northern, seaward side of the 'spine' although still linked intimately with it through the mountain pass of San Glorio.

This is the green side of Spain. Only 15 kilometres (9½ miles) from the Costa Verde, Picos de Europa receives most of its weather from the Atlantic; the climate is cool and moist, the valleys lush, and mists occur so frequently that travellers may never see the tops of the mountains.

In contrast to the slates and shales of the Cordillera Cantábrica, Picos de Europa consists of pale limestones, laid down in the Lower Carboniferous. Localized glacial activity during the Ice Ages created the typical frost-shattered topography of today, with its ancient hanging valleys and

glacial *cirque* lakes. There are huge circular hollows, known as *hoyos* or *jous*, in the mountain plateaux: lunar landscapes filled with the shattered limestone rubble, relics of former Ice Ages. Percolating ground waters and underground streams have created huge caverns and galleries decorated with stalagmites and stalactites. You can enter them via sinks of swallow-holes, known as dolines, some of which extend vertically for hundreds of metres.

Picos de Europa comprises three towering massifs separated from one another by steep gorges. The western boundary is the Desfiladero de los Beyos, a narrow ravine carved out by the Río Sella. The adjacent massif, Cornión, which includes the Peña Santa de Castilla (2,596 metres/8,515 feet), receives much of the rain and snow carried by depressions over the Atlantic. Urrieles, the central massif, is the most awe-inspiring; it includes a number of peaks over 2,600 metres (8,500 feet) high – notably Torre Cerredo, at 2,648 metres (8,687 feet), the highest peak in Cordillera Cantábrica, Llambrión and Peña Vieja. But the star is Naranjo de Bulnes (2,519 metres/8,262 feet). This almost conical block of limestone, known to the local people as Picu Urriellu, is something of a Spanish Matterhorn and was not conquered by man until 1904.

Urrieles is divided from Cornión by the most spectacular gorge in Picos de Europa:

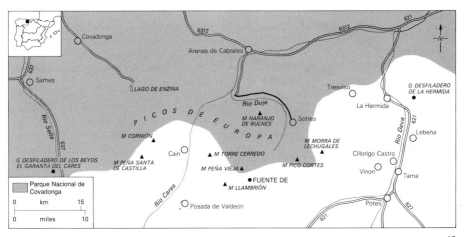

45

This hay meadow at Sesanes in the Picos de Europa is not annually mown, and so provides a haven for wild flowers and butterflies

la Garganta Divina, formed by the fast-flowing Río Cares. The walls are almost sheer, rising in places to over 2,000 metres (6,500 feet); these cliffs are a favourite haunt of that elusive bird, the wallcreeper. If you look up from the depths of the gorge you may see a group of griffon vultures drifting lazily across the narrow band of blue sky, and peregrine falcons, crag martins and the occasional eagle may also be spotted. La Garganta Divina stretches for some 12 kilometres (7½ miles) from Caín in the south to Puente Poncebos. This is one of the most famous walks in Picos de Europa, along a narrow mule track that has been carved from the wall of the gorge, high above the spray of the thundering river. You cross from side to side over

46

fragile bridges, in some places walking inside the mountain itself, where the roar of the river is just an echo.

The gorges of Picos de Europa are so sheltered from climatic extremes that many of the trees and shrubs clinging to their walls are typically Mediterranean. Wild jasmine and barberry grow among the glossy evergreen foliage of strawberry trees and Spanish laurel, and the turpentine tree, a close relative of the pistachio, spreads its leaves in the sunniest spots, together with wild figs, walnuts and olives.

Andara is the smallest and easternmost of the massifs. The peaks are less imposing, and are certainly less well-explored. The massif is separated from Urrieles by the Río Duje and from lesser mountains towards Santander by the Liébana valley, home of the Río Deva. Spring comes earlier to this valley; because it lies in the rain-shadow of the Urrieles peaks, the weather is rather warmer and sunnier.

Covadonga, in Asturias, was the site of a decisive battle fought in AD722, in which the Spanish turned back the Moorish invaders, reputedly with divine help: an avalanche crushed the Muslim forces. From here the Christian reconquest of Spain began. Covadonga, according to King Juan Carlos II, is 'the primary and eternal source of the nation'. In 1918, almost 1,200 years after the Battle of Covadonga, the Parque Nacional de la Montaña de Covadonga was created, to commemorate 'the moment in which we consider Spain to have been conceived'. The park covers almost the whole of the western massif.

There are botanical treasures high in the Picos de Europa, but my own idea of heaven is their gloriously colourful hay meadows. Managed in a traditional manner since they were first reclaimed from the primeval forest, these meadows are among the most floristically rich Atlantic grass-lands in Europe. Over 40 species of orchid have been recorded here, including the evocatively named pink-butterfly, lizard, man, woodcock, fly and bee orchids. Dark, exotic tongue orchids, towering white asphodels and Pyrenean lilies decorate these meadows, and the montane grasslands are renowned for their daffodils, dog's-tooth violets and fritillaries that burst into flower at the edges of melting snow-fields. The tiny Asturian jonquil and hoop-petticoat daffodil form yellow-studded sheets in the *vegas* in early summer.

The highly endangered Pyrenean desman (a kind of mole), for which Picos de Europa is an international stronghold, has declined more in the last 25 years than in all the previous centuries, due mainly to increasing human interference with and destruction of the natural environment. If you venture even a short way into the mountains, you will undoubtedly encounter the king of that realm: the chamois. Now present in quite large numbers, these wonderfully agile creatures spring up almost vertical cliffs and balance on the most inaccessible ledges. Wild boar forage for underground tubers in the deciduous woodlands, but are wary of intruders; the best time to see them is at the onset of cold weather in the autumn, when they come into the villages to forage for potatoes in the fields. One of the rarest animals to be found here is the *asturcón* wild horse, a few of which run free in the Vega de Enol around the glacial lakes of Covadonga.

Pride of place among the birds must go to the raptors, or birds of prey. The rocky cliffs and gorges are the favoured haunts of golden eagles, both griffon and Egyptian vultures, and short-toed and booted eagles soar in the thermal updrafts over the passes in search of their prey. Their numbers are never large and several species are still sadly in decline, despite official protection. Nevertheless, Spain remains the principal country in Europe for birds of prey and these mountains are renowned as one of their strongholds. Hen harriers inhabit the rough heathland areas, goshawks and sparrowhawks patrol the woodlands and buzzards are ten-a-penny. Nesting on the rocky ledges in the heart of the peaks, kestrels and the noisy, gregarious – but, sadly, declining – lesser kestrels swoop overhead; occasionally, a peregrine dives past you like a dark arrow.

Small birds include pied flycatchers,

black redstarts, tree pipits, nuthatches and short-toed treecreepers, black wood-peckers as well as their great, middle and lesser spotted cousins, and no less than six species of owl. Outstanding among these is the magnificent eagle owl, the most powerful predatory bird in the whole of Europe. Their deep 'oo-oo' calls are far-carrying but never loud, even when nearby. They nest in deep caves often near cliff tops but also in quite low buttresses. Their prime need is shelter from sun, wind and rain, so narrow gorges are often favoured. Despite being quite numerous they are very difficult to see and chance sightings are rare. The determined eagle owl watcher will explore these mountains deep in the winter when the birds call by night. Later, in the spring, follow-up visits to likely cliffs may reveal the location of the nesting caves.

The high peaks are favoured by a number

Magnificent beechwoods clothe the slopes of the Covodonga national park from 800–1,500m (2,600-5,000ft), some 40m (130ft) high

of specialized montane birds, including snow finches, alpine accentors and rock thrushes, while flocks of choughs and alpine choughs fly tirelessly overhead. Bee-eaters, hoopoes and golden orioles are not uncommon in the southern and eastern reaches of Picos de Europa, and red-backed shrikes can be seen in many of the valley meadows.

The butterflies that occur in these mountains represent over a third of the entire European fauna. In addition, there are many races which occur nowhere else in the world, and many threatened and endangered species.

Rare and vulnerable species include the scarce swallowtail (*Iphiclides podalarius feistamelii*), a Spanish and North African race, and the Spanish argus (*Aricia morro-* *nensis*). More specific rarities include the Asturian race of the Gavarnie blue (*Agriades pyrenaicus asturiensis*), a yellow-brown lycaenid whose type locality is Picos de Europa, and which is recorded sporadically in the Cordillera Cantábrica, but from nowhere else in the world. Its larval food plant is a rock-jasmine (*Androsace vilosa*), and the adult flies in July over meadows and pastures above 1,800 metres (6,000 feet). The type locality for the *astur* race of Chapman's ringlet (*Erebia lefebvrei*) is also Picos de Europa, the whole species being endemic to the Pyrenees and the Cordillera Cantábrica. It, too, flies at altitudes in excess of 1,800 metres (6,000 feet) at the end of June and July; it is a small, dark butterfly with virtually no ocelli on either upper or lower surface.

BEFORE YOU GO
Maps: SGE 1:50,000 Nos. 55, 56, 80 (15-6) and 81 (16-6).
Guidebooks:*Picos de Europa – Northern Spain* by Robin Collomb (Goring, 1983); *Por los Picos de Europa (de Andara al Cornión)* by Cayetano Enríquez de Salamanca (Madrid).

GETTING THERE
By car: Picos de Europa can be approached from the main

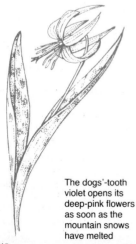

The dogs'-tooth violet opens its deep-pink flowers as soon as the mountain snows have melted

Oviedo–Santander highway, the E40, heading south down either the N621, Unquera–Potes road, or the C637, Arriondas–Cangas de Onís road.

The main roads in Picos de Europa circumnavigate the mountains and are confined to the river valleys; no metalled thoroughfares for vehicles traverse the 3 massifs.
By rail: from Santander the narrow-gauge FEVE line runs to Oviedo through some of the most beautiful scenery on the entire length of Spain's Atlantic coastline. Or alight at Unquera, where you can get a bus into the heart of Picos de Europa. From Bilbao, the same line will take you to Santander; alternatively you can travel in a south-westerly direction to León and take a bus to Posada de Valdeón.
By bus: there is a daily service to Potes, on the eastern side of Picos de Europa, from Santander and Unquera. From León there is a bus which runs northwards into Picos de Europa to the village of Posada de Valdeón, via Riaño. In addition, a daily bus runs

between Cangas de Onís and Arenas de Cabrales along the northern edge of the range. There are also buses between León and Santander which stop at Portilla de la Reina, not far from Posada.

WHERE TO STAY
In almost every village in Picos de Europa there will be at least one *fonda*, pension or hostel in which to spend the night, and more usually a wide array from which to choose. Three centres which make good bases are Cangas de Onís, Potes and Posada de Valdeón. Try, in Cangas de Onís, the 2-star Ventura, T: (985) 84 82 00; and in Potes, the Hostal Residencía Valentino, T: (942) 73 04 58.
Outdoor living: there are several official campsites, the best of which is Camping Naranjo de Bulnes, 1km (½ mile) east of Arenas de Cabrales on the lower reaches of the Río Cares, T: (985) 84 51 78.

Ask at the tourist office for a list of places where you are allowed to camp within the park; you may have to obtain

In spring and summer chamois live around the tree line but in summer climb higher to feed on grasses and alpine herbs

a permit from a park warden.
Refuges: the eastern massif is lacking in *refugios*, but they are frequent elsewhere in Picos. Size and facilities vary from Cabaña Verónica (2,325m/7,625ft), a 4-person hut, to the relative luxury of 46 beds and a restaurant at Aliva (1,667m/5,470ft). For up-to-date information on which huts are open contact the Federación Asturiana Montañismo (see below).

ACTIVITIES
Walking: a fairly tough, 6-hr walk is that from the Refugio de Vega Redonda to the Refugio de Vega Huerta and back again, taking you through the Macizo Occidental; this route crosses 5 passes, through fields and lakes and provides brilliant views and scenery. It takes at least 1hr to walk from the end of the road – at Vega de la Piedra – to Refugio de Vega Redonda.

Another classic walk is through the Cares gorge, a walk 24km (15 miles) long, half of which is through sheer limestone gorge, along a path hewn out of the rock high above the thundering river; the usual approach is from Posada de Valdeón to Poncebos and it takes a day, although it is possible to go by Landrover from Posada to

Caín where the gorge proper begins.
Guides: climbing guides are available at Posada de Valdeón and Sotres.
Viewpoints: from Mirador del Tombo at Cordiñanes, Valle de Valdeón, there is a superb view over the central massif; a better vantage point is Mirador del Puerto de Panderruedas (1,450m/4,750ft) in the south west. Mirador de la Reina looks towards the sea from the road between Covadonga and the famous glacial lakes on the Vega de Enol. Mirador del Corzo and Mirador del Puerto de San Glorio, both of which are situated on the road between Potes and Riaño, looking north east.

There are several notable viewpoints which are a little way off the main roads. Mirador del Naranjo above Puente Poncebos, deep in the heart of the Garganta del Cares, is reached after a 20-min scramble up from the river and the reward is a superb view of the famous Naranjo de Bulnes. A brisk stroll (or short car ride) north of the Puerto de San Glorio takes you to Mirador de Llesba and the *monumento al oso* – a life-size statue of the brown bear. One last viewpoint, from which there is a splendid panorama of the

eastern and southern mountain ranges, is that at the top of the Teleférico: the Mirador del Cable. The only things that spoil it are the crowds of people in peak season, and the piles of rubbish lying around.
Cable-car: a hair-raising, 10-min trip in the Teleférico from Fuente Dé takes you up to a wilderness of shattered limestone.
Caves: at Buxu, just west of Cangas de Onís, where palaeolithic paintings can be seen; closed Mon.
Fishing: excellent trout and salmon fishing in the clear rivers of Picos de Europa; these are the southernmost spawning grounds for salmon in Europe. Contact the ICONA office at Uria-Oviedo 10, T: (985) 22 25 47 for details and permits.
Monasteries: the Monasterio de Santo Toribio de Liébana is near Potes; the hermitage and church are interesting, and there is also a magnificent view over the Liébana valley. And the monastery at Covadonga is built on the site where the legendary King Pelayo fended off the Moors in AD722; the road to the monastery leads to the 2 glacial lakes of Enol and Ercina, some 1,700m (5,580ft) above sea level.
Museum: there is a museum of ethnology just off the main road near Tama, north of Potes.
Riding: horseback treks can be arranged at Turieno near Potes; for information, contact La Isla campsite (see above).

FURTHER INFORMATION
Tourist information: Pl. Jesùs del Monasterio, Potes; Emilio Lara 2, Cangas de Onís, T: (985) 84 80 43; and Ctra General, Arenas de Cabrales, T: (985) 84 41 88.

Somiedo & Pajares

Remote national park south of Oviedo, a haven for the typical vertebrate fauna of the Cordillera

Lying south west of Oviedo, the capital of Asturias, and straddling the crest of the Cordillera Cantábrica, is the Reserva Nacional de Somiedo. The ancient Palaeozoic rocks, well-faulted in a north-south direction, have weathered to provide fertile valleys and slopes, and consequently the area was favoured by early settlers as far back as pre-Roman times.

There is much evidence of Roman civilization here in Somiedo, notably at Saliencia, which was one of the most important fortresses of the Emperor Augustus in the north of Spain. More famous today, though, are the lakes of Saliencia. There is said to be treasure hidden at the bottom of the lakes, guarded jealously by *xanas*, or nymphs, of Asturian mythology. The lakes, of glacial origin, are imprisoned between the twin peaks of the Peña de la Cueva (1,681m/5,515ft) and El Canto de la Almagrera (1,758m/5,766ft), and until recently were inaccessible except on foot.

The northern slopes of the Puerto de Pajares to the east are mantled with extensive beech and oak forests, the southern slopes with secondary heathland and pastoral communities. These latter, especially on bare, slatey areas, have a population of *Teesdaliopsis conferta* – an endemic of the Cordillera Cantábrica – and support

other such interesting species as *Viola bubanii*, *Ajuga pyramidalis*, the leafy lousewort *Pedicularis verticillata* and the white-flowered buttercup *Ranunculus aconitifolius*, none of which are found in Spain away from this northern area.

To the east of the pass, in the sub-alpine snow-melt areas, the verdant pastures are dotted with dog's-tooth violet (*Erythronium dens-canis*), amplexicaule buttercups (*Ranunculus amplexicaulis*) and 2 tiny daffodil species – the Asturian jonquil (*Narcissus asturiensis*) and angel's tears (*N. triandrus*). Two other species occur in this mountain pass that are found only on the extreme western edge of Europe – Ireland and the Atlantic seaboard of Iberia: large butterwort (*Pinguicula grandiflora*), an attractive, purple-flowered carnivorous plant, and St Dabeoc's heath (*Daboecia cantabrica*), a heather-like small shrub heavily laden with pink, bell-shaped flowers.

The absence of roads in Somiedo has ensured that the typical vertebrate fauna of the Cordillera has remained undisturbed and the Somiedo reserve is one of the Spanish strongholds of the Iberian brown bear. Of 77 in Asturias in 1962, 70 could be found here, although just 10 years later only 28 remained. This animal must surely be one of the most threatened mammal species in Spain, with a total Iberian population of between 85 and 120. Other species which are typical of Somiedo include red and roe deer, chamois, wild boar and capercaillie.

Before you go *Maps:* SGE 1:50,000 Nos. 52, 53 and 76; and Instituto Geográfico y Catastral, Nos. 51, 52, 76 and 77.

Getting there *By car:* from the N634 Oviedo–Luarca highway, take the N633 south from Doriga to Somiedo. From the pass at Somiedo down to La Vega, the road is closed Dec–Mar. From the south, approach along the C623 from León.
By bus: there is a service which runs between Oviedo and Pola de Somiedo; ask at the Oviedo tourist office for further details concerning routes, times, etc.
Where to stay: it is difficult to find accommodation in this remote area. Salas has a 1-star hotel, the San Roque. If you are stuck for somewhere to stay, ask at the tourist office in Salas for addresses of *casas particulares*, where you may be able to find a room for the night.
Activities *Walking:* from Pola de Somiedo, north of the Puerto de Somiedo, follow the river to Lago de la Cueva, Lago Negro and Lago del Valle, a walk which takes about 4hrs. Another option is to approach the lakes from the pass. This does take a little longer, though, and is a more strenuous walk.

Peña Ubiña is the most interesting mountain in this region for walking. There are several refuges in the vicinity; get in touch with the Federación Asturiana de Montañismo, Melquíades Alvarez 16, Oviedo for details.
Further information *Tourist information:* Salas, T: (985) 83 08 67; and Pl. de la Catedral 6, Oviedo, T: (985) 21 33 85. ICONA, Uría 10, Oviedo, T: (985) 22 25 47.

Rocky outcrops and scant scrub in Las Médulas suggest the drier south

50

El Bierzo

Including Sierra de Ancares, Las Médulas de Carucedo, Degaña and El Bosque de Muniellos (the last 2 are part of western Cordillera Cantábrica) Mountain range; red rock landscape; hunting reserve

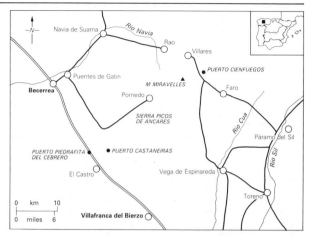

To get to the southern foothills of the Sierra de Ancares, follow the meandering road from the sleepy market town of Cacabelos, through small plots of flowering tobacco plants, tumbling vines and orchards, until the fertile lowlands are left behind and the wilderness begins.

This southern face of Ancares has a dry and inhospitable aspect; patches of eroded soil show through the sparse, shrubby heath. Many of the plants bear vicious spines or produce pungent oils to deter grazing animals. Narrow-leaved and sage-leaved cistus bloom amid a bewildering variety of gorses, heathers and brooms. There are stunted evergreen oaks and every so often tall trunks of the most typical and prized tree of these mountains: the sweet chestnut. In the summer in these grasslands you can lie in the sun and listen to the calls of a thousand grasshoppers, or stroll through the flowers preceded by the flashing blue or red wings of these insects.

The Sierra de Ancares extends over some 5,000ha (12,355 acres) of mountainous terrain which, although lacking the ruggedness of 52

Picos de Europa, holds a certain quiet beauty all its own. The outlines are less severe, the contours more rounded – a legacy of the extreme antiquity of the rocks here. Often you will find yourself in a place that feels as if it had never been seen before.

This forgotten land teems with animal life, especially in the western part of the range, which is known as Cervantes (literally, 'the land of the red deer'). Despite the name, it is the roe deer which is most abundant here, although red deer and fallow deer are also found. Their smaller relative, the chamois, was hunted to extinction by soldiers stationed nearby during the Civil War, and is only now becoming re-established from other colonies in nearby areas of Cordillera Cantábrica.

The woodlands provide the best habitat for the typical species of the Sierra de Ancares. That between Suárbol and Piornedo, for instance, comprises lichen-covered oaks on an outcrop of granite, together with holly, bilberry, bracken, Cantábrian broom and alder buckthorn. Other woods here feature beech as a major component,

together with hazel, silver birch, yew, sycamore and the ubiquitous sweet chestnut. In the cover provided by these primeval habitats live wild boar, genets, beech martens, wild cats, red squirrels and foxes, as well as the most characteristic bird of these mountains, the capercaillie. The last native brown bear was killed in Monte Buixicedo some 40 years ago, but occasionally animals wander into the area from Somiedo, to the east. Wolves still thrive in the Sierra de Ancares, their main prey – the roe deer –

The capercaillie is restricted to woodlands of the Western Cordillera

being wildly abundant.

Almost due north of the rounded contours of Ancares lies the region of Degaña and El Bosque de Muniellos. Degaña, one of the smaller hunting reserves of the Cordillera Cantábrica, totalling only 8,274ha (20,450 acres), has managed to maintain its small brown bear population despite a drastic reduction generally in the numbers of this animal in recent years. This is largely due to the heavily forested nature of the park, which includes the beech wood of Navariegos. Another attraction is several unspoiled glacial lakes on the southern border of the reserve – Las Lagunas de Fasgueo – but the north-eastern section has been somewhat scarred by coal-mining activities.

El Bosque de Muniellos is one of the largest oak woods in Europe; it is made up of some 3,000ha (7,415 acres) of superlative natural vegetation and lies between the *puertos* of Connio and Rañadoiro – the latter pass is the birthplace of the Río Muniellos, a tributary of the Narcea. The highest point of the Muniellos is La Bobia de Teleyerba (1,685m/5,530ft), from which radiate 3 valleys: Candanosa, which contains 4 glacial lakes; Las Berzas, also known as Las Gallegas; and La Cerezal. The rivers flowing through these .

valleys are supplied by a wealth of clean, crystalline streams.

The woodland canopy is comprised of pedunculate and Pyrenean oak (*Quercus robur* and *Q. pyrenaica*), birch, alder and hazel, with a dense understorey of holly, hawthorn and strawberry tree. The autumn fruits of these shrubs attract large numbers of passerines and small mammals, and consequently the predatory vertebrates are also well-represented. As in Degaña, brown bears are frequent, together with wolves, wild cats and foxes. Avian predators include goshawk, sparrowhawk, peregrine, kestrel, golden eagle and short-toed and Bonelli's eagles, although the latter are scarce. Chamois and roe deer are also common, as are wild boar, and this dense woodland is the most favoured breeding site in the whole Cordillera Cantábrica for the capercaillie.

By some strange miracle, in this day and age, the woodland has been little interfered with. Its status, now it is owned by the state, is close enough to that of a national park: its official designation is Coto Nacional de Muniellos. But what is important is that considerable care is being taken to ensure that the trees are regenerating, and to control

The great yellow gentian grows in pockets of marsh and damp grassland in hilly regions

hunting and poaching in the woodland.

To the north of Degaña and east of Muniellos lies another great woodland, this time of beech, which surrounds the Monasterio de Huermo. This is the largest beech forest in Asturias, although it has no legal protection.

On the opposite side of Ancares, separated from its sunny slopes by the Río Sil and the market town of Ponferrada, lie the Montes Aquilianos and the Sierra del Teleno. At the western end of this narrow mountain chain you come across a landscape scene more typical of the African desert: the weather-scarred cliffs of Las Médulas de Carucedo.

The shy, nocturnal genet can easily be mistaken for a cat, but in fact is a close relative of the mongoose

53

In the late afternoon sun, Las Médulas appeared to be on fire. Its pillars and pinnacles of ruddy-coloured rock have been etched into extraordinary shapes and forms by wind and water, and, strangest of all, by humans. In the 1st century AD when this part of Spain was under Roman rule, these mountains were mined for gold. Canals were built to bring water from Río Cabrera, some 28km (17 miles) away, and underground galleries were dug until the whole plateau, as it then was, became riddled with holes. Gradually the upland was reduced to a series of peaks, which today rise from a sea of sweet chestnut trees. The mines have long since been abandoned, but a labyrinth of galleries remains to be explored. Of these the Mina de Orellán and the Galería de Yeres figure among the most famous and extensive.

What really struck me, as I sat looking down on this incredible landscape, was the sound of swifts' wings ripping through the air close to my head, the noise strangely mirrored by the rasping of the scythes as the local people harvested their wheat and barley in the valley below. And the dome-shaped stacks of straw gradually taking shape around their central poles looked rather like the convex peaks of Las Médulas – in both their colour and their form.

Before you go *Maps:* (Sierra de Ancares) SGE 1:50,000 Nos. 126 and 158, and IGN 1:50,000 Nos. 99, 100, 125, 126, 157 and 158; (Las Médulas de Carucedo) SGE 1:50,000 Nos. 75 and 100; (Degaña and El Bosque de Muniellos) SGE 1:50,000 Nos. 100 and 101, and IGN 1:50,000 Nos. 75, 76, 100, 101.

Guidebooks: Alfredo Sánchez (Arro), *El Parque Natural de Ancares* (1985); David Gustavo López, *Las Médulas* (1983); and Luis Pastrana, *El Bierzo* (1981).

Getting there *By car:* from León take the N120 to Astorga and the N-IV to Ponferrada and/or Pedrafita to Cebreiro; alternatively, take the C623 to Villager, turning right on to the C631 and first left on the small road to Degaña.

By rail: the railway is an unsatisfactory method of travel for the Ancares area, the nearest stations being at Lugo or Ponferrada.

By bus: 2 bus lines take you into the heart of Ancares: Lugo to Degrada; and Ponferrada to Candín.

Where to stay: within Ancares itself, there are *fondas* and hostels at Degrada, Candín, Donis and Balouta. Just outside the town, along the main Ponferrada–Lugo road, is the Parador Nacional de Villafranca del Bierzo, T: (987) 54 01 75.

Outdoor living: south of Ancares, but well-situated if you plan to visit Las Médulas as well, is Camping El Bierzo at Villamartín de la Abadia, T: (978) 54 67 00; space for 240 and open Jun–Sep.

Refuges: the Albergue del Club Ancares at Degrada is recently opened; it lies between the peaks of Mustallar and Peñarrubia.

Activities: Ancares is made up of 2 main conservation areas: the region in Galicia now known as the Parque Natural de Ancares, which was formerly a national hunting reserve; and the part of León known as the Reserva Nacional de los Ancares-

The clear blue water and shining white sands of Las Islas Cíes remain unspoiled by man

Leoneses – 38,300ha (95,000 acres) of hunting reserve for red deer and roe deer; formerly bear and capercaillie were also legal prey here. *Climbing:* contact Federación Leonesa de Montañismo, Alcázar de Toledo 16 (Casa del Deporte), León, T: (987) 22 73 00, for information on climbing and walking in the area.

Fishing: there are numerous stretches of river good for fishing. Permits and further information can be obtained from ICONA offices in Lugo and León (see below for addresses).
Tours: you can arrange Landrover excursions around the mountains from Degrada, Castillo de Doiras, Candín and Vega de Espinareda. Ask

at the tourist offices (see below) for details.
Further information *Tourist information:* Pl. de Regla 4, León, T: (978) 23 70 82; and Pl. de España 27, Lugo, T: (982) 21 13 61. ICONA, Avda Ramón y Cajal 17, León, T: (978) 22 69 17; and Ronda del General Primo de Rivera 38, Lugo, T: (982) 21 49 40.

Islas Cíes

Archipelago just off the north-western coast by the city of Vigo; an important site for marine breeding birds

First impressions are supposed to be the most important. It was mid-July and raining when I left Vigo. Mist had closed down around the hills that ring that city's estuary and I could not even see my destination.

I was lucky to visit Las Islas Cíes on a rainy day. I wandered for hours among the eucalyptus trees without ever seeing another person. I spent a happy half-hour following a sparrowhawk from tree to tree in a small Monterrey pine forest on Punta Muxeiro; despite having been planted the woodland was full of native shrubs and herbs, such as sage-leaved cistus and heath lobelia – the fragrance on this wet day was wonderful. Another half-hour was spent watching the shags diving for fish in the choppy waves around a rock near Playa Cantareira; at any one time there was an equal number of avian spectators perched out of reach of the sea, like so many penguins waiting patiently on an ice-floe.

If I had approached the islands from the west, I might have formed a very different opinion. Here the granite cliffs receive the full force of the Atlantic Ocean; although the cliffs tower above the sea, the waves have carved out numerous caves at the base, some of which are enormous.

Las Islas Cíes are made up of three main

islands, with two northern ones linked artificially by a road and a sand bar: from north to south, Isla del Norte, Isla del Faro and Isla del Sur o de San Martín. They lie at the mouth of the Ría de Vigo, some 14.5 kilometres (nine miles) from the city itself. It amazes me that they remain so unspoiled despite being so close to 300,000 people. The archipelago also includes many smaller islets and rocky outcrops. The four main ones are El Beriero o Agoeiro, Viños, Popa Fragata and Pinelón da Cortella; the former lies 1.3 kilometres (¾ mile) from the southern island, is topped by a small tower, and supports only about ten plant species on its barren surface.

Since the declaration of Las Islas Cíes as a *parque natural* in 1980, there has been no access to the whole precipitous western side of Isla del Norte, the cliffs which harbour the highest density of nesting gulls and shags. Similarly, there is no access to the triangular Isla del Sur, and consequently optimal conditions exist for wildlife.

The botanical highlight of Las Islas Cíes is the beach and sand-dune vegetation. The Galician rarity *camariña* (*Corema album*) thrives on both Rodas and Figueiras beaches; this dwarf shrub is endemic to the Iberian peninsula and produces separate male and female plants. With it flourish sea rocket, saltwort, sea knotgrass, cottonweed, sea immortelle and the sea daffodil.

Much of the interior of the islands consists of pine and eucalyptus plantations, boasting an understorey of European gorse, blackthorn, bracken and Pyrenean oak. Here and there the monotonous green is relieved by the pink of round-headed leek, sky-blue sheep's-bit, purple foxgloves and white asphodels. Native tree species are few and far between, but a number of ornamental and orchard trees persist in abandoned domestic gardens. It is strange that the heaths and lings so common in similar habitats on the mainland are virtually absent here. A total of 260 plant species have been recorded on Las Islas Cíes, of which 232 are of European origin.

There is little fresh water on the islands and the sole amphibian found here is the black-and-gold fire salamander, which is only to be seen after rain or at night. Of the reptiles, both Bocage's wall lizard and the Iberian wall lizard occur (the former being endemic to north-west Spain and Portugal), as well as the larger, blunt-headed ocellated and Schreiber's lizards.

But it is the birds that command most attention in Las Islas Cíes – and justly so. At the height of the breeding season, even the most inattentive day-tripper could not fail to notice the clamour of the gulls as they fight for nesting space on precarious ledges in the cliff-faces. The most important marine breeding birds here are herring and lesser black-backed gulls (the latter occupying their most southerly colony in the world), as well as shags and guillemots. The cave and cliff-nesting shags had decreased to 300 pairs by 1981; this colony, much the largest in the Iberian peninsula, is one of the prime reasons for the establishment of the natural park.

Of even greater significance, though, is the Iberian guillemot that breeds here. It is on the verge of extinction on Las Islas Cíes, with only two or three pairs returning to nest each year. Not only is this tiny enclave endangered, but the bird is very rare on the entire Atlantic coastline, and thus merits the greatest possible protection, although Iberia is right at the southern edge of the bird's range.

There is also an abundance of pelagic bird life, although they do not nest here. Gannets are a frequent sight, accompanied in winter by razorbills, puffins and kittiwakes. Although migrant seabirds such as Manx, Cory's and great shearwaters may be seen offshore in late summer, these birds are more regularly found off Cape Finisterre to the north.

Between two and four thousand ducks winter in the Ría de Vigo every year – mostly mallard, wigeon, pochard and common scoter – and these are a frequent sight in the more sheltered bays of the islands in bad weather. Grey herons can also be seen fishing, and in 1977 a group of 25 flamingoes visited in winter. Waders which winter in the area include a few bar-tailed godwits and grey plovers, along with turnstones and the oystercatcher; the latter used to breed here, but has not done so for a number of years. It is thought that the only shore-nesting bird on the islands is the Kentish plover.

BEFORE YOU GO
Maps: SGE 1:50,000 Nos. 222, 223 and 261.
Guidebooks: *Islas Cíes, Parque Natural de Galicia* by Estánislao Fernández de la Cigoña-Núñez.

GETTING THERE
By sea: the only way to get across to Las Islas Cíes from Vigo is by the ferry from the Estación Marítima de Ría, T: (986) 43 77 77.

WHERE TO STAY
There is no shortage of hotel or *fonda* accommodation in Vigo – for instance, the 3-star Ipanema, T: (986) 47 13 44; and the 1-star Lepanto, T: (986) 21 46 08. For listings for the islands themselves, ask at the tourist office (see below).
Outdoor living: there is a campsite on the Isla del Faro, open from mid-Jun–mid-Sep, T: (986) 42 16 22. Camping is forbidden elsewhere on the island.

ACTIVITIES
Birdwatching: Observatorio del Faro do Peito (Isla del Norte) for watching the shag colonies; and Observatorio de la Campana (Isla de Faro) for observing herring gulls and shags.
Fishing: for licences and information contact the tourist offices (see below) or ICONA, Michelena 1, Pontevedra, T: (986) 85 19 50.

FURTHER INFORMATION
Tourist offices: Estacíon Marítima, Vigo, T: (986) 21 30 57; and Michelena 1, Pontevedra, T: (986) 85 19 50. ICONA, Michelena 1, Pontevedra, T: (986) 85 19 50.

CHAPTER 3

North Meseta

The central plateau, or Meseta, covers nearly half the entire area of Spain. It is a high tableland with an average altitude of 700 metres (2,300 feet) in the northern portion, 600 metres (2,000 feet) in the south. Surrounding it is a series of mountain ranges that separate the Meseta from the Costa Verde, the Ebro valley, the Mediterranean and the valleys of Andalucía.

The Meseta is a vast and curiously deceptive region. I have flown over it many times and wondered where the people were hiding; from the air much of it resembles a trackless desert without roads, rivers or villages. But the picture changes dramatically as soon as you travel across the Meseta at ground level. Farmhouses and wheat-fields make their appearance; the brown and grey earth is veined with narrow roads and cart tracks. In summer much of the land is sunbaked to the consistency of terra cotta but there are also some surprizingly fertile regions that have clearly benefited from modern agricultural technology. Yet the Meseta still has more than its share of half-wild lands that are suitable only for sheep-grazing – or for wanderers and nature-seekers looking for remnants of pre-technological Spain. Its very emptiness strikes me as one of its principal attractions, but I know from experience that not everyone shares my predilection for such landscapes. A New York friend once asked me to recommend a place in the Castilian countryside which he could visit on a sidetrip from Madrid,

An eroded gorge near Zaragoza bakes in the summer heat. Although inhospitable-looking, this is a likely habitat for birds such as rock thrush and black wheatear

and I gave him the name of a small decaying town in the midst of a wonderfully bare region of wheat-fields. When I saw him again some months later he took me to task for having wasted his time on this out-of-the-way destination. 'What do you see in it?' he asked me, looking thoroughly mystified. 'There isn't anything there!'

The northern Meseta is separated from the southern by a long, irregular chain of mountain ranges, the Sistema Central, that runs diagonally just to the north of Madrid, stretching from the Sierra de Peña de Francia in the west to the Sierra de Ayllón in the east. This is no mere range of hills. Indeed, to my mind there are no more dramatic mountains in Spain than the Sierra de Gredos, which forms a giant escarpment above the valley of the Río Tiétar, about 140 kilometres (87 miles) west of Madrid. From the southern rim of the Gredos, at well over 2,000 metres (6,500 feet), you can look out across a vast expanse of farms and forested hills, some 1,700 metres (5,500 feet) beneath your feet. In the mountain meadows the ecosystem is alpine, and ibex spring from ledge to ledge; in the Tiétar valley the flora is semi-tropical, with palms and lemon trees. A four-hour climb will take you from the sub-tropical plains to the snow-covered mountains. There is skiing in the Gredos during the winter months and serious mountain climbing at all times of the year, but this is also an immensely rewarding region for travellers who want to wander on foot through a superb massif which, except for one or two familiar points, is still largely unknown to international tourism.

In the western outlies of this mountain range you will feel yourself at the edge of the known world. Pilgrims visit the shrine of the Madonna atop the Peña de Francia, but ordinary tourists almost never come this way. Perhaps it was the sense of isolation which induced the emperor Charles v to retire to Yuste when he abdicated his throne in favour of his son.

The Sierra de Guadarrama, the eastern continuation of the Gredos, lies just above Madrid and is thus crowded with *madrileño* skiers during the winter and holiday-makers during the summer. These cool, green peaks have always served as the summer 'hill stations' of the sweltering inhabitants of the capital. Even the kings and their royal families used the Guadarrama as an escape hatch. While wandering through its high-altitude forests you might do well to visit the 140-hectare (350-acre) garden of La Granja de San Ildefonso, the royal pleasure park that contains the world's finest sculptured fountains. Philip v loved capturing the cold springs that pour down from these mountains, and this was his way of improving on nature – 26 fountains that incorporate hundreds of sculptures, ponds, cascades, sprays and *jets d'eau*. Although surrounded by wild Spain, this is Baroque Spain with a vengeance, and not even Versailles can hold a candle to it. In the baths of Diana, for example, 20 naked nymphs dance in attendance on the goddess of the hunt, while her tame lions roar out great streams of water and cascades splash down a series of marble tiers. There is a fountain that leaps 40 metres (130 feet) into the air; the *fuente del Canastillo* weaves a basket of interlacing jets; a sea-god drives his horses through the fountain of *la Carrera de Caballos*; Apollo slays the python, which bleeds a foaming stream of water. Be sure that your visit coincides with the announced schedule of days and hours when the fountains are turned on for visitors.

The Sierra de Ayllón, still further to the east, lies far off the beaten track and boasts some of the finest rural landscapes of northern Spain. One of the Sierra's chief talking points is the beech forest known as the Hayedo de Tejera Negra, but for me its special fascination lies in its rolling hills and flower-bedecked hay meadows. The whole region was once more densely populated than it is today, and in the middle of some peasant village you'll suddenly come upon the ruins of a medieval church of truly magnificent proportions.

Apart from these central mountains the northern Meseta usually runs to wheatfields and vineyards, sheep pastures and low hills covered with forests of pine, beech and oak. The walled city of Avila suggests itself as a natural base of operation in the southern part of this zone, with Salamanca as a possible alternative. Soria, Valladolid and Zamora are the principal cities of the central region.

The classic way to see the countryside of northern Castilla between Logroño and Ponferrada is to follow the way of the medieval pilgrims, the Camino de Santiago. I first walked along the pilgrims' road in the 1960s and found it indescribably beautiful. It was early summer and the nights were still chilly, but in the morning the whole chorus of resident and visiting birds were in full voice, and as the day warmed up the crickets formed an impromptu orchestra. We wandered through wheatfields, marched along remnants of the old Roman roads and crossed rivers by means of medieval bridges. Often the villages *en route* still had hospices and monasteries – vestiges of the first great 'mass tourism'

enterprise in the western world – and in some cases the monasteries were still inhabited by monks who were busy doing more or less the same things their predecessors had been doing a thousand years before.

It struck me at the time that this retracing of an ancient route was just as adventurous as striking out on your own through an uncharted wilderness; indeed, this particular admixture of nature and history is more akin to what one can find in India than in Europe. As Walter Starkie writes in *The Road to Santiago*, 'a reflective pilgrim on the road to Santiago always makes a double journey . . . the backward journey through Time and the forward journey through Space.' When the historical dimension is added to this journey, and to the whole experience of walking through fertile fields and semi-deserts, across rolling hills and deeply scarred *arroyos*, every step the pilgrim takes 'evokes memories of those who passed that way century after century.'

It used to be that people would trudge all the way to Santiago de Compostela and back, hanging up their tattered shoes in their local church as proof of their piety – to say nothing of their endurance. Today few people will go as far as this, and many hikers are content with covering just a small part of the Camino (a sign of the short attention span prevalent in the twentieth century). If I had time for only one segment I would probably choose the 90 kilometres (55 miles) between Nájera and Burgos – a superb and thoroughly characteristic sector of the Camino that leads from one of the old royal cities of Navarre to the erstwhile capital of Castilla. The way traverses a variety of plains and hills, including the oak-forested mountains of Oca, and takes in a dozen medieval towns and villages: Santo Domingo de la Calzada with its twelfth-century cathedral; Villafranca de los Montes de Oca, with its 600-year old hospice for pilgrims; and Valdefuentes, once a mountainous hiding place for both monks and bandits (the monks left the more interesting memento, the ruined monastery of San Félix de Oca).

All along the Camino there are opportunities for observing the flora and fauna of the northern Meseta. Certainly you'll see the white storks nesting in the church towers, but it is more difficult to spot some of the endangered species of the region: the imperial eagle with its great wing-span (up to 2.25 metres/7½ feet) and vast hunting territory (around 27,500 hectares/68,000 acres); the peregrine falcon, whose hunting dives have been clocked at 400 kilometres (250 miles)

per hour; and the eagle owl, known locally as the *buho real* or the *gran duque*, the most powerful of all European birds of prey. Smaller birds, however, are well provided for in the ecosystems of the northern Meseta, and they also abound in the monastery gardens along the Camino. At Silos, John Gooders once recorded storks breeding in the bell tower and rock bunting nesting in the buildings themselves; spotless starling and melodious warbler in the gardens; yellow wagtail in the water-meadows of the nearby valley, with woodchat shrike, golden oriole and serin in the poplars that grow there; azure-winged magpie and roller on the pine-clad hillsides; rock thrush and black wheatear above the treeline; and in the crags above the valley, griffon and Egyptian vultures, alpine swift, crag martin and chough. He also found the eagle owl, red-necked nightjar and the wallcreeper, 'which should not be in this part of Spain at all'.

Among the olive trees of Sierra de Peña de Francia, the pattern of pastoral life has remained unchanged for centuries

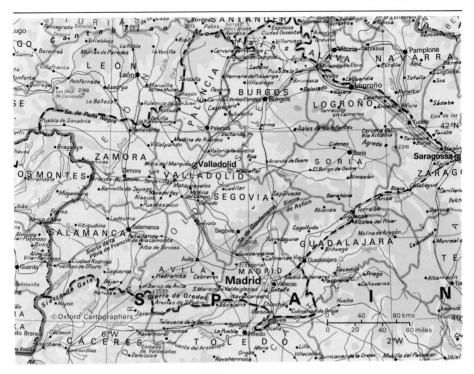

GETTING THERE
By air: Madrid is well
connected by air to all
European capitals and other
parts of the world, as well as
being the central point of the
Spanish internal network.
There are no other major
airports in the Meseta, either
north or south, and the
nearest cities served by
Iberia's domestic network are
all outside the perimeter of
the Meseta: Vitoria,
Santander, Oviedo, Valencia
and Alicante.
By car: the motorway network
radiates from Madrid like the
spokes of a wheel, providing
high-speed access to the Sierra
de Guadarrama, for example.
But further from Madrid the
national routes are mainly
2-lane highways; whenever
possible, take the alternative
roads marked in yellow on the
maps. By far the best way to
travel throughout the Meseta

is on these secondary and
tertiary roads that take you
through the most remote
places.
By rail: there are excellent
RENFE connections between
Madrid and the cities of the
northern Meseta: 5 trains a
day to Soria and Castejón; 2
to Logroño; 9 to Aranda de
Duero, Burgos, Miranda del
Ebro and Vitoria; 10 a day to
Valladolid, Palencia, León and
other stations on the line to
Astorga and Ponferrada; and
6 to Salamanca and other
points north-west of Madrid.
RENFE's special reservation
telephones in Madrid are
staffed every day from
9am–9pm, T: (91) 429 82 28.
By bus: an elaborate network
of local companies covers
most of the cities, towns and
villages of the Meseta. For
current schedules and
information, call the Estación
de Autobuses, T: (91) 46 84 00.

WHEN TO GO
The temperatures in Madrid,
which is situated on the
central plateau at about 600m
(2,000ft) above sea level, are
admittedly extreme but still
typical of this region. It has
freezing winters and burning
summers that average out to a
mean annual temperature of
15°C (59°F).

WHERE TO STAY
For suggested accommodation
in the region, refer to the
individual entries. For a
detailed list of hotels, contact
the Madrid tourist office or
any of the regional offices
mentioned below.

ACTIVITIES
Mountaineering clubs:
Federación Castellana de
Montañismo, Apodaca 16,
Madrid 4, T: (91) 448 07 24.
Skiing: the main ski fields in
the northern Meseta are:

63

Madrid – Puerto de Navacerrada, Valcotos and Valdesquí; Segovia – La Pinilla.

FURTHER INFORMATION
Avila (918): tourist office, Pl. de la Catedral 4, T: 21 13 87. Red Cross, T: 22 48 48. Highway information, San Roque 34–36, T: 22 01 00.
Burgos (947): tourist office, Pl. Alonso Martínez 7, T: 20 16 10. Red Cross, T: 21 23 11. Highway information, Avda del Cid 52–54, T: 22 45 00.
Guadalajara (911): tourist office, Travesía de Beládiez 1, T: 22 06 98. Red Cross, T: 22 17 88. Highway information, Cuesta de San Miguel 1, T: 22 30 66.
León (987): tourist office, Pl. de la Regla 3, T: 22 00 18; and C. General Sanjurjo 15, T: 22 77 12. Red Cross, T: 25 25 35. Highway information, Ordoño II 27, T: 25 02 12.
Logroño (941): tourist office,

C. Miguel Villanueva 10, T: 25 54 97, and C. Portales 1, T: 25 60 60.
Palencia (988): tourist office, C. Mayor 105, T: 72 00 68. Red Cross, T: 74 41 46. Highway information, Avda de Castilla 23, T: 75 45 00.
Salamanca (923): tourist office, Gran Vía 41, T: 24 37 30. Red Cross, T: 21 56 42. Highway information, La Rúa 20, T: 21 90 03/05.
Segovia (911): tourist office, Pl. Mayor 10, T: 41 16 02; and Pl. de San Facundo 1, T: 41 17 92. Red Cross, T: 41 14 30. Highway information, Alhóndiga 4, T: 41 42 90.
Soria (975): tourist offices, Pl. Ramón y Cajal, T: 21 20 52; and C. Alfonso VIII 1, T: 22 48 55. Red Cross, T: 21 26 36. Highway information, Mosquera de Barnuevo sn, T: 22 12 50.
Valladolid (983): tourist office, Pl. de Zorrilla 3, T: 45 18 01.

Red Cross, T: 26 19 82. Highway information, José Luis Arrese 3, T: 33 91 00/66
Zamora (988): tourist offices, C. Santa Clara 20, T: 51 18 45; and Avda de Italia 25, T: 52 20 20. Red Cross, T: 52 33 00. Highway information, Avda de Italia 20, T: 52 24 00.

FURTHER READING
P. Barrett and J. N. Gurgand, *La Aventura del Camino de Santiago* (Vigo, 1982); Alistair Boyd, *The Companion Guide to Madrid and Central Spain* (London, 1974); Robin Collomb, *Gredos Mountains and Sierra Nevada* (Reading, 1987); Eusebio Goicechea Arrondo, *El Camino de Santiago* (Madrid, 1982); Ernest Hemingway, *For Whom the Bell Tolls* (New York, 1940); and Walter Starkie, *The Road to Santiago: Pilgrims of St James* (London, 1957).

Sierra de Gredos

Massive range of mountains running west from Madrid,
one of Spain's major strongholds for birds of prey

There was no path as such, only a few stone markers placed at desultory intervals atop some of the more prominent boulders. Very gradually I was ascending a broad valley strewn with great rocks that had fallen from the flanking heights, their rough-hewn surfaces covered with lichen in delicate shades of green, yellow and pink. There was hardly a cloud in the sky but with a pleasant breeze and the temperature perfect for walking. As a counterpoint to the omnipresent sound of birds there was the sweetly tangy frangrance of thyme and lavender; clearly all was right with the world. Finally, I crossed the main brook

flowing down the centre of the valley, ascended a steep slope and reached the high southern ridge, my aim for the last hour. To my left rose the peaks of Los Campanarios (2,152 metres/7,059 feet). But suddenly there was nothing beneath my feet except a yawning abyss that fell away for more than 1,000 metres (3,280 feet).

I had discovered the not-so-discreet charm of the Gredos, the majestic range of mountains lying athwart the centre of Spain like a titanic rampart. Until recently, the beauties of the Gredos were a fairly well-kept secret, known mainly to hunters, mountaineers and cross-country skiers. During the past decade, however – since the building of a road to a place appropriately known as the Plataforma – the very centre of the range has been opened up to just about anyone capable of putting one foot in front of the other. As a result, there are summer Sundays when the path up the highest mountain (Pico Almanzor; 2,592 metres/8,500 feet) is almost as crowded as the Ramblas of Barcelona.

The Circo justifies all the superlatives that have been written about it; that, of course, is one of the reasons why so many weekenders make the trip. It's worth noting, however, that this is virtually the only place in the Gredos where you'll find a surfeit of people.

On the east, the crooked elbow formed by the Río Alberche on its way to meet the Tajo divides the Gredos from the Sierra de Guadarrama; on the west, the trench of

The black stork, unlike the white, nests in forest treetops far from human habitation

Aravalle separates the Gredos from the Sierra de Béjar (sometimes regarded as the western extension of the Gredos). The peaks of the Sierra grow progressively higher from east to west – Cerro Guisando, 1,320 metres (4,330 feet); El Cabrero, 2,188 metres (7,176 feet); La Mira, 2,348 metres (7,700 feet); Almanzor, 2,592 metres (8,500 feet) – then they decline slightly before ending abruptly with the majestic Covacha, overlooking the Sierra de Tormantos at 2,399 metres/(7,870 feet). Like second-year Latin, the Gredos are usually divided into three parts: the Eastern Massif, between the Peña del Cadalso and the Puerto del Pico; the Central Massif, which includes Almanzor, a favourite haunt of griffon and black vultures; and the Western Massif, comprising the mountains

west of the Puerto de Tornavacas.

The most striking differences, however, are not between east and west but between the northern slope of the Sierra and the south face, which plunges so abruptly from the highest peaks (over 2,100–2,500 metres/ 6,890–8,200 feet) to the 300 metres (984 feet) of the Tiétar valley. The north side of the Gredos consists of hills that rise by easy steps from 1,400 metres (4,590 feet).

Although the altitude is not especially great, the Cordillera happens to lie in one of the coldest zones in Spain, and temperatures resemble those of much more alpine regions. Curiously, the northern slope supports a sub-alpine flora, with great stands of pine (especially in Hoyos de Espino, Navarredonda, Hoyo Casero and

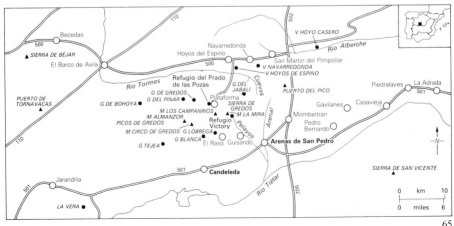

the whole Eastern Massif), large tracts of *Genista purgans* and the rich meadows that a Brown Swiss cow would instantly recognize as home, while the southern slope borrows its sub-tropical flora from the Valle del Tiétar and La Vera (the so-called 'Andalucía of Avila'), what with holm oaks, olives, citrus trees and such. In the Gredos, in other words, the sure-footed botanist can have the best of both worlds.

The Central Massif begins at Arenas de San Pedro, the real capital of the Sierra de Gredos – a much-besieged town whose history is written into its coat of arms: 'Always burning and always faithful'. It stands at the confluence of the rivers Arenal and Cuevas, and is surrounded by an immense circle of mountains.

In the Central Massif some 23,000 hectares (56,835 acres) are set aside as a

The Rio Arbillas begins life as a shallow, rocky stream near Arenas de San Pedro in the central part of the Sierra de Gredos, then flows south to join the Rio Tietar

coto nacional, but hunting is strictly controlled and only a few selected animals are culled every year. Originally this was a royal preserve, the Coto Real de Gredos, established by Alfonso XIII in 1905 as a means of saving the local ibex from extinction. Successive governments have succeeded so well in this endeavour that the ibex population is currently estimated at 5,000, and you can hardly walk through the high Gredos without seeing them at close range.

Three hundred metres (984 feet) above La Apretura – a narrow defile between the Galayos and Risco Enebro, where a high waterfall marks the birth of the Río Pelayos – rises the peak of La Mira (2,343 metres/ 7,685 feet). Here you can often see numbers of ibex with their young in the high meadows called *cervunales*. La Mira is known as the best observation point of the entire range; the ruined tower on its summit is a relic of an old optical telegraph station which sent and received messages at enormous distances thanks to its immense field of view.

The Gredos can be enjoyed in innumerable ways that are not always overly strenuous. In every part of the Cordillera there are ancient towns and villages from which you can make short excursions into the neighbouring fields and meadows. At the eastern end there is the Cerro de Guisando (1,303 metres/4,274 feet) and one of the oldest thoroughfares in Spain, the 'Pass of the Horses', connecting Toledo and Valladolid. Nearby stand the mysterious stone bulls that must have belonged to some Celtic rite – the famous Toros de Guisando. The Río Tiétar rises some distance to the west, and you can make an idyllic detour through the villages of its valley, keeping an eye – and an ear – out for the warblers that frequent this area, including Cetti's melodious, Orphean and Dartford. Other birds found here include quail and stone-curlew, bee-eater, spotless starling, golden oriole and the azure-winged magpie.

Above all, however, the Sierra de Gredos is known as one of the major strongholds of birds of prey in the whole of Spain. Here the rare and endangered Spanish sub-species of the imperial eagle

In the Coto Nacional de Gredos, ibex live above 2,000m (6,500ft) on mountain crags, feeding on tufts of grass and lichens

may be seen soaring on flat, broad wings. It has developed a white crown and mantle that extends across the forewings, making identification simple for a bird of prey. These are denizens of large forested hillsides, although they soar over the mountain tops as easily as the vultures.

Also with a stronghold in Gredos is the equally elusive Bonelli's eagle, a cliff and buttress nester almost as large as the imperial. Here, too, are golden, short-toed and booted eagles, so that all five Spanish eagles may possibly be seen in a single day. The road between Avila and Arenas via the Puerto del Pico is a good starting point, but the remote valleys should also be explored.

Eagles apart, Gredos has both red and black kites, goshawk, chough and, hidden away on its most remote cliffs, the highly elusive black stork. Vastly outnumbered by their white cousin, these are mainly forest birds which cross the straits of Gibraltar to winter in sub-Saharan Africa.

The relatively high rainfall and the mild winters of the Sierra de Gredos have produced a thick cover of Pyrenean oak (*Quercus pyrenaica*) and maritime pine (*Pinus pinaster*) woodlands, especially in the area of Arenas de San Pedro.

One of the more interesting species endemic to western-central Spain is *Echium lusitanicum* ssp *polycaulon*, which has soft, hairy stems and leaves to guard against ultra-violet radiation, and small, pale blue flowers. Similarly, the Spanish lupin (*Lupinus hispanicus*) is known only from Portugal and western Spain; its pale cream flowers turn lilac-pink as they mature.

The highly acidic soils of the granite uplands support a wide range of heathland scrub species, such as gum cistus (*Cistus ladanifer*), poplar-leaved cistus (*C. populifolius*) and *C. psilosepalus*. Leguminous shrubs include the silver-leaved *Genista florida*, and the two broom species, *Cytisus multiflorus* and *C. striatus*; the former has white pea-like flowers, the latter the more characteristic yellow blooms.

In the Scots pine woods at Hoyocasero,

the pale yellow race of the alpine pasque-flower (*Pulsatilla alpina* ssp *apiifolia*) is found. Later on, the colour in these woods is provided by two crimson peony species and the less conspicuous but deliciously scented lily-of-the-valley (*Convallaria majalis*). This forest is most renowned, however, for the huge summer-flowering knapweed, *Centaurea rhaponticoides*, with purple florets extruded from a husk-like calyx; this is its type locality. Also occurring here are St Bernard's lily (*Anthericum liliago*), martagon lily (*Lilium martagon*) and the endemic pink, *Dianthus laricifolius*, which is restricted to central Spain.

The short-toed eagle is a specialist hunter of snakes and lizards

Other interesting plants in the Sierra de Gredos include the highly localized composite *Hispidella hispanica*, with flat yellow flowers with purple hearts, and a star-of-Bethlehem (*Ornithogalum concinnum*) more usually found in Portugal, as well as the blue-and-white columbine *Aquilegia dichroa*, known from mountains in north-west Spain and Portugal. Two species endemic to the Sierra de Gredos range itself are the pale yellow-flowered snapdragon, *Antirrhinum grosii*, and *Reseda gredensis*, with slender white-flowered spikes; the only other known locality for this latter plant is the Sierra de Estrëla in Portugal, again in mountain pastures. One of the more attractive grassland species found here is the storksbill *Erodium carvi-*folium, with flowers of deep crimson, two petals larger than the other three.

The Spanish argus butterfly (*Aricia morronensis navarredondae*) is a race specific to the Sierra de Gredos. Other races in Spain include *ramburi* from the Sierra Nevada; *elsae* from Riaño, south of Picos de Europa; and *ordesiae* from Valle de Ordesa in the Pyrenees. The type locality of *Aricia morronensis morronensis* is in the Sierra de Espuña.

BEFORE YOU GO
Maps: SGE 1:50,000 Nos. 530, 531, 554, 555, 556, 577, 578, 579; IGN 1:200,000 Mapa provincial of Avila; and Sierra de Gredos, Cordillera Central, 1:40,000 (Editorial Alpina).
Guidebooks: *Gredos, por dentro y por fuera* by C. Enríquez (Madrid 1981); *La Sierra de Gredos* by M. A. Adrados et al (Madrid 1981); and *La ruta de Yuste* by E. Sánchez (1981).

GETTING THERE
By car: highway C501 from Madrid to Plasencia takes you to the south side of the Central Massif, to Arenas de
68

San Pedro, by way of the Tiétar valley. To enter the Cordillera from the north, take the Madrid–Avila highway, then highway N110 to El Barco de Avila or C502, and turn right at the junction with C500, towards El Barco de Avila: this is the road to the highest villages of the range, as well as the *parador nacional*.
By rail: there is an extensive service from centres throughout Spain to Avila. From there, take a bus to Arenas de San Pedro or El Barco de Avila (see below).
By bus: a daily service connects Madrid to El Barco

de Avila, with stops at Navarredonda and Navacepeda; it takes about 4hrs to reach the heights of the Sierra de Gredos. The bus leaves from the Estación de Autobuses Sur, in C. Palos de la Frontera, Madrid.
From Avila on Mon–Fri, there is a bus to Arenas de San Pedro taking about 2½hrs; also one to El Barco de Avila, which takes a little under 3hrs and stops at Venta del Obispo and Parador de Gredos. Another bus runs from Avila to El Barco by way of Piedrahita.

WHERE TO STAY

There is a wide choice of accommodation in the Sierra de Gredos, including 2 *paradors* – the 3-star Parador Nacional de Gredos, T: (918) 34 80 48, at Navarredonda de Gredos, also at Jarandilla de la Vera, T: (976) 56 01 17. Many hotels are open only during the summer, however. In the Tiétar valley and the adjoining area there are hotels in La Adrada, Piedralaves, Casavieja, Pedro Bernardo, Mombeltrán, Arenas de San Pedro, Candeleda, Gavilanes and Guisando; and the northern slope, at Navarredonda de Gredos, Navacepeda, El Barco de Avila and at Hoyos del Espino. And there are 5 hotels in Béjar, including the Colón, T: (923) 40 06 50.

Outdoor living: permitted throughout the *coto nacional* and at a number of official sites: details available from the tourist office in Avila.

Refuges: sometimes in semi-ruined condition but still

Hispidella hispanica thrives on the arid mountain slopes of the Gredos

useful in a pinch. The better ones are carefully tended by sponsoring mountaineering clubs: Albergue José Antonio Elola, on the Laguna Grande; property of the Federación Española de Montañismo. Refugio Victory (2,000m/6,560ft), at La Apretura, at the foot of La Mira and Los Galayos. Refugio de La Mira (2,250m/7,380ft), in the meadow of Los Pelaos, 800m (2,624ft) from the peak of La Mira; in poor condition. Refugio-Hermitage of Nuestra Senora de la Nieves, in the Collado Alto, Guijo de Santa Bárbara. The refuge in the Prado de las Pozas is in very poor condition. All the other mountain refuges indicated on existing maps, including the Refugio del Rey in Majasomera, are in ruins.

ACTIVITIES

Walking: this is beautiful country for nature walks, although there are relatively few walking trails. Apart from the old *trocha real* built by Alfonso XIII as a footpath from Candeleda to the Venteadero across the Central Massif, there are only marked trails up the Gargantas de Gredos, del Pinar and de Bohoyo, and one recently opened by ICONA, which starts at El Raso (near Candeleda) and leads up the Garganta de Chilla to the pass known as the Portilla Bermeja, just below Almanzor.

Climbing: good rock climbing. By the village of Guisando, a forest path traverses the Nogal del Barranco and ascends to La Apretura; the refuge here is used as a base-camp for climbing the nearby Galayar, an imposing array of granite 'needles' that rise from a 300m (984ft) base to an average of over 2,200m (7,216ft). Among the more daunting needles are the Punta Amezua, the Aguja

Negra, the Diedro de la María Luisa, the Risco de la Ventana (which offers the best view of the Galayar) and the fiendishly difficult Torreón.

Candeleda, just south of the Central Massif, makes an ideal starting point for those who want to assault the highest peaks from the lowest base. Several paths lead from the village into the mountains: local points of interest include the natural swimming pool formed by the Garganta de Santa María and a Roman bridge, the Puente del Puerto.

The following organizations provide detailed information on many other walks and climbs in the region: Federación Castellana de Montañismo, Apodaca 16, Madrid 4, T: (91) 448 07 24; Federación Española de Montañismo, Alberto Aguilera 3, 4izda, Madrid 15, T: (91) 445 13 82; Real Sociedad Española de Alpinismo Peñalara, Avda José Antonio 27, Madrid 13, T: (91) 222 87 43.

Caves: the Aguila caves are 4km (2½ miles) south of the village of Ramacastañas; guided tours from 10.30–6pm.

Fishing: there is excellent trout fishing in the waters around Arenas de San Pedro; permits can be obtained from the ICONA office at Méndez Vigo 6/8, Avila, T: (918) 22 16 86.

Riding: one way of seeing the Cordillera is on horseback. Several local livery stables offer tours lasting from 4–8hrs.

For information and reservation phone (91) 416 65 92 in Madrid, or the Hostal Almanzor in Navarredonda, T: (918) 34 80 10.

FURTHER INFORMATION

Tourist information: Pl. de la Catedral, Avila, T: (918) 21 13 87. ICONA, Méndez Vigo 6/8, Avila, T: (918) 22 16 86.

Sierra de Guadarrama

A continuation of the Central Cordillera, to the north west of Madrid, famous for its forests and streams and nesting birds of prey

The Sierra de Guadarrama with its uplands of wild herbs lies 56km (35 miles) from Madrid

The Guadarrama appears on topographic maps as a sort of gable above Madrid. It rises from the central plateau and stretches across Castilla for about 100 kilometres (60 miles), from the Puerto de Somosierra to the peak of San Benito, situated between the mighty watercourses of the Tagus (Río Tajo) and Duero, separating Castilla-Neuva and Castilla-Vieja. In summer, coming up from the sweltering Meseta on either side of it, you are greeted by the cool almost alpine air of a range of mountains rich in forests and spring water. Here Felipe v, the first Bourbon monarch of Spain, built the summer palace, whose gardens contain the world's greatest array of fountains and *jets d'eaux*, La Granja de San Ildefonso.

The sierra was known in ancient times as Mons Carpetani – the sentinel and protector of Madrid – although the effect it has on the city's climate is less than beneficial. Northerly gales sweep down from the heights of the Guadarrama in winter causing intense cold, and often bringing snow, while in summer the ridge intercepts the moisture carried by the Atlantic air currents, keeping the city hot and dry. Madrid in August has more than once been likened to a cement oven.

Those areas that are not easily reached by car are still in the ecological golden age. Off on the less accessible peaks, with their forests and fields full of thyme, rock roses and lavender, it is the wild animals that predominate: roe deer, wild boar, foxes, otter, badger – even wolves and eagles uphold their end of the ecological balance.

The Sierra de Guadarrama is subdivided naturally into three separate zones converging at Siete Picos (really seven peaks), between the passes of Navacerrada

and Fuenfría. The western one begins in the Sierra de la Mujer Muerta ('the dead woman') and runs south west toward the Risco San Benito. The eastern region is formed by Cabezas de Hierro ('iron heads'), Cuerda Larga ('long string [of peaks]') and La Najarra, as far as the Morcuera pass. The north-eastern salient

forms a spine of 2,000 metres (6,560 feet) or more between the Valsaín valley, with its Río Eresma, and the valley of the Río Lozoya. These forested peaks create an important watershed, for the Lozoya, Guadalix, Manzanares and Guadarrama rivers are all tributaries of the Tagus, while the Eresma, Pirón, Cega and Duratón, born in the same massif, eventually flow into the Duero.

The highest peak is Peñalara (2,430 metres/7,970 feet), decorated at the summit by a megalith, and the most famous pass, Navacerrada, which links Segovia and Madrid. The general appearance is less rugged than the Sierra de Gredos, but the Guadarrama is almost as high. This mountain chain is renowned for its numerous nesting birds of prey, including black and griffon vultures; golden, booted, Bonelli's and imperial eagles; goshawk; red and black kites; and honey buzzard.

There are extensive Scots pine forests on both the northern and southern slopes, with the shrub layer typically comprising *Genista florida* and another legume, *Adenocarpus telonensis*, as well as juniper and tree heather. The pine forests abound with herbs revelling in the more humid microclimate in the shade of the trees, and include three toadflax species (*Linaria nivea*, *L. incarnata*, and *L. triornithophora*), a cut-leaved ragwort (*Senecio adonidifolius*), Spanish bluebells (*Endymion hispanicus*), woodrushes, bedstraws, and the sweet-scented, spherical pink flowerheads of a mountain valerian (*Valeriana tuberosa*). The dry, acid soils above the forest level are a stronghold of Pyrenean broom (*Cytisus purgans*).

There are no villages within the sierra: except for the recently built ski resorts, the human settlements were all, for good reason, built in the peripheral valleys. It seems that only hermits and bandits could cope with the rigours of Guadarrama, but they certainly made the most of it.

Of course, many of the most spectacular views of the sierra can be enjoyed without any of the muscular exertions that can make the going tough. But the motorized visitor to these hills would be missing the hard-won hiker's pleasure afforded by this rugged range of mountains.

BEFORE YOU GO

Maps: SGE 1:50,000 Nos. 483, 484, 485, 486, 507, 508, 509, 511, 532 and 533; IGN 1:200,000 Mapas provinciales of Madrid and Segovia; and Sierra de Guadarrama, Mapa montañero 1:50,000 by Cayetano Enríquez de Salamanca.

Guidebooks: *Guía del Guadarrama* (Ministerio de Transportes, Madrid); *Por la Sierra de Guadarrama* by C. Enríquez de Salamanca (Madrid, 1981); and *Guadarrama, Paraíso Olvidado* by J. Benítez and M. Cortés (Madrid, 1984).

GETTING THERE

By car: the southern slope of the Guadarrama is just 50km (31 miles) from Madrid, from where there are 2 main highways: A6 Madrid–León, turning north at N601 toward Navacerrada; and C607, which heads almost due north from Madrid before turning west towards Navacerrada. The latter also affords access to Manzanares el Real and Miraflores de la Sierra, then to Rascafría via the Puerto de la Morcuera. From Segovia the heart of the Sierra can be approached on N601, which follows the valley of Valsaín to the Puerto de Navacerrada.

By rail: Cercedilla, the village just below the pass of Navacerrada and the Siete Picos, is a stop on the Madrid–Segovia line. From there, a funicular ascends to the Puerto de Cotos, with a stop at Navacerrada; this is a most beautiful train ride.

WHERE TO STAY

Only the Navacerrada ski resort offers hotel accommodation: at the 3-star Venta Arias, T: (91) 852 11 00, and the 1-star Hotel Pasadoiro, T: (91) 856 02 97; they are open all year. The nearby villages of Navacerrada and Guadarrama, however, offer a wide choice of accommodation. There are also hotels in Guadarrama, Rascafría, Buitrago de Lozoya and Cercedilla.

Outdoor living: there is a camping ground just out of Segovia on the road to La Granja.

Refuges: a whole series of

The imperial eagle builds its bulky nest in tall, often isolated trees

refuges are scattered through the Sierra: Albergue del Club Alpino Español, A. de la R.S.E.A. Peñalara, A. del Club Alpino Guadarrama, A. 'Dos Castillas', A. 'Cumbres' and Residencia José Antonio. Are all near Navacerrada at about 1,800m (6,000ft). The Albergue Coppel (1,870m/ 6,133ft) is located at Puerto de Cotos, the Refugio Zabala (2,100m/6,888ft) near the Laguna de Peñalara, the Refugio de Navafría in the Puerto de Navafría, and the Refugio Diego de Ordás in the Valdesquí.

ACTIVITIES
Walking/climbing: the Valle de la Acebada, with its streams and pine forests, offers some beautiful walks. The route along the ridge of the Sierra de Guadarrama runs from Cercedilla to Estación del Espinar over 5 major summits offering stunning views. Taking approximately 9hrs 1-way, you can end up at a train station on the Segovia–Madrid line.
Fishing: the Río Angostura is a well-known trout stream. For more detailed information regarding fishing permits, etc., contact the tourist office in Madrid.
Historic trails: the ancient trail from Miraflores de la Sierra, on the southern slope of the range, to the Monasterio El Paular ('the poplar') in the valley is a 5hr hike used for centuries by the Cartusian monks for whom Juan I built the first Chartreuse in Spain. The monastery stood in ruins for the better part of 2 centuries but has now been meticulously restored as a *parador nacional* where you can have sherry and biscuits on the patio after arriving, footsore but still smelling of wild flowers, from the 1,800-m (5,900-ft)

Puerto de la Morcuera.
Another historic hiking route crosses the Malagosto (or Reventón) pass which, in the Middle Ages, constituted the main avenue of communication between the 2 Castillas, Castilla-Neuva and Castilla-Vieja..

FURTHER INFORMATION
Tourist information: C. Floridablanca, El Escorial, T: (91) 896 07 09; Pl. Mayor, Segovia, T: (911) 43 03 28; Torre de Madrid, Pl. de España, Madrid, T: (91) 241 23 25. ICONA, Pl. de Guevara 1, Segovia, T: (911) 41 25 95; and General Sanjurjo 47, Madrid 1, T: (91) 442 05 00.

La Cuenca Alta del Manzanares

Parque natural *(4,000ha/ 9,885 acres)*

La Cuenca Alta del Manzanares contains an amazing range of limestone mountains that have been gradually eroded into a breathtaking variety of abstract shapes. If the park were located deep in rural Spain it would probably be regarded as a geological wonderland – which it is – but since the Pedriza del Manzanares (as it is generally known) lies only 50km (31 miles) from Madrid it has become a popular weekend excursion area for *madrileños* who seem quite unaware that this is more than just a range of mountains.
Bounded by the Sierra de los Porrones, the peak known as La Maliciosa and the range called La Cuerda Larga, the

parque natural divides into 2 distinctive zones: the Pedriza Anterior and the Circo Posterior, which are separated by the hills known as the Collado de la Dehesilla and the Hoya Calderón. Vegetation is sparse, and some areas could be used as backdrops for a film on lunar life. On the lower slopes grow holm and dwarfed holm oaks; in the higher reaches, juniper, holly and the newly planted pines of the state forestry service, notably in the Sierra de los Porrones and the Cabezas de Hierro.
But it is the bare rocks that steal the show from the flora and fauna, such as it is. The Yelmo, for example, is a huge mass of bare-scrubbed limestone in the shape of a helmet (or, for that matter, a bald pate) which rises straight into the air for 150m (500ft); on a clear day it can be seen from the northern outskirts of Madrid. Or there is the crumpled escarpment known as Las Buitreras ('the vultures' roost'), whose highest caves and fissures are stained white with the *guano* of the many pairs of griffon vultures that build their nests in them. The whole massif is shot through with cracks, cavities and caves, with giant boulders poised dramatically as if to crash into the abyss at any moment, and limestone 'statues' resembling Rodin's 'Balzac' or even the heroic entanglements of Gustav Vigeland.
The Río Manzanares snakes through the adjoining valleys, blithely unaware that it has been responsible for creating one of the world's great outdoor art galleries. It receives help from tributary streams such as the Garganta, Cuervo, Majadilla and Hoya Calderón. Once the Manzanares has united all these waters, it enters the

Garganta de la Camorza, flows past the Peña Sacra, rushes through the village of Manzanares and forms an artificial lake at the Embalse de Santillana.

Many steep paths lead upward through the rocks from the Arroyo de la Dehesilla, and if you follow one of them to the heights of La Pedriza you encounter dozens of strangely contorted rock formations. Fallen rocks sometimes block the way, and occasionally there are bramble thickets to be circumvented, but small meadows also make their appearance; in the springtime they are covered with wild flowers such as irises and narcissi.

Before you go *Maps:* SGE 1:50,000 Nos. 508 and 509; IGN 1:200,000 Mapa provincial of Madrid.
Getting there *By car:* the simplest way to get there from Madrid is on the road to Colmenar Viejo, continuing on to Manzanares; 1km (½ mile) past the village an access road leads to the control post at the gates of La Pedriza.
By bus: there is a regular service from Madrid to the village, but no public transport to the gates of the park, however.
Where to stay: there is 1 hotel in Manzanares el Real – El Tranco, T: (91) 853 00 63 – and an old hermitage on the Peña Sacra.
Outdoor living: permitted only in the special camping zone near the Embalse de Santillana.
Refuges: there is a small refuge within the park, beyond the Canto Cochino.
Activities *Walking/climbing:* until recently it was quite difficult to get to the heart of La Pedriza; the only access was an unpaved track that follows the Río Manzanares and leads up to the hermitage

on the Peña Sacra, and a footpath that leads through the Garganta Camorza to the Pradera de los Lobos ('meadow of wolves') and Canto Cochino.

Nowadays you can drive to the Canto Cochino in a matter of minutes, thanks to the paved road that crosses the Collado de Quebrantaherraduras ('the horseshoe-breakers' pass'). On the far side of this settlement are paths that lead beyond civilisation, to the Peña Siro, the imposing peaks of El Pájaro ('the bird'), Las Buiteras and El Cocodrilo ('the crocodile'); in the further distance lies the summit of Las Torres ('the towers').

For climbing information contact the Real Sociedad Española de Alpinismo Peñalara, Avda José Antonio 27, Madrid 13, T: (91) 222 87 43.
Further information: avoid visiting the park at weekends and fiestas, when the number of admissions is limited by the park wardens.

Sierra de Ayllón

30km (19 miles) south of Ayllón, comprising the parque natural of Hayedo de Tejera Negra

The Sierra de Ayllón begins a long way south of the medieval walled city it is named after, which is one of the historic showplaces of the province of Segovia. Much of the Sierra, in fact, lies in the province of Guadalajara, and large tracts of land in the Sierra used to belong to the feudal rulers of Ayllón, 30km

(19 miles) to the north.

Perhaps the most convenient base for a reconaissance tour of this still unspoiled and half-forgotten Sierra is the village of Galve de Sorbe, a sleepy community of shepherds and wheat farmers at the eastern edge of the Sierra de Ayllón. The village and its ruined hilltop castle belong to Guadalajara – and also to another world. Architecturally speaking it is still in the Middle Ages, and life goes on as it did before the machine age.

You can walk for miles into the open countryside, through flowering meadows and into forests that ascend the adjoining hills. These are low, and the highest point in the range is the Pico de Ocejón (2,056m/6,743ft).

From the naturalist's point of view, the most important part of the Sierra is the Hayedo de Tejera Negra, a *parque natural* made up of a 1,391-ha (3,440-acre) beech forest. The park lies within the township of Cantalojas and includes portions of the Sorbe river valley and the valley of the Río Lillas. Its northern limit is the Pico de la Buitrera ('the vulture's peak'), which is just over 2,000m (6,560ft) above sea level. The beeches, however, are confined to the cooler, wetter slopes of the Sierra, between 1,300–1,800m (4,260–5,900ft). Elsewhere in the same range are 2 other significant stands of beech trees – the Hayedo de Puerto de la Quesera and the Hayedo de Montejo.
Before you go *Maps:* SGE 1:50,000 Nos. 432 and 459; IGN 1:200,000 Mapas provinciales of Segovia and Guadalajara.
Guidebooks: Guía del Macizo de Ayllón by Miguel Angel López Miguel (Madrid, 1982).
Getting there *By car:*

The Sierra de la Demanda rises above the valley of the stately Río Najerilla in the wine region of Ríoja

Cantalojas, the village nearest the Hayedo de Tejera Negra, is just south of highway C114.

Within the park, an unpaved forest road leads from Cantalojas to the *parque natural*, 12km (7½ miles) from the village, though it may be impassable after heavy rains or snows.

By bus: there is a daily service to Guadalajara and Madrid; the bus stops at every small village.

Where to stay: 2 hotels are near the park: in Cantalojas – Hayedo de Tejera Negra, T: (911) 30 30 28; and in Galve de Sorbe (10km/6¼ miles to the east) – Nuestra Señora del Pinar, T: (911) 30 30 24.

Further information *Tourist information:* Guadalajara, T: (911) 22 19 00; Ayuntamiento, Cantalojas, T: (911) 30 30 78. ICONA, C. Marqués Villaverde 2, Guadalajara, T: (911) 22 33 04.

At night the gates to the park are kept locked.

Sierra de la Demanda

Sierra running east-west with mountains rising to 2,000m (6,500ft)

La Rioja has the best wine and some of the most magical places in Spain. Driving south from Nájera, where the remains of some medieval kings of Navarra lie in a church (equipped with its own cave), I stopped off to see another historic cave, on a hillside in the Cerro de San Lorenzo, where the C6th saint, San Millán de la Congolla, passed 40 years saying prayers and performing miracles. His cave, known as the Suso monastery, holds his empty sarcophagus, the dry bones of some monks, and a row of magnificent Moorish arches.

A little further on the rolling hills of grape and wheat suddenly come to a stop, and a line of peaks a thousand metres (3,200ft) higher than the hills rears up and blocks the way. This is the Sierra de la Demanda, whose 2,000m (6,560ft) mountains are as imposing as they are unexpected. You pass 2 villages that cling to the slopes of the outermost peaks in the range, then the road plunges into a shadowy wood of birches, beeches, poplars and pine. For 15km (9 miles) you won't meet a soul along this forest track, which has the Pancrudos mountain looming

75

over it: the track leads to the most important stand of beech trees in the province of La Rioja. If you wanted to get lost, you could hardly find a wilder and less inhabited spot in the Iberian peninsula.

The Sierra de la Demanda runs from east to west: San Lorenzo (2,265m/7,420ft) is the highest peak in La Rioja, and San Millán (2,131m/ 6,980ft), the highest mountain in the neighbouring province of Burgos. This is a very old range – over 500 million years – and for this reason the peaks are more rounded than usual.

Ideally, this is a region for quiet hikes and for wandering from village to village through unbroken forests. Toward the east the forests thin out and give way to *matorral*, but even the scrub country contains many points of interest to the naturalist. The road along the Río Najerilla towards Anguiano, for instance, is a tangle of broad-leaved shrubs over the shales of the Sierra. The lilac-striped flowers of the pale toadflax (*Linaria repens*) resemble miniature rabbits' heads, although the stems that bear them can reach up to a metre (3 feet) in height. The Lusitanian pink (*Dianthus*

lusitanus) forms cushions of grey and pink beneath the silver-yellow-flowered bushes of *Genista florida*.

At Enciso, just beyond the eastern edge of the Reserva de Cameros, you can follow in the footsteps of the dinosaurs: the so-called Ruta de los Dinosaurios exhibits a series of dinosaur tracks made about 130 million years ago.

Before you go: *Maps:* SGE 1:50,000 Nos. 200, 201 and 239; SGE 1:150,000 Mapa provincial of La Rioja; SGE 1:200,000 Mapa provincial of Burgos; and IGN 1:50,000 Nos 202, 240 and 277.

Guidebooks: Las Sierras de la Demanda y de Neila by Leopoldo Valdivielso Gómez (Federación Española de Montañismo, Madrid, 1982).

Getting there *By car:* 2 highways cross the Sierra de la Demanda from north to south. From the N120 (Logroño–Burgos) you can either turn south at Nájera on C113, which follows the valley of the Najerilla to Tierra de Cameros or turn off N120 at Santo Domingo de la Calzada, and follow a secondary road along the Oja river valley to Ezcaray and the peak of San Lorenzo, which lies at the heart of the Sierra. Another

alternative is the Logroño–Soria highway, which takes you to Sierra de Cameros through the Iregua valley.

By bus: a regular service connects Logroño to all of the villages in the region. For Valle del Iregua information, T: (941) 23 71 68; for Valle del Oja, including Ezcaray and San Lorenzo, T: (941) 24 35 72 and 22 70 45; for San Millán, T: (941) 22 42 78; and for Valle del Leza, T: (941) 23 81 49 and 22 26 53.

Where to stay: Santo Domingo de la Calzada has a 3-star *parador nacional*, T: (941) 34 03 00. In Excaray there is a hotel and 4 hostels. The Monasterio de Valvanera, near Anguiano, offers accommodation in its 2-star Hostal Abadía de Valvanera, T: (941) 37 70 44.

Activities *Walking:* the Sierra de la Demanda is a very pretty area with many walks, ranging from the gentle to the strenuous. For information, ask at the tourist offices in Burgos or Logroño.

Further information *Tourist information:* Pl. de Alonso Martínez 7, Burgos, T: (947) 20 18 46; Miguel Villanueva 10, Logroño (941) 25 54 97. ICONA, Belchite 2–1, Logroño, T: (941) 23 66 00.

Sierra de Peña de Francia

The isolated western edge of the Central Cordillera which stretches east from Béjar to Cuidad Rodrigo

These so-called 'French' mountains are the westernmost segment of the Spanish central system (the other four parts

are Ayllón, Guadarrama, Gredos and Béjar). Portugal lies 50 kilometres (31 miles) to the west, France 600 kilometres (370 miles) to the north-east. The range is called the Sierra de Peña de Francia because in the eleventh century, after the Christian reconquest, it was repopulated with settlers from France. This rather attenuated French connection is recalled in such place names as Río Francia, Soto de Francia, and Peña de Francia.

The Sierra de Peña de Francia is off the beaten track in many respects: agricultural development was slow to arrive in this obscure corner of Spain, and for centuries it remained an isolated and rather mysterious region of impenetrable forests and small peasant villages. Today, however, it offers an extraordinary mixture of nature and folklore: vast forest reserves, mountain pastures, villages with half-timbered medieval houses, Stone Age sites decorated with cave paintings, and hunting reserves where deer, wild boar and small game are abundant.

Between Salamanca and the inner core of the sierra rises an outer range of mountains, of which the highest is Pico Cervero (1,463 metres/4,800 feet). Here meadows and peaks alternate with dense forests like that of La Honfría, in the *municipio* of Linares de Ríofrío, which is traversed only by footpaths and an unpaved forest road. On the southern slope the underbrush is so thick as to make the forests of Las Quilanas almost impassable; they are prime examples of Iberian vegetation in an untouched state of nature. This is the watershed of the Río Quilana, which flows into the Alagón, one of the many rivers in this region which are tributaries of the River Tagus (Río Tajo).

At 1,723 metres (5,650 feet) the Peña de Francia is the highest peak in the sierra, looming above the rest like a giant pyramid and affording superb views in every direction.

Much of the peak is bare granite, here and there sprouting a deep yellow rock daffodil (*Narcissus rupicola*), but the lower slopes are covered with the forests of oak,

The Spanish lynx or pardel hunts at dusk, lying in ambush or stalking its prey, mainly rabbits

poplar and fern that are characteristic of the zone. The surrounding valleys are carpeted in yellow and purple flowers in late spring. Past the memorable medieval village of La Alberca begins the valley of Las Batuecas, a *reserva nacional* of 20,976 hectares (51,832 acres). Carmelite nuns chose this remote spot for one of their convents in 1599. Today, their erstwhile retreat, San José de Batuecas, is a hermitage for Carmelite monks (who do not admit visitors either). It is said that there are 18 hermitages scattered throughout the mountains, and 24 in the valley, but every one that I've ever come across is in ruins. There are wolves and lynx deep in the reserve, as well as roe deer and wild boar, the imperial eagle and black vultures.

BEFORE YOU GO
Maps: SGE 1:50,000 Nos. 526, 527, 551 and 552; and IGN 1:200,000 Mapa provincial of Salamanca.
Guidebooks: *La Alberca, monumento nacional* by J M. Cervantes (1981), and *La Casa Albercana* by L. González (Salamanca, 1982).

GETTING THERE
By car: from the north, take highway N620, Salamanca– Ciudad Rodrigo, turning south on C525 in the direction of

Tamames, the first village in the Sierra. The eastern approach, from Béjar, is via highway C515 to San Esteban de la Sierra and Sequeros, which brings you to the centre of the Sierra; or you can turn off on C512 to Linares de Ríofrío, in the north east.
By bus: on weekdays a daily bus connects Salamanca to La Alberca – the trip takes 1½hrs; for information, contact the Estación de Autobuses, Avda Filiberto Villalobos 79, in Salamanca.

WHERE TO STAY
In La Alberca, the 2-star Las Batuecas, T: (923) 43 70 09; and the 1-star París, T: (923) 43 70 56. Cepeda has San Marcos, T: (923) 43 22 32; Condado de Miranda, T: (923) 43 20 26, is in Miranda del Castañar; and Los Alamos, T: (923) 43 75 22, is in Sequeros.

FURTHER INFORMATION
Tourist information: Arco de las Amayuelas 6, Cuidad Rodrigo, T: (923) 46 05 61; in Béjar: Pl. Mayor.

Camino de Santiago

Clumps of broom flower enhance a fortress of rock in the valley of Las Batuecas

Medieval pilgrims' route that wends its way along the northern boundaries of the Meseta to Santiago de Compostela in Galicia

The way from Roncesvalles, in the Pyrenees, to Santiago de Compostela in distant Galicia, is a matter of some 800 kilometres (500 miles). In the Middle Ages it was one of the great pilgrimage routes, which many people covered on foot and the most pious on their knees. For centuries there were miracles and apparitions to be seen at every turn of the road

to Santiago: you could meet angels, beggars, kings and status-seekers – the Plantagenet king Edward I on horseback, St Francis of Assisi walking barefoot, and a certain Flemish wayfarer who is reputed to have carried a mermaid around with him, in a tub.

You don't meet many pilgrims of the old-fashioned sort on the Camino de Santiago nowadays, but more than half a million people travel along the route each year. And it is still one of the most beautiful journeys in Europe. The miracle is that so little seems to have changed since the Middle Ages; that you can still cover large parts of the route on unpaved tracks leading through fields and forests – or occasionally on paved section of road that were built by the Romans to facilitate the movement of their legions through the endless expanse of their Iberian colony. The road enters Spain from France in the high Pyrenees and winds across unforgettable countryside to the western edge of the continent. According to the old chronicles, this was where the bones of the apostle James were discovered early in the ninth century, by a local bishop who was amazed to see bright light emanating from the ground and a star pointing to the spot where the saint lay buried.

When news of the saint's whereabouts reached the rest of Europe, thousands of devout pilgrims began converging on the cathedral that was built over his tomb – after Rome, the holiest place in medieval Europe. It was a spot so sacred, it was 'honoured by miracles never ceasing, and with a plenty of candles from Heaven that burn day and night, and godly Angels who serve without end'. At the beginning of the

Many valleys of the Sierra de la Demanda are planted with mixed woodland, the finest growing here in the Reserva de Cameros

eleventh century a progressive-minded king of Navarra built a new road from the French border – Roncesvalles to Pamplona, Logroño, Burgos, León and points west. Several competing monastic orders, notably the Benedictines of Cluny, established hospices and priories along this 'French road'. Some of their more elaborate hospices had facilities for a thousand guests, and traffic along the Camino reached truly formidable proportions, especially during the summer months when the pilgrim season was at its height and the road was jammed with the devout (and more than a few sensation seekers, I do not hesitate to add).

They came, led by their dukes and bishops, from France, Britain and Germany; from Italy, the Lowlands and the Balkans. Inevitably there were a certain number of camp followers 'having neither office nor profession', and these were accused of bringing the pox to Santiago. Yet despite the many hazards it was considered imperative to make the journey. As Dante puts it in *La Vita Nuova*, 'He is no pilgrim who does not make his way to the tomb of St James and return therefrom.'

In the 1960s I travelled the entire length of the Camino, partly by car and frequently on foot, and was enchanted by this slow intensive way of getting to know the northern third of the Iberian peninsula. I travelled with a portable tape-recorder, taking down vestiges of the folk music of this incredibly musical country. Indeed, pockets of ancient music had survived along the more remote stretches of the road, and I was lucky enough to hear peasants in the fields singing the old reaping and threshing songs. A Castilian wheat farmer in his 70s sang an old harvesting song that must have been new in Columbus's day. 'The land is poor and the crop is bad and we have nothing to sing about,' his daughter complained, but the old man went on singing anyway, an endless chant about sailors and kings and how we shall all be equal in the grave.

The Camino of today entails crossing many major urban centres, but some of the open country between is absolutely magnificent. The road descends from the hills of Navarra and crosses the plains of Castilla-León, then negotiates the hill country of Galicia before entering the city of Santiago – a Renaissance town with wall-to-wall streets and a twelfth-century cathedral that has a Baroque façade. Such striking contrasts are commonplace all along the pilgrims' way.

The pilgrims' road combines glimpses of a vanished medieval way of life, with long rambles through the great outdoors. The route itself is not fixed and offers many alternatives and detours, such as the one to the monastery of Santo Domingo de Silos, for example, which takes you about 50 kilometres (31 miles) south of the 'standard' Camino. As a way of discovering the heartbeat of this astonishing land, there is no more satisfying means than to travel on foot along a portion, if not all, of the Pilgrim's way, the historic Camino de Santiago.

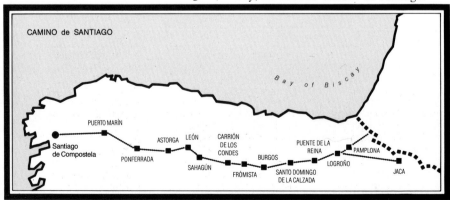

CAMINO de SANTIAGO

Bay of Biscay

Santiago de Compostela · PUERTO MARÍN · ASTORGA · LEÓN · CARRIÓN DE LOS CONDES · PUENTE DE LA REINA · PAMPLONA · JACA · PONFERRADA · SAHAGÚN · FRÓMISTA · BURGOS · LOGROÑO · SANTO DOMINGO DE LA CALZADA

BEFORE YOU GO

Maps: Ministerio de Obras Públicas y Urbanismo: España, Mapa Official de Carreteras, 1:400,000; and Firestone España/Portugal 1:1,1000,000.

Guidebooks: P. Barret and J. N. Gurgand, *La Aventura del Camino de Santiago* (Vigo, 1982); Eusebio Goicoechea Arrondo, *El Camino de Santiago* (Madrid, 1982); Walter Starkie, *The Road to Santiago: Pilgrims of St James* (London, 1957); and (Codex Calixtinus) *Ruta de Santiago* with notes by Enrique Barco Teruel and drawings by Juan Commerleran (Barcelona, 1965).

GETTING THERE

Traditionally there were 4 main points of departure in France for the Camino de Santiago: Paris, Vezelay, Le Puy and Arles. Pilgrims from the 3 northern cities entered Spain via Roncesvalles; those from Arles travelled by way of Toulouse, Auch and Oloron; entered Spain via the pass of Somport and Canfranc; descended the Pyrenees to Jaca; and joined the main route of the Camino at Puente la Reina, 24 km (15 miles) west of Pamplona, the first major town on the northern route. The other main points of the road are Logroño, Santo Domingo de la Calzada, Burgos, Frómista, Carrión de los Condes, Sahagún, León, Astorga, Ponferrada, Puerto Marín and finally, Santiago de Compostela.

By air: modern airborne pilgrims can, of course, fly directly to Santiago, which is the westernmost airport of Iberia's peninsula network, or they could begin the walking tour from either end of the Camino. It hardly matters which way you are headed – except that the historical sense of the thing is lost if you start at the destination!

By sea: ferries to Santander offer a convenient entrance to the Camino; Santander is 156km (97 miles) from Burgos.

By car: you can still drive along the ancient routes from France using the Roncesvalles or Somport passes as crossing points. All the towns and villages along the Camino have road signs and historical markers pointing the way to significant monuments associated with its history; this is the one route in Spain where it is impossible to lose your way.

By rail: RENFE's railway network intersects with the Camino at several points. From Madrid, 4 trains a day (3 from Chamartín, 1 from Atocha station) make the Navarre run – 2 to Pamplona, 2 to Logroño; there are 9 trains a day from Madrid (Chamartín) to Burgos. And from P. Pío Station, Madrid, there are 2 fast trains daily to Santiago de Compostela.

By bus: a number of public and private buses connect the major cities of the Camino, so that you could travel the whole route by relays of buses, stopping off in small towns and villages as well as terminal points such as Logroño, Burgos or León. Travel agencies in Madrid and Barcelona also offer charter sightseeing and/or pilgrimage buses that cover part of the road to Santiago.

WHERE TO STAY

There is ample accommodation along the Camino; contact the relevant tourist office (see below) for listings. Pamplona has 6 hotels, 9 hostels and 4 pensions; Burgos has at least twice this number. Logroño is also well endowed, while the nearby Santo Domingo de la Calzada has a *parador nacional*, T: (941) 34 03 00 and 2 hostels. At Fromista there is a pension and a hostel; at Carrión de los Condes 3 pensions.

Sahagún, in the Castilla-León, has 2 hostels – as do Astorga and Ponferrada – and several hotels, while León, with its 5-star San Marcos Hotel and a large number of other hotels, hostels and pensions, offers the full gamut of choice. At Puerto Marín there is a *parador nacional*, T: (982) 54 50 25. Finally, Santiago offers a wide range of accommodation to suit every pocketbook.

FURTHER INFORMATION

Burgos: Paseo del Espolón 1, T: (947) 20 18 46.
Canfranc: Avda de Fernando el Católico 3, T: (974) 37 31 41.
La Coruña: Darsena de la Marina, T: (981) 22 18 22.
Irún: Estación del Norte, T: (943) 61 15 24; and Puente de Santiago, T: (943) 61 22 22.
Jaca: Pl. de Calvo Sotelo, T: (974) 36 00 98.
León: Pl. de la Catedral 4, T: (987) 21 10 83.
Logroño: Miguel Villanueva 10 (Shopping Arcade), T: (941) 21 54 97.
Lugo: Pl. de España 27, T: (982) 21 13 61.
Oviedo: Cabo Novál 5, T: (985) 21 33 85.
Pamplona: Duque de Ahumada 3, T: (948) 21 12 87.
Port-Bou: Estación Internacional, T: (972) 25 00 81.
Sangüesa: Mercado 2, T: (948) 87 03 39.
Santiago de Compostela: Rúa del Villar 43, T: (981) 58 11 32.
Tuy: Customs Post, T: (986) 252.
Viana: Apr–Sep, T: (988) 64 51 02.

CHAPTER 4

South Meseta

'**S**o, like a good knight, he decided to add the name of his country to his own and call himself Don Quixote de la Mancha.'

The adventures of Don Quixote hold the same symbolic significance for the southern Meseta as the pilgrims' road has for the northern. La Mancha – originally Al Mansha, 'the dry land' or 'the wilderness' – was the Moorish name for the vast, parched plain that stretches from the mountains of Toledo to the Sierra Morena. Modern maps indicate it as a rather vague stretch of territory south of Madrid and east of Ciudad Real. Historically, it never was a province or any other formal territorial unit, but under the new Spanish constitution the five provinces of Cuenca, Ciudad Real, Toledo, Guadalajara and Albacete have come together as the autonomous region of Castilla-La Mancha, and this is the main administrative component of the great topographical region known as the south Meseta.

Cervantes chose La Mancha as the setting for his masterpiece not only because he knew it very well personally but because it was then a backward peasant region whose very name was calculated to bring a smile to the lips of his sophisticated urban readers. But the twentieth-century La Mancha is very different from the seventeenth-century one, for what was once a wilderness has become one of the great wheat-growing and wine-making regions of Spain, even though there are hardly any cities to speak of, only some farm villages and a scattering of six or

The plains of La Mancha stretch to the horizon beyond this group of olive trees on the flat tableland of the south Meseta

seven market towns. Although the highway south from Madrid traverses it, tourists rarely bother to stop here as they race through Don Quixote's country on the way through to Jaén in Andalucía.

Needless to say, the true Manchegan would not trade the monotonous landscape for all the hanging gardens of Granada. But as readers of Cervantes are aware, the land is not invariably flat. Here and there the Meseta is broken by a chance row of hills, occasionally topped by the famous windmills that Don Quixote mistook for giants. Except for *literati,* however, it doesn't draw many visitors.

The windmills of La Mancha are not an ancient and immutable part of the landscape. The first ones had been introduced to Spain from the low countries in the 1570s, about 20 years before Cervantes began writing his book, and they represented a great leap forward for Spanish technology. When Don Quixote charged the windmills he was, therefore, doing battle with the menace of the machine.

Of the hundreds of windmills built in La Mancha during the sixteenth and seventeenth centuries, only a handful are still in existence, most near the town of Campo de Criptana, where Quixote's encounter is supposed to have taken place. Ever since they stopped turning at the end of last century they have served a purely decorative purpose. If you want to see a far more authentic collection of windmills, take the road that runs northwest from Campo de Criptana to the town of Consuegra in the province of Toledo.

Three or four really first-rate wines are produced in the vineyards of the southern Meseta. A bottle of Valdepeñas blanco, lightly chilled by being hung in a well, is a proven antidote to the mid-afternoon heat that melts the marrow in your bones.

'"I'll bet," said Sancho, "that before long there won't be a wineshop or a tavern, an inn or a barber's shop, where the history of our exploits won't be painted up."'

The tourist ministry has gone one better by erecting a monument to Sancho and Quixote in every town and village even remotely connected with their wanderings. There is the tavern of Don Quixote, the inn of Sancho Panza and the wineshop of Dulcinea. In the village of El Toboso the inhabitants take great pride in showing you their '*casa de Dulcinea*', despite the fact that Cervantes' Dulcinea passes through his book as the great unattainable ideal, the eternal feminine mirage. It is, however, a perfectly good excuse for going to see the village which, though it has only one windmill, is one of the most beautiful in La Mancha.

By following in the footsteps of the ingenious Spanish gentleman, you can wander through some of the wilder and more forgotten landscapes of the south Meseta. But, as elsewhere in Spain, the real wilderness begins where the mountains commence, at the periphery of the plains and valleys. In the west, the Parque Natural de Monfragüe straddles the banks of the now dammed Tagus (Tajo) as it flows between two mountain ranges, the Sierra de Gredos and the north slope of the Sierra de Guadalupe, before commencing its descent through Portugal to the Atlantic. In the east there is the Parque Natural del Alto Tajo, which embraces the river's swift-flowing headwaters in Guadalajara province. Further to the south the Serranía de Cuenca forms part of the Meseta's eastern margin: it is a moutain range full of mineral springs and the beginnings of streams such as the Río Cuervo, which tumbles over mossy banks and small caves before beginning its journey to the Guadiela and the Tagus.

By contrast, the nearby Montes Universales are more like a Jules Verne conception of the mountains of Mars or Jupiter; although the Tagus rises here (in the form of a barely discernable trickle), these are noticeably dry mountains often devoid of topsoil. Thanks to the absence of human habitation, however, it is a region that provides a favourable habitat for eagles, vultures, kites and falcons. The neighbouring Sierra de Albarracin is also full of wild places and mountain villages almost high enough to have you panting for oxygen; this was once part of a tiny Arab kingdom and it still strikes me as a world apart. Unfortunately, it is not enough for a nature reserve to be off the beaten track in order for it to survive; Las Tablas de Daimiel, a wetland ecosystem considered important enough to qualify as the one national park in the south Meseta, is in danger of drying up owing to agricultural depletion of the underground waters that used to fill these lakes and marshes to overflowing. Which only goes to prove that nowadays even the wilderness has to be managed.

GETTING THERE

By air: Madrid is well served by flights to Europe and the rest of the world. There are regional airports at Seville, Granada, Murcia, Alicante and Valencia, all part of Iberia's domestic network, except Murcia which is serviced mainly by Aviaco airlines.

By car: the motorway system from Madrid to points south is still in the making. Superhighway E25 takes you speedily to Aranjuez and, a little further on, to Ocaña, and there are also some short segments of 4-lane motorway on E4, towards Navalcarnero, and E101, on the way to Tarancón.

The rest of the south Meseta's main roads are all 2-lane highways, and are apt to have heavy traffic: it is better to take minor roads, as you will undoubtedly end up at your destination much more quickly.

A few of the high mountain passes in the Serranía de Cuenca area are sometimes snowed-in during the winter: for information about road conditions, phone Madrid (91) 254 28 00 or 254 50 05 for round-the-clock taped announcements. Special road information operators can be reached at (91) 253 16 00 from 8.30am–8.30pm in winter and till 10pm in the summer months.

By rail: RENFE's lines to the south are less useful to the explorers of the Meseta than the northern ones, but a good part of the region can be covered by rail. From Madrid, there are frequent trains to Cuenca (on the Valencia line), to Albacete (on the Alicante line), to Ciudad Real, and to Cáceres and Badajoz (on the Extremadura line). There is also a useful express train south from Barcelona–Ciudad Real–Mérida–Badajoz.

For nationwide RENFE reservations, call (91) 429 82 28, open 9am–9pm daily, year round.

By bus: there are long-distance buses from Madrid to the major cities of the southern Meseta, and many local bus lines providing service to the villages and towns of the region. Schedules vary with the seasons; for up-to-date information, call the Estación de Autobuses located in Madrid, T: (91) 46 84 00.

WHERE TO STAY

The *paradores nacionales* of the south Meseta are particularly welcome because the region is not overly well supplied with accommodation and in many instances the *parador* is the only good hotel around.

For detailed lists of accommodation, contact the local tourist information offices (see below for addresses and telephone nos.).

ACTIVITIES

Mountaineering clubs: Federación Castellana de Montañismo, Apodaca 16, Madrid 4, T: (91) 448 07 24. The national mountaineering federation has its offices in Madrid: Federación Española de Montañismo (FEM), Alberto Aguilera 3–4° izda, Madrid 15, T: (91) 445 13 82.

Guided walks/adventure holiday: Club de Viatjers, Rodríguez San Pedro 2, Madrid 15, T: (91) 445 11 45 and 445 59 62.

FURTHER INFORMATION

Albacete (967): tourist offices, C. Virrey Morcillo 1, T: 21 56 11; and C. Teodoro Camino 2, T: 21 25 68 and 21 19 38. Red Cross, T: 22 50 02. Highway information, Tinte 35, T: 21 38 87.

Aranjuez (910): tourist office, Pl. de Santiago Rusiñol, T: 891 04 27.

Badajoz (924): tourist office, Pasaje de San Juan, T: 22 27 63. Red Cross, T: 23 33 91. Highway information, Avda General Rodrigo 10, T: 23 24 90.

Cáceres (927): tourist office, Pl. Mayor, T: 24 63 47. Red Cross, T: 21 14 50. Highway information, Pl. de los

Golfines 4, T: 21 40 97.

Ciudad Real (926): tourist office, Avda Alarcos 31, T: 21 29 25. Red Cross, T: 22 33 22. Highway information, Edificio Servicios Múltiples, T: 21 22 00.

Cuenca (966): tourist offices, C. Colón 34, T: 22 22 31; and C. Dalmacio García Izcarra 8, T: 22 00 62 and 22 06 17. Red Cross, T: 21 11 45. Highway information, Colón 67, T: 22 00 50.

Guadalajara (911): tourist office, Travesía de Beladiez 1, T: 22 06 98. Red Cross, T: 22 17 88. Highway information, Cuesta de San Miguel 1, T: 22 30 66.

Madrid (91): tourist office, Princesa 1, Edificio Torre de Madrid, T: 241 23 25; tourist information also available in Atocha train station, T: 228 52 37, and Chamartín station, T: 733 11 22. Red Cross,

T: 279 99 00. Highway information, Raimundo Fernández Villaverde 54, T: 233 11 00.

Mérida (924): tourist office, C. Puente 9, T: 31 53 53.

Monfragüe (927): tourist office, Avda Gral Primo de Rivera 2, T: 22 76 01, 22 05 04 and 22 46 62.

Toledo (925): tourist offices, Puerta de Bisagra, T: 22 08 43, and Pl. de Zocodover 11, T: 22 14 00 and 22 10 52. Red Cross, T: 22 29 00. Highway information, Pl. de Santa Clara 6, T: 22 44 04. Weather information, T: (91) 232 35 00.

FURTHER READING

Alister Boyd, *The Companion Guide to Madrid and Central Spain* (London, 1974); Fernando Chueca Goitia, *Madrid and Toledo* (London).

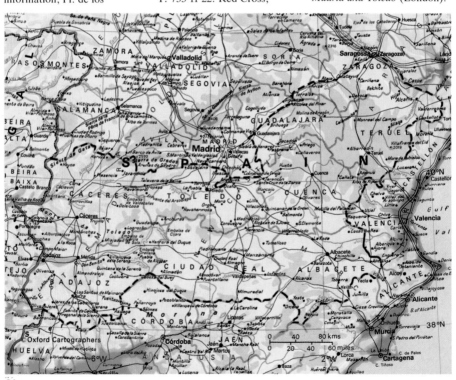

Serranía de Cuenca

The Río Cuervo is the most magical of the many rivers that spring from the 'enchanted' rocks of the Serranía de Cuenca

Mountain range to the east of Madrid, including the Ciudad Encantada and several protected areas

High above the headwaters of the Tagus rise the peaks of the Serranía de Cuenca, a chain of mountains occupying the north-east corner of the province of Cuenca. They form the western rampart of a major massif that also includes the Montes Universales and the Sierra de Albarracín. A number of subordinate sierras are contained within the Serranía de Cuenca: the Sierra de Tragacete, de los Palancares, de las Cuerdas, de Mira and de Bascuñana. The highest peak in the system is the Cerro de San Felipe (1,839 metres/6,030 feet), near Tragacete.

The range is full of quirks and surprises: hot springs, caves, cliff-hanging villages, an 'enchanted city' of natural sculptures, and rivers that pour out of fissures in the mountainside. The Ciudad Encantada resembles the ruins of some prehistoric city: huge blocks of limestone sculpted into weird shapes by erosion lie scattered through a 2,000-hectare (4,940-acre) forest where you can exercise your imagination identifying 'El Teatro', the 'Roman Bridge', 'The Ships' and whatnot. But apart from this famous tourist attraction, the Serranía de Cuenca will reward patient study and quiet walking tours.

Plants of interest include *Antirrhinum pulverulentum*, a hairy, pale-yellow snapdragon with leathery leaves that grows from rock crevices; *Saxifraga corbariensis*, a cushion-forming saxifrage with glaucous, tough leaves; *Tanacetum pallidum*, a composite with silvery-haired leaves from which rise slender flowering stems, each with a pale-yellow bloom; and the strange crucifer, *Sarcocapnos enneaphylla*, which creeps across sheer rock faces, a bundle of irregular yellow-white flowers in a nest of blue-green trifoliate leaves.

The Serranía de Cuenca generally is rich in orchid species, with woodcock and late spider orchids (*Ophrys scolopax* and *O. sphegodes*) numbering among the more exotic. There are seven helleborine species from a range of habitats, including the marsh helleborine (*Epipactis palustris*) and the red helleborine (*Cephalanthera rubra*), which is highly restricted to calcareous woodlands. Burnt-tip orchids (*Orchis ustulata*) and frog orchids (*Coeloglossum viride*) also favour lime-rich soils, as does the violet bird's-nest orchid (*Limodorum abortivum*). Three rare butterflies have been recorded here: the large blue (*Maculinea arion*), the spring ringlet (*Erebia epistygne* ssp *andera*) and iolas blue (*Iolana iolas*).

One day at the village of Beteta – the word means 'splendid' in Arabic – I went looking for one of the local mineral springs that reportedly issues from beneath a hermitage-shrine to La Virgen del Rosal, the Madonna of the Rosebush. I finally found it, too, at an abandoned farm near the village, steadily pouring forth its medicinal waters that were being used further downhill to irrigate an orchard. Nearby there is a second spring, no less therapeutic, of rose-tinted ferruginous water said to be a cure for anaemia. Higher up on the mountain stand the ruins of the hermitage and a tangled forest of pine.

There are mineral springs throughout the region, and even one or two spas that are still in operation, notably the one at Solán de Cabras. The Río Cuervo, which eventually flows into the Guadiela and the Tagus, also begins as a mineral spring; its birth high in the Serranía is a far more interesting spot than the place where the Tagus rises across the way in the Montes Universales. Part of the river comes pouring out of a cave in the mountain; another cascades over a series of rocks and caverns, covering their entrances with a curtain of rivulets. This specially protected area is not far from another of the Serranía's main talking-points, the Parque Cinegético del Hosquillo, which occupies about 1,000 hectares (2,410 acres) in the centre of the immense area known as the Reserva Nacional de la Serranía de Cuenca.

The Hosquillo park is in a valley flanked by Cerro Gordo, El Pajarero and El Barranco, and traversed by the Río Escabas; it has become one of the country's main deer-breeding stations and is separated from the rest of the reserve by a high wire fence (park entrance is restricted). Within it live red, fallow and roe deer, bear and wild boar; the area is also known for its otters, eagles and griffon vultures. More accessible is the Serranía's *reserva nacional*, adjoining the Montes Universales. It comprises superb forests and deep valleys inhabited by deer, boar and several species of raptor; its mountains and ravines are virtually untrodden by tourist feet but known to specialists for their geological and ecological interest.

BEFORE YOU GO

Maps: SGE 1:50,000 Nos. 565, 587, 588, 610, 611 and 612; and IGN 1:200,000 Mapa Provincial of Cuenca.

GETTING THERE

By car: there is no single preferred route to the Serranía, which can be approached from Guadalajara and Priego as well as from Molina de Aragón or Cuenca.
By rail: from Madrid, there are daily connections with Guadalajara and Cuenca, and with Teruel.
By bus: daily buses connect Cuenca to the villages of the Serranía. Buses to Beteta are operated by Empresa Campi, T: (966) 22 14 65; to Tragacete by Empresa Rodríguez, T: (966) 22 64 87; and to Cañete by Empresa La Rápida, T: (966) 22 27 51.

There is no public transport to more remote areas such as El Hosquillo or the birthplace of the Río Cuervo.

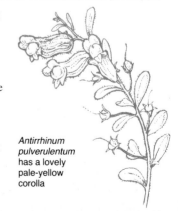

Antirrhinum pulverulentum has a lovely pale-yellow corolla

The large blue flies in June and July high on the bare Montes Universales

WHERE TO STAY

The city of Cuenca offers a wide range of accommodation, from the 4-star Hotel Torremangana, T: (966) 22 33 51, to simple pensions, but is at least an hour's drive from the heart of the Serranía.

Beteta has the comfortable 2-star Hotel Los Tilos, T: (966) 31 80 98, and the 2-star Balneario Solán de Cabras, just south of the city, one of the area's traditional spa hotels. Both Tragacete and Priego have several good small hotels.

Outdoor living: not prohibited, but if you plan to spend more than a day in any one spot, check first with ICONA in Cuenca (see below).

ACTIVITIES

Walking: paths that traverse the Serranía are not marked but there is plenty of scope here for easy walking through pine forests and strange rock formations. From the mountains above Cuenca, there is a splendid view of the adjoining plains of La Mancha. For details of routes contact the Federación

Castellana de Montañismo (see below).

The best way to see the Ciudad Encantada, open sunrise to sunset, is to get as far away from the tourists as possible. It is an extraordinary area littered with some gigantic rocks, wind-blown and water-worn into intriguing shapes and forms.

Caves: near the little village of Villar del Humo are some interesting paleolithic cave paintings.

FURTHER INFORMATION

Tourist information: C. Fermín Caballero, 3 blocks north of the train station, at the corner of García Izcara, Cuenca, T: (966) 22 22 31. ICONA, 18 de Julio, Cuenca, T: (966) 21 15 00.

For information on mountaineering, cave exploration and trekking contact: Federación Castellana de Montañismo, Apodaca 16, Madrid 4, T: (91) 448 07 24.

Montes Universales

Birthplace of the River Tagus
Bare mountains, snow-covered for up to 8 months in the year

An immensely pompous monument more suited to the Rockefeller Center marks the spot, but no matter: just behind the *nacimiento del Tajo* lies a wonderful area, a happy tableland for sheep, designed as though by a Japanese master in the art of landscape architecture. Low shrubs grow in dark-green circles against a grey limestone background, like polka-dots in a giant *bata de lunares*, the dress of the *flamenco bailadora*. Here and

there a red-roofed shepherd's hut is outlined against the green polka-dots, or an equally cubist sheep corral.

The mountains are bare, windswept and beautiful, rising to about 1,800m (5,900ft). Here you may find the large blue butterfly (*Maculinea arion*), which has the most famous and well-studied symbiotic relationship with ants (of the species *Myrmica sabuleti* in Spain): the larval butterflies are carried into the nest by the ants when they reach their final instar, where they spend the winter. Above the beginnings of the Tagus looms the massive Muela de San Juan ('St John's Jaw'), whose heights are snow-covered for 8 months of the year. ICONA has planted pine forests on the Montes Universales, but the most fascinating landscapes are the half-bare mountainsides with their fragrant herbs and wild flowers. They are inhabited by deer, wild boar, hares, rabbits, partridges and large raptors. This is one of the few places in the world (apart from Alaska) where I have seen an eagle feasting on a hare, not far from a path regularly used by human beings. For lovers of solitude this quasi-Tibetan landscape is a veritable godsend.

Before you go *Maps:* SGE 1:50,000 Nos. 565, 566, 588 and 589; and IGN 1:200,000 Mapas provinciales of Teruel and Cuenca.

Getting there: there is no way to get into the mountains by public transport.

By car: the Montes Universales can be approached from either Albarracín or Guadalaviar in the province of Teruel, or Tragacete in Cuenca. The Tragacete–Frías de Albarracín road leads through the Montes and past the birthplace of the Tagus; many of ICONA's forestry tracks are along this highway.

Only 1 road actually traverses the Montes, although others lead up to its slopes and then come to a stop. Among such dead-end roads is the one leading from Toril (south of Albarracín, in the province of Teruel) to the villages of Masegoso and El Vallecillo, where carefully tilled fields alternate with wild mountain scenery. Halfway between the 2 villages a road takes you to the falls of the Río Cabriel, beside the Molino de San Pedro. Nearby

stand some of the oldest pines in the sierra, with enormous trunks that are nearly 4m (13ft) in circumference.

Where to stay: hotel accommodation can be found in Albarracín, Frías de Albarracín and Bronchales. For instance, try the 1-star Montes Universales, T: (974) 71 01 58, in Albarracín, or El Gallo, T: (974) 71 00 32.

Activities *Walking:* many of ICONA's forestry tracks lead off the Tragacete–Frías de Albarracín road. Paths are not marked; for information, contact either the Federación Castellana de Montañismo or the Federación Aragonesa de

Montañismo (see below for addresses).

Further information *Tourist information:* C. Tomás Nogues, Teruel, T: (974) 60 22 79; and C. Fermín Caballero, Cuenca, T: (966) 22 22 31. ICONA, San Francisco 29, Teruel, T: (974) 60 22 50; and 18 de Julio, Cuenca, T: (966) 21 15 00.

For information about mountaineering, walking routes and cave exploration, contact Federación Aragonesa de Montañismo, Albareda 7, 4°, Zaragoza, T: (976) 22 79 71; and Federación Castellana de Montañismo, Apodaca 16, Madrid 4, T: (91) 448 07 24.

Sierra de Albarracín

Rugged reserva nacional *with ancient pine forests and meadowlands near the city of Teruel*

The Sierra de Albarracín always was a world apart, as much in its history as its geography. In Muslim Spain, Albarracín was ruled as an independent kingdom by the family of Aben Racin – hence the name

– as a vassal state of the khalifate of Córdoba. Today it is part of the province of Teruel, in Aragón, yet it seems to be a separate enclave, neither quite Aragonese nor Castilian. The sierra extends roughly from the Cuenca border to the town of Gea de Albarracín, but its focal point is the town of Albarracín itself – an almost perfectly preserved walled city of the Middle Ages.

Tramacastilla, 18 kilometres (11 miles) to the west of the town, is the point of departure for excursions into pine-clad mountains and the valley of Noguera, to the north, or the fieldstone villages of Villar del Cobo and Griegos, both of which claim to be even higher than Trevélez in the Alpujarras (Andalucía). To reach them you pass through some of the steepest ravines and most rugged landscape in the whole of Spain.

Toward Orihuela del Tremedal stretches a great tableland at over 1,600 metres (5,250 feet) that contains ancient pine forests and fertile meadows in which red deer are a common sight. The land gradually rises to the Sierra Alta (1,855 metres/6,085 feet). Here the bare limestone screes take on a mantle of pink-purple in

The contrasting wildernesses of the Montes Universales (left) and the Sierra de Albarracín (opposite page) are both easily reached from the medieval city of Albarracín

summer from the flowers of the storksbill *Erodium daucoides*. *Ranunculus gregarious*, a yellow buttercup with kidney-shaped leaves in a basal rosette, also grows at this height. More unusual is *Astragalus turolensis*, a milk-vetch normally found in North Africa. This is the only population in Spain of the low-growing yellow-flowered legume and it supports the larvae of the rare violet-suffused zephyr blue butterfly (of the race *hespericus* in Albarracín). The zephyr blue flies in May on gentle slopes, usually over limestone, between 400–1,100 metres (1,300–3,600 feet) in altitude, and lives in extremely small colonies. Other rare or endangered species found in the sierra include the American painted lady (*Cynthia virginiensis*), which thrives on flowery mountain slopes and is thought to breed here; and the Iolas blue (*Iolana iolas thomasi*), a large butterfly with silver underwings and lustrous azure upperwings – it has a symbiotic relationship with ants of the genus *Myrmica*, sometimes in conjunction with the larvae of the more common long-tailed blue.

From the Sierra Alta there is a panoramic view of the 59,000-hectare (145,790-acre) *reserva nacional* of the sierra establshed by ICONA in 1973 as a means of protecting the forest and meadowlands of 11 villages. But the inhabitants of some of these villages are far from happy with the result. The farmers of Guadalaviar and Villar del Cobo complain that the deer are destroying their crops and vegetable gardens. In a referendum on the question, '*Reserva sí, reserva no*', 98 per cent of the villagers voted against it, and the issue remains a political football. The local shepherds point out that the law forbids them to leave their goats untended lest they destroy young pines – but the pines, they say, are being destroyed anyway by young deer. Whatever the rights and wrongs of this situation, a walk through the Sierra de Albarracín is almost like a visit back to the Middle Ages, when peasant communities were still working out what ecological compromises they could make with the natural environment out beyond their doorstep.

BEFORE YOU GO
Maps: SGE 1:50,000 Nos. 565, 566, 588, 589; and IGN 1:200,000 Mapa provincial of Teruel.
Guidebook: *Albarracín y su Serranía* by J. Albi (Everest, 1976).

GETTING THERE
By car: the most direct approach is to follow the Teruel–Albarracín road if approaching from the west.
By rail: the nearest train station is Teruel on the main Madrid–Valencia and Alicante–Irún lines.
By bus: there is a daily service from Teruel to Albarracín and a circuit of the sierra; for information, T: (974) 60 20 72.

WHERE TO STAY
Only 3 communities in the area offer hotel accommodation: Albarracín,

Frías de Albarracín and Bronchales.

ACTIVITIES
Walking: there is an endless variety of trails in the area. Contact the Federación Aragonesa de Montañismo (see below).

The lilac-coloured *Erodium daucoides* colonizes barren mountain scree

FURTHER INFORMATION
Tourist information: C. Tomás Nogues, Teruel, T: (974) 60 22 79. ICONA, 18 de Julio, Cuenca, T: (966) 21 15 00.
For information about mountaineering, walking routes, etc, contact the Federación Aragonesa de Montañismo, Albareda 7–4°, Zaragoza, T: (976) 22 79 71.

Parque Natural del Alto Tajo

16,940 ha (41,860 acres) of parque natural just outside Molina de Aragón

One evening I drove from Sacecorbo to Molina de Aragón, a distance of well

over 100km (60 miles), and did not meet so much as one other car on the road until I came to the outskirts of Molina. I felt utterly alone, surrounded only by trees and sky, in this virtually unknown provincial park of the Alto Tajo – the upper Tagus.

The Tagus rises, in fact, in the Montes Universales, south-east of the *parque natural*, but when it reaches this part of Guadalajara it already has the strength of a young giant, and sufficient force to cut great gorges into the limestone cliffs that once impeded its passage. Collecting fresh tributaries at every turn, it soon acquires such power that it can carry heavy timbers downstream, from Peralejos to the royal river port at Aranjuez. Building rafts of up-country logs and poling them downriver used to be the dangerous occupation of the men known as *gancheros del Tajo* – the *gancho* was the long-staved grappling hook they used to shepherd their logs through the narrows.

The full length of the upper Tagus can be an unforgettable experience for hikers with thick boots and strong legs. Most of the countryside is as pristine and unspoiled as it was on the 8th day of Creation, with mountains, valleys, meadows and rivers, and countless hiking paths that rarely receive the imprint of an alien foot. Beyond the park is an ancient spa, the Balneario, called La Esperanza ('hope'). At this point, the Tagus enters a reservoir, the Embalse de Entrepeñas.

Before you go *Maps:* SGE 1:50,000 Nos. 488, 489, 513, 514 and 539; and IGN 1:200,000 Mapa provincial of Guadalajara.

Note: none of the above

maps shows the recently completed highway that leads from Peralejos de las Truchas (supposedly at the end of a 1-way road) across the Tagus and up the Serranía de Cuenca on the other side of the river, connecting with the high mountain road that leads to Beteta in the north and Poyatos in the south.

Getting there *By car:* Molina de Aragón is best reached via N211, which branches off the Madrid–Barcelona road at Alcolea del Pinar.

By bus: there is a regular service from Barcelona and Lerída (Lleida) to Molina de Aragón via Zaragoza. For details, T: (93) 318 38 95.

From the point of view of public transport, this is one of the most isolated areas of Spain. The long distances between one village and the next are best covered by car, and these simple farm communities usually lack even the most modest accommodation for tourists.

Where to stay: Molina de Aragón has 4 1-star hostelries – including Rosanz, T: (911) 83 08 36. At Cifuentes there is a 2-star hotel – San Roque, T: (911) 81 00 28. An alternative overnight stop is provided by Priego, in the province of Cuenca but just south of the park boundary: it has 2 1-star hostels.

Activities *Walking:* the 2 base-camp towns from which explorations are best undertaken are Cifuentes, just to the west of the park, and Molina de Aragón, not far from the north-east corner.

You can follow the route of the river, starting at the southern extremity of the park and walking northwards until the Tagus swings westward in a great arc. Peralejos de las Truchas (the *truchas* are the mountain trout for which the village is famous) can be

reached in a 2-day hike from Molina de Aragón, the county seat, but you may want to detour an extra day to visit the Barranco de la Hoz ('the sickle gorge'), where high cliffs loom above the poplars lining the Río Gallo. There is a small shrine to the Virgin de la Hoz here, a simple image of the Madonna that stands in a sanctuary that is half-cave, half-chapel.

If you have time for just a single day's excursion, a good place to spend it is at or near Villanueva de Alcorón, which is known for its local peak, La Zapatilla ('the slipper') – an easy climb – and for the waterfall called El Hundido de Armallones, another outstanding bit of scenery. There is no inn at Villanueva de Alcorón.

Further information *Tourist information:* Paseo Doctor F. Iparraguirre 24, Guadalajara, T: (911) 22 86 14. ICONA, Marqués Villaverde 2, Bloque B, Guadalajara, T: (911) 22 33 00.

A word of caution: for some reason this magnificent landscape is rather more insect-ridden than the rest of Spain; be sure to bring a bottle of mosquito repellent.

Laguna de Gallocanta

Largest natural inland lake in Spain (1,400ha/3,500 acres) in the southernmost part of Zaragoza

Situated in an otherwise fairly desolate landscape, this is 1 of the Iberian peninsula's great birdwatching sites. During the

great winter waterfowl migrations the sky above the lake of Gallocanta is often black with birds. Eighty different species have been recorded here, and Gallocanta is particularly noted as one of the major wintering haunts of the European crane. Feeding during the day on the surrounding fields, up to 8,000 of these great birds come to roost each evening from Nov–Feb. By the beginning of Mar they are on their way northwards along a traditional route that eventually leads them to the southern shores of the Baltic.

The *laguna* is also the main watering-ground in Europe of the red-crested pochard, plus there are hen and marsh harriers in the reed beds and red kites soaring overhead. Pin-tailed sandgrouse, pigeon-like birds of the arid regions, with needle-like tail feathers that trail somewhat in flight, come to drink, and the whole area is alive with larks.

The number of birds fluctuates dramatically from 1 year to the next. In 1978 some 200,000 birds were estimated to have used the lake as a stopover point; by 1981 the number had dropped to 50,000.

Located at 1,000m (3,280ft) above sea level in the southernmost part of the privince of Zaragoza, not far from Daroca, the Laguna de Gallocanta is of geological interest, too. It covers about 1,400ha (3,460 acres) – which makes it the largest natural inland lake in Spain. It is connected to a subsidiary *lagunazo* at the northern end, and, on the opposite side, to a labyrinthine appendix of reeds

The remote region of the Alto Tajo preserves primitive rugged landscapes and an equally primitive way of life

The waters of the Ruidera lagoons abound in eels and other fish, food for the herons and egrets that stalk the dense reed beds

and ponds known as the Lagunazos de Tornos. The local farmers grow sunflowers and wheat in the surrounding fields, although there is also a lot of dry pasture land and some fields of thyme. The trees that once surrounded the lake have vanished, but there are pines and holm oaks in the nearby hills.

Before you go *Maps:* SGE 1:50,000 Nos. 464, 465, 490 and 491; and IGN Mapa provincial of Zaragoza.

Getting there *By car:* Daroca is 86km (53 miles) south-west of Zaragoza near the intersection of highway N330, from Zaragoza, and N234, which runs north-south from Soria to Teruel. From Daroca take C211 toward Molina de Aragón as far as Santedo, from where a road leads to the Laguna de Gallocanta.

By bus: there are regular services from Barcelona and Lerida to Molina de Aragón by way of Zaragoza. For information, T: (93) 318 38 95 (Barcelona).

Where to stay: Daroca has a range of 2-star accommodation – the Hotel Daroca, T: (976) 80 00 00, and the hostels Agiria, T: (976) 80 07 31, and Legido, T: (976) 80 02 28, as well as the Pensión El Ruejo, T: (976) 80 03 35.

Further information *Tourist information:* Paseo Doctor F. Iparraguirre 24, Guadalajara, T: (911) 22 86 14. ICONA, Marqués Villaverde 2, Bloque B, Guadalajara, T: (911) 22 33 00.

Parque Natural de Las Lagunas de Ruidera

Group of 11 lakes centred around the town of Ruidera

Cervantes, in *Don Quixote*, says that there are seven of these small lakes; in actual fact there are 11. You sense their presence even before you finally see them, after driving through some of the driest countryside in Spain. This, indeed, is Don Quixote country – La Mancha, the sun-baked Arabic 'wilderness' whose heat-waves had a notoriously hallucinogenic effect on the wits. The road from Argamasilla de Alba to Ruidera is lined with poplars and there are gentle undulations in the flat Manchegan landscape announcing an imminent change of scenery.

At the Embalse de Peñarroya the plain turns into hills and you find yourself in another, friendlier, habitat. The first natural lake along the route is Cenagosa, accompanied by an incessant clamour of birds, for whom this *zona húmeda manchega* is an oasis in the desert (the more so since the Tablas de Daimiel are drying up). The reeds along its shore provide perfect cover for many kinds of duck. A little further on, already accustomed to the cooling air that rises from these unexpected bodies of water, you come across another *laguna*, La Colgadilla, which receives much of its water via subterranean filtration from the great cave-cum-storage deposit known as the Cueva de la Morenilla.

Not far from the sleepy village of Ruidera are the two largest lakes, the Laguna del Rey and La Gran Colgada. The fell hand of tourism has lately made itself felt hereabouts in the form of small hotels, camping grounds and private villas; even so, they have not driven away the birds that flock to these remarkably clear lakes.

The road from Ruidera winds along their banks and gradually ascends from one lake to the next, for each is just a step higher

than its neighbour. Just after several small *lagunas* – Batana, Santo Amorcillo and Salvadora – is La Lengua, which is sausage-shaped and full of fish, hence much frequented by anglers. It receives most of its water via a row of small falls and rivulets that pour into it from the next link up in the chain, Redondilla. This, in turn, receives water from San Pedro, whose shore is partly lined with houses and plant nurseries. At last you reach the highest and least visited, the Laguna Conceja, with its marshy shoreline and wooded surrounding hills.

I have spent some extremely pleasant nights on the shores of Laguna Redondilla, and woken up at dawn to hear a philharmonic chorus of birds such as I have rarely encountered anywhere else, even in the remotest of bird sanctuaries. Their vocal enthusiasm is perfectly understandable, for these crystalline lakes are in such stark contrast with the parched *maquis* of the encircling hills.

The name Ruidera is said to derive from the noise (*ruido*) made by the water running from lake to lake, which stretch

Under cover of the reeds, the great crested grebe builds a nest surrounded by water

96

along a total of 25 kilometres (15½ miles), with a difference of 128 metres (420 feet) in height between the southernmost pool, La Blanca, and Cenagosa at the northern end. Geologists have demonstrated that while some of the water runs from one lake to the other along surface streams and cascades, it also flows underground, through layers of clay and gypsum or sandstone.

The protected area of the Parque Natural de Ruidera includes not only the lakes but also the tributary valley of San Pedro, and its cave of Montesinos, which plays such an important part in the second part of *Don Quixote*. Close by, the ruins of Rochafrida castle are perched atop a limestone redoubt that overlooks a cultivated field that must also have been a shallow pool before it was subdued by mules and a plough.

These are literary landmarks. Rochafrida is mentioned in Spanish medieval romances, although it was already in ruins when Cervantes roamed this district as a tithe proctor for the Knights of St John at Argamasilla. Hence Don Quixote must go underground to meet the heroes of his ever romantic imagination: Montesinos, Belerma, Durandarte. Here he learns that the inhabitants of the cave, Guadiana and Ruidera, together with their seven daughters and two nieces, have been transformed into a river and several lakes by Merlin the magician.

Indeed, the traditional explanation is that the lake at the bottom of Montesinos's cave, which is said to communicate with the Laguna de San Pedro via an underground stream, constitutes the real source of the Río Guadiana. The Lagunas de Ruidera, as a group, were reputed to be the headwaters of an eccentric and recalcitrant stream that went underground again after the Cenagosa, only to reappear 40 kilometres (25 miles) to the west, at Daimiel. Some geologists have recently questioned the hypothesis that this really is the subterranean Guadiana, and the argument continues to exercise some of the best scientific minds of Spain. The great subterranean reservoir, through which the river supposedly flowed westward, has been tapped by the pumps of the wine-growers of Tomelloso, and the wetlands of Daimiel have ceased to be the great national park they once were. But the Lagunas de Ruidera are upstream from the pumps, and thus more precious than ever.

BEFORE YOU GO
Maps: SGE 1:50,000 Nos. 762, 763, 787 and 788; and IGN 1:200,000 Mapas provinciales of Albacete and Ciudad Real.

GETTING THERE
By car: the village of Ruidera is on the highway N430, halfway between Albacete and Manzanares. From Madrid, take highway N-IV towards Andalucía. At Puerto Lápice turn east on to highway N420 to Alcázar de San Juan and then C400 towards Tomelloso and Ruidera.
By bus: regular daily services connect Albacete to Ossa de Montiel, the nearest village to the easternmost lagoons. For information, T: (967) 21 60 12 in Albacete.
There is no public transport for the *lagunas* route.

WHERE TO STAY
There are a number of modest hotels in the area, mainly on the shores of the larger lakes. The 1-star Hotel La Colgada, T: (926) 52 80 25, adjoins the *laguna* of the same name; the 1-star El Molino, T: (926) 52 80 81, is just across the road from the Laguna Redondilla and at the Laguna de San Pedro there is the 3-star Hotel Albamanjon, T: (926) 52 80 88. Ruidera itself has 3 1-star hotels. Near Ossa de Montiel, the largest town near the *lagunas*, there is the 1-star Hotel Montesinos, T: (926) 37 71 05.

ACTIVITIES
Fishing: licences for fishing can be obtained at the tourist offices in Ciudad Real and Albacete.
Cave: the road to Montesinos's cave begins at the Laguna de San Pedro and takes you almost to its mouth, which a thoughtful government has kindly supplied with steps for a troublefree descent into the depths. At one time there was internal lighting, too, at selected times of the day, but that seems to have come to an end: bring your own electric torch.

FURTHER INFORMATION
Tourist offices: Avda de los Mártires 31, Ciudad Real, T: (926) 21 33 02; and Tesifonte Gallego 1, Albacete (967) 21 33 90.

Tablas de Daimiel

Parque nacional *that was once one of the great wetlands of Europe; 40km (25 miles) from Ciudad Real*

The Tablas de Daimiel have achieved an international reputation as one of the most important wetland reserves of Spain. But the fact that the *tablas* were declared a *reserva nacional* in 1966, then a *parque nacional* in 1973, has not managed to save them from the consequences of sweeping ecological and economic change.

As you approach the village of Daimiel from any point of the compass, you pass vast areas of newly planted vineyards that are irrigated with water pumped up from artesian wells. The vineyards are thriving

under the blazing sun of La Mancha, and there are signs of flourishing modern farms and agricultural co-operatives. The cumulative result, however, is that the Río Guadiana has been pumped dry and the Cigüela has been both diverted and polluted. In 1982 the Guadiana dried up for the first time; now, the Tablas de Daimiel have almost ceased to exist as a way station or a breeding ground for wildfowl. At the beginning of summer, there is no sign in the park that this had been one of the great marshlands of Europe – only a few stagnant pools remain to suggest that this was not entirely a wilderness of thistles and scrub.

The authorities responsible for the national park have declared an environmental emergency and are attempting to impose water conservation measures that will restore the *tablas* to something approaching their original state.

The Manchegans use the word *tablas* for the shallow lagoons that form when the river overflows its banks in winter. Most of the *tablas* always did dry up during the summer droughts, but there were several lagoons that survived year round and saw the birds through until the autumn rains

The shrunken lagoons of the Tablas de Daimiel, once the Venice of La Mancha, were formerly a magnet for red-breasted pochard and other mainly surface-feeding duck

replenished the river. Actually the *tablas* were fed by four sources: the Guadiana, Cigüela, Zancares and Riansares, with the first two providing the lion's share of the water. The Cigüela's slightly salty waters come from the Serranía de Cuenca, whereas the Guadiana emerges from its underground course some 15 kilometres (nine miles) north of the *tablas* to form the pools known as *ojos* (eyes), from which the village of Villarrubia de los Ojos takes its name.

The park's rugged landscape is composed of five major elements: the *tablas*; the surrounding reed beds; the *masiegal*, consisting of slightly higher ground covered with saltwort and low scrub; the islands; and finally the small, relatively fertile dales known as *vegas*. Of these the *masiegal* is the one element that has remained untouched by the drought: this is one of the most extensive areas of its type in Western Europe, and walking through it is a decidedly prickly experience.

You can still see the series of small islands dotted throughout the marshes: the Isla de Pan ('bread'), Isla de los Asnos ('donkeys'), Isla de los Generales, Isla de Algeciras, Isla del Descanso ('repose') and so on. To find the *vegas* is more difficult; they occur at the south-west corner of the park's 1,812 hectares (4,480 acres) between the areas known as Prado Ancho and Suerte de Don Felix, and are (or were) subject to brief annual inundations.

If the waters return to Las Tablas, an army of birds will surely put in an appearance once more. Among the breeding group, mallards and red-crested pollards have traditionally predominated. Gadwalls and pochards also used to breed here, and a few pairs of ferruginous duck. The reed beds of Rosaleo were famous for their purple herons, as well as coots, moorhens, water rails and great-crested grebes.

The long list of wintering birds was headed by pintails and shovelers, as well as contingents of northern mallards and pochards that joined their live-in relatives every year. The migratory population also included black-tailed godwit, snipe and even black kites and imperial eagles. The mammals were headed by wild boar, red foxes and large families of otters.

BEFORE YOU GO
Maps: SGE 1:50,000 Nos. 737, 738 and 760; IGN 1:200,000 Mapa provincial of Ciudad Real; and ICONA 1:20,000 Mapa del Parque Nacional de Las Tablas de Daimiel.

GETTING THERE
The Parque Nacional de Las Tablas de Daimiel is situated about 180km (112 miles) from Madrid and 40km (25 miles) from Ciudad Real, capital of the province.
By car: the usual route from Madrid entails the N-IV (Madrid–Cádiz) as far as Puerto Lápice, then on to Villarrubia de los Ojos or Daimiel. The only way to get to the heart of the *tablas* is to take the road from Daimiel to the park's visitors' information centre, 11km (7 miles) to the north-west.

By bus: there is no public transport from Daimiel to the park, but there are regular bus connections to Daimiel from Ciudad Real and Madrid.

WHERE TO STAY
Local accommodation is plentiful. At Almagro, 23km (14 miles) from Daimiel, there is a 4-star *parador nacional*, T: (926) 86 01 00. Ciudad Real has 2 3-star hotels and several 2-star hostelries. At Daimiel there are 2-star hotels and a pension. Fuente del Fresno, west of the park, has a 2-star hotel.

FURTHER INFORMATION
The park is open every day 9am–8pm in summer and 10am–5pm in winter. The Centro de Visitantes remains closed on Mon and Tues. For further information, phone ICONA in Ciudad Real, T: (926) 21 37 40.

Daimiel's climate is fiercely hot in summer and bitterly cold in winter. It is also subject to violent diurnal fluctuations.

The black-tailed godwit has suffered from the drying up of the *tablas*

Monfragüe

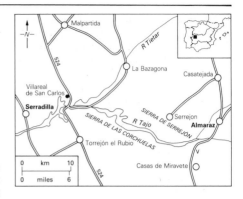

Parque natural, *about 25km (14 miles) south of Plasencia*
Breeding ground for an extraordinary 218 vertebrate species

Early one morning I went for a walk through the cork-oak *dehesa* that surrounds the *cortijo*, or farmstead, of Las Cansinas in the heart of Monfragüe. It was hot already. The air was filled with the hum of insect wings, hoopoes and golden orioles were uttering their first notes of the morning, and a woodchat shrike flitted from tree to tree. Then I noticed the short-toed eagle (known here as *águila culebrera*, the snake eagle) perched on a rocky mound not far away. I crouched down and studied the broad grey, almost owl-like head, with prominent brows and unusually large eyes; strangely, the toes seemed to be a normal length! The *águila* never moved, save to flinch as half-a-dozen azure-winged magpies dive-bombed it from the branches of a nearby tree, a situation of David taking on Goliath if ever there was one.

Later I learned that this bird had been released, somewhat prematurely, the day before from Las Cansinas after having been nursed back to apparent health subsequent to sustaining an injury in the wild. Since it was apparently unable to adjust to freedom just yet, a warden was duly dispatched to find it. It took him nearly two days to gain its confidence, when we were finally rewarded with the sight of a somewhat humiliated and indignant bird, blindfolded and carried by those ferocious talons, head down like a trussed-up chicken. Freedom had been cancelled, at least for the time being.

The Parque Natural de Monfragüe gets its name from the Castillo y Ermita de Monfragüe, which overlooks the western end of the reserve. The castle was built on the top of the Sierra de las Corchuelas by the Berbers as a lookout over the ancient

crossing point of the River Tagus at Puente Cardenal, and given the name Al-Mofrag. To the Romans, this difficult, uneven and somewhat inhospitable terrain was known as Monsfragorum.

The origin and composition of the rock formation here is mirrored almost exactly in the Sierra de Ancares, at the western end of the Cordillera Cantábrica. The land consists of a Palaeozoic platform, much elevated and faulted during the Hercynian and Caledonian orogenies, or upliftings. It now forms a slightly dissected plateau, which tilts towards the west and the Atlantic Ocean. The valleys are composed of slates of Silurian age, bisected at more or less regular intervals by ridges of quartzite running in a north-west to south-east direction. The two most commanding and prominent ridges are the Sierra de las Corchuelas, south of the rivers, and the Sierra de Serrejón, to the north, just outside the park.

The crystalline parent rocks have weathered slowly, producing dry, acid soils that are highly erodible, making it very important that the natural vegetation cover is maintained. Sadly, almost 20 per cent of the park has been afforested with non-native maritime pine and eucalyptus; however, the authorities have now committed themselves to restoring the more stable *dehesa* and woodland habitats, which are of infinitely greater value to wildlife.

Dehesa habitats are restricted to the Iberian peninsula and north-west Africa; they are composed of sparse plantations of cork and holm oak, traditionally harvested for acorns, firewood, cork and charcoal. The high-quality land beneath is used as pasture, a centuries-old practice that is acknowledged to be the best way to use this harsh terrain. Consequently, a totally characteristic fauna and flora has evolved, one that is unknown anywhere else in the world.

The second major habitat is virtually the only remaining original Mediterranean woodland. It is dominated by evergreen shrubs and trees, often species that produce aromatic oils to deter would-be herbivores. Looking down the northern slopes from the Castillo y Ermita de Monfragüe, you can see a wonderous tangle of mastic and turpentine trees, wild olives, laurustinus, strawberry trees, stone pines and the holly (or Kermes) oak. Beneath this green canopy are the cistus which are so typical of Monfragüe – the gum, grey-leaved and popular-leaved varieties – together with pink Spanish heath, fragrant French lavender, yellow-flowered broom and bladder senna.

Two hundred and eighteen vertebrate species breed within the Parque Natural de Monfragüe, and many more drop in on their long migratory journeys. Some 20 species of raptor nest and raise their young here, with substantial proportions of the global populations of black vultures and Spanish imperial eagles. Both these species are severely threatened with extinction, and the presence of this last redoubt is one

of the prime reasons for the existence of the natural park: the imperial eagles make their homes and breed more successfully here than in their better known refuge on the Coto Doñana.

The black vulture and Spanish imperial eagle nest in the tops of ancient cork and holm oaks as do goshawks, sparrowhawks, booted eagles and most of the owl species that occur here. Other raptors make their homes on remote rocky ledges, such as the griffon vultures at Peñfalcon, a huge crag by the Puente Cardenal, which is also inhabited by their small cousins, the Egyptian vultures. Both the common species of kite nest in the park, and can frequently be seen quartering more open ground, controlling direction with a deft twist of their forked tails. Golden eagles, Bonelli's and short-toed eagles, peregrines and both species of kestrel have also found Monfragüe greatly to their liking, as have marsh and Montagu's harriers, and those other great masters of the air, the ravens and the choughs.

The assemblage of smaller birds which typifies *dehesa* and Mediterranean woodland must be one of the most colourful anywhere. Hoopoes and woodchat shrikes represent the more conservative members of a clan which includes such brightly plumaged fellows as the bee-eater, golden oriole, azure-winged magpie and roller. With the exception of the last, which is a rather uncommon sight, the other birds are present in such numbers that you can fully immerse yourself in their fluting calls and flashing colours as they go about their business almost – but not quite – indifferent to your presence.

It is the black stork, however, that emerges as the truly memorable bird of Monfragüe. Again, it is a species threatened continually by human activities, and is suffering a great contraction in its former range; that said, some seven pairs choose to return to Monfragüe every summer to rear their young.

Many of these birds can be seen simply by parking at the roadside opposite Peñfalcon and watching the vultures circle overhead to land on the great buttress

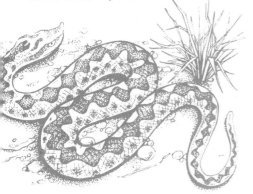

The range of the snub-nosed Lataste's viper extends from Tunisia to the Pyrenees

opposite. Among them may be an eagle, a peregrine or a black stork returning to its nest in one of the clefts near the dammed waters below. Black vultures sometimes join them, but are more common over the oak forests to the south on the road to Trujillo. Eagles, too, are more abundant elsewhere. Try the road after it has crossed the dam to the east where all five eagles and the three vultures occurring in Spain may be seen. One of the special birds of Monfragüe is the black-winged kite. One of the most beautiful and rarest of all Euro-

pean raptors, it nests among the cork oaks to the north and south of the great river systems, but is always difficult to locate. In areas where they occur it is definitely worth the effort of investigating every bird that hovers, for, like the kestrel, these splendid birds spy out most of their food by this technique.

The mammals of Monfragüe are no less exciting, the speciality of the park being the Spanish lynx, although the retiring nature of this animal makes it unlikely that you will see it. No less elusive in the night air are the 15 species of bat found here.

Red deer and the smaller, palmately horned fallow deer are among the permitted targets of game hunters, the

The display of the great bustard (below) is one of the natural wonders of Monfragüe, while Peñfalcon (opposite) is, as the name suggests, home to many birds of prey

authorities reasoning that limited hunting of these sustainable resources will bring in extra money for conservation of other species. The numerous wild boar, *jabali*, of the *dehesa* are also popular with hunters.

Wild cats, Egyptian mongeese and genets inhabit the Mediterranean woodland, all of them frightened away by the least noise, and otters patrol the *arroyos*, or streams, leading into the reservoirs. Foxes, badgers, roe deer, polecats and beech martens, as well as the introduced *mouflon*, are also resident in Monfragüe, as is the garden dormouse, a tree-dweller, and the subterranean mole, every niche has been exploited.

The 19 species of reptile that breed in the *parque natural* include such exotic creatures as the moorish gecko, often seen clinging adhesively to the wall beside a window at night, feeding on the insects which have been attracted to the light. Less frequently encountered is the *amphisbaenian* or worm lizard, resembling nothing so much as a large pink earthworm, and occupying a similar territory. Three-toed and Bedriaga's skinks, the latter limited to Iberia in its worldwide distribution, also occur in Monfragüe, their tiny vestigial legs an evolutionary leftover from the days when they resembled true lizards and had not adapted to their current burrowing habit.

The Moorish gecko is most likely to be seen in villages at night, lured on to walls by street lamps that form brilliant insect traps

Nine species of snake lurk in the undergrowth; three are poisonous – Lataste's viper, the false smooth snake and the Montpellier snake. None is fatal, and the former two have fangs positioned right at the back of their mouths and so cannot inject their venom unless they have a really good grip. Other, somewhat less threatening, species include the horseshoe whip snake, and ladder snakes, too.

The wetter habitats of Monfragüe – the reservoirs of the dammed Tagus and Tiétar rivers and their minor tributaries – support an equally diverse animal community, particularly with respect to amphibians and wintering and migratory birds. Great crested grebes and the beautifully marked collared pratincole can be seen during the summer months, the former with its cargo of fluffy chicks aboard, the latter swooping noisily around the mud flats that become exposed as the water levels drop. These same mud flats are swarming with house martins during May, as they gather material from which to construct their little mud igloos under the lip of the dam of the River Tagus. The wintering avifauna includes cattle egrets, spoonbills and greylag geese, as well as both grey and night herons, stalking though the shallows, while regimental ranks of cormorants perch on the rotting remains of partially submerged trees.

The amphibians at home in the creeks and gullies surrounding the reservoirs include livid black- and yellow-fire salamanders and the khaki-camouflaged marbled newt. Bright green tree frogs perch on their arboreal vantage points, while natterjacks, spadefoots and midwife toads go about their chores. Other species include painted and parsley frogs, and the sharp-ribbed salamander, an ugly, warty creature confined to Iberia, and one of the largest tailed amphibians in Europe, reaching almost 30 centimetres (12 inches) in length.

BEFORE YOU GO
Maps: SGE 1:50,000 Nos. 651, 652, 678 and 679; Michelin Map No. 447 1:400,000.
Guidebook: *Guía del Parque Natural de Monfragüe* by José-Luis Rodríguez (Ediciones Fondo Natural, 1985).

GETTING THERE
By car: from Plasencia or Trujillo, take the C524, which leads to the villages of Castillo de Monfragüe and Villarreal de San Carlos. There is an eastbound minor road which branches off the C524 just north of Villareal de San Carlos.
By rail: the nearest station is Palazuelo, just south of Plasencia, and some 20km (12 miles) from the nearest section of Monfragüe. There are few trains to Palazuelo, as the station is on a sideline to the main Madrid-Cáceres line; the best idea is probably to travel to Cáceres first, and then by bus to Plasencia (see below for details).

To Cáceres, there are 5 trains daily from Madrid and one from Seville; both journeys take about 7hrs. The station in Cáceres is quite a hefty walk from the centre of the city, but it is connected with the main square by bus which stops here every 20min or so.
By bus: from Madrid, buses to Cáceres take between 3–5hrs, and there are 5 daily. The bus station in Cáceres is located outside the main city centre, in the new town on C. Gil Cordero, T: (927) 22 06 00.

All the main towns of this region have a reasonable interconnecting bus service, notably to Guadalupe from Talavera, Navalmoral and Cáceres, via Trujillo; Plasencia to Cáceres; as well as north to Salamanca, and Cáceres to Trujillo.

WHERE TO STAY
This is one of the least populated parts of Spain and only a few towns are large enough to boast even a bar, let alone a hotel. Plasencia has several; try the Rincón Extremeño, T: (927) 41 11 50, or the 3-star Alfonso VIII, T: (927) 41 02 50. There is accommodation of varying quality in the nearby villages of Torrejón el Rubio (only a few km from Monfragüe) and Malpartida de Plasencia, as well as in Trujillo. However, there are 4 *paradores nacionales* in the area: the 4-star Parador de Trujillo, T: (927) 32 13 50; the 3-star Parador Zurbarán, T: (976) 36 70 75, in Guadalupe; the 3-star Parador Carlos V, T: (976) 56 01 17 in Jarandilla de la Vera; and in Oropesa, Parador Virrey Toledo, T: (923) 43 00 00.
Outdoor living: permitted within the park in strictly designated areas. Ask for details at the information centre in Villareal de San Carlos. There is also a campsite at Jarandilla, north of the park.

ACTIVITIES
Walking: several tracks and pathways lead to the interior of the park. The route to the summit of Castillo y Ermita de Monfragüe starts at the bridge over the River Tagus (Puente Cardenal); from there follow the small winding footpath up to the castle. There is a small cave nearby, which contains a few Bronze Age paintings of archers and mountain goats; unfortunately you cannot see very much as there is now a grille across the entrance to the cave, which has been put there to protect the drawings from graffiti.

Southwards from Castillo, there is a narrow cleft in the quartzite and sandstone ridge, through which road and river both squeeze, albeit on different levels. A magnificent quartzite pinnacle rises steeply from the water to your right – this is Peñafalcon, one of the most visited and popular sites in the park, largely because of its bird population. At almost any daylight hour the sky teems with birds such as the griffon vultures, passing overhead to the Sierra de las Corchuelas. On warm sunny days, if you have your binoculars handy, you will be able to see several of Monfragüe's half-dozen or so pairs of breeding black storks, perched on the south side of the rock face and reviewing the scene below them with a regal air.
Fishing: for a permit allowing you to take any of the 9 species which frequent the reservoirs, apply to ICONA in Cáceres (see below).

FURTHER INFORMATION
Tourist information: Pl. General Mola, Cáceres, T: (927) 24 63 47; C. Trujillo 17, Casa de la Cultura, Plasencia, T: (927) 41 27 66; and Pl. de España, Trujillo, T: (927) 32 06 53. ICONA, Argentina 1, Cáceres, T: (927) 22 51 30.

A park information centre is located at Villareal de San Carlos. Within the boundaries of the park is a *reserva integral*, which is closed to the public at all times, so the rarer Monfragüe birds can breed and rear their young in peace. The exact location of this closed area is unknown, so as not to attract undue attention. Respect all fences within the park – you can get spectacular views of all the bird species from well within the open-access area.

The Mediterranean Coast

Spain's Mediterranean coast has had a decisive and incalculable effect on the country's history. It was the 'middle sea' that brought the Greeks, Carthaginians and Romans to this siren shore in ancient times. Later, after the Moorish invaders had finally been ejected, Spain became, for a time, the foremost maritime power in the western Mediterranean. Columbus's discovery of America changed all that: for economic reasons, Spain's interest shifted to the Atlantic, and the Mediterranean became something of a backwater.

But in our own day the sleepy fishing villages and farming communities along this coast have been engulfed by a new but hardly less problematic invasion, this time of northern sun-seekers and vacationers, who come to these latitudes for the sunshine and pleasantly warmed saltwater they lack at home. Thus many of the once-pristine beaches of the Spanish Mediterranean have been turned into mass bronzing beds, with just enough space beside each over-exposed body to accommodate a bottle of suntan lotion, a paperback best-seller and a pair of sandals. Beyond the beaches rise the serried rows of shoebox hotels that house the sun worshippers when they're not on the beach: the consensus seems to be that these hotels are not a pretty sight, but that it's too late to do anything about it.

The sands and salt marsh and saline lagoons of the Delta del Ebro, between Barcelona and Valencia, form the largest unspoiled area of the Spanish Mediterranean

Yet there are wild places, and often they begin just behind the seaside resorts, on the landward side of the mountains that usually form a sort of rampart to the west of the beaches separating the real Spain from the land of the bikini bottom and the beach umbrella. Often it is only a short drive – or even a hike, although not in the broiling August heat if you can help it – from some of the busiest cities of the strand to some of the most deserted landscapes of the sierra. A case in point is the Sierra del Maestrazgo, which begins hardly 30 kilometres (18 miles) from the crowded beaches of Castellón de la Plana and yet belongs among the most forgotten parts of Spain, a Shangri-la of hilltop towns and fortified villages, windswept highlands and vast Mediterranean forests.

Murcia, which used to be one of the poorest provinces of Spain, has become remarkably prosperous thanks to its new-found status as *el huerto de Europa*, the fruit orchard of the European Economic Community. Not far from its capital city rises the Sierra Espuña, a part of the coastal range that contains some astonishingly wild landscapes and a *reserva nacional*. For a real sense of what the Mediterranean hinterland used to be like, you could do worse than to camp out in the Sierra Espuña for a few days.

Those who live on the shores of this great sea have always had good and sundry reasons for climbing the peaks of the nearby mountains. In Roman times there was a temple of Venus on Montserrat, the sacred mountain that rises almost sheer from the lowlands of the Catalan plain to reach a height of 1,237 metres (4,057 feet). Since the ninth century there has been a shrine to the Black Madonna at the same spot, and every year tens of thousands of pilgrims visit the sanctuary and the adjoining Benedictine monastery. But the mountain is also used by climbers from Barcelona and other nearby cities, who practise their rapelling techniques on the fantastically shaped cliffs of the Montserrat massif. Thus, while the monastery is besieged by a constant stream of visitors arriving by car and bus, the adjoining mountains are as daunting and unspoiled as any range in the further interior.

Montserrat can best be seen, incidentally, from the town of Vich (Vic), far to the north of the mountain itself. It is one of the special characteristics of this 'most Catalan of mountains' that it presents a fantastic shape from whichever side it is viewed from – a series of irregular silhouettes. From its summit you can see as far as the mountains of Aragón as well as much of nearby Cataluña; on especially clear days you may be able to discern Mallorca on the distant horizon. Two geological cataclysms account for the startling rock formations of this famous range: the first plunged the whole region to the bottom of a vast Eocene lake; the second pushed it up above what is now the valley of the Río Llobregat. Quaternary glacial action sculpted it into a series of bulging cliffs and gorges so that its outlines suggested the name Montserrat, the saw-toothed mountain.

Farther north, between Granollers and La Selva and also quite close to the coast, the Sierra de Montseny offers a less dramatic landscape but even more varied opportunities for hikers, campers and climbers. Indeed the whole coastal range behind the Costa Brava of Cataluña has summits and escarpments that afford spectacular views across the wine-dark Mediterranean, from which it is rarely separated by more than 30–40 kilometres (18–25 miles) of coastal plain.

South-west of Tortosa lies a different kind of exploration zone, the Puertos de Tortosa and Beceite (Beseit) – a region of wooded mountains and gentle valleys that is part orchard and part wilderness. This is another of the wholly unknown corners of Spain, and a walking tour of the forests and peasant villages of the Puertos de Beceite might well be combined with a birdwatching excursion to the Delta del Ebro, less than 50 kilometres (30 miles) to the east. The delta is unlike any other region of Spain, except the nearby Albufera de Valencia. Much of it consists of a succession of shallow basins for growing rice, and these, of course, make ideal feeding troughs and swimming pools for wintering birds and passage migrants. For human beings, too, the delta can hardly be bettered as an island of psychological calm light-years removed from the madding beach belt that extends endlessly north and south along almost the entire coast.

From the mouth of the Ebro to La Albufera, south of Valencia, is only 180 kilometres (112 miles) as the mallard flies, and this famous freshwater *laguna* at the edge of the Mediterranean also offers an inviting habitat for waterfowl – both for those who like to breed among its reeds and rushes, and for birds who only use it *en passant*. La Albufera and its environs cannot be said to be truly 'wild', but it does constitute an extremely important birdwatching area and is included here for that reason.

Essentially there are two Spains, the wet one and the dry one, and it is all the more remarkable to find these two great wetlands here on the Mediterranean coast, which belongs emphati-

cally to the dry Spain. In both instances, however, the water comes from the upland regions that receive far more rainfall than the coastal strip itself. In any case, the vegetation on this shore has learned to live with what the French call *la grande chaleur* – the hot, dry period from June to September, when virtually no rain falls and the sun burns down for an average of more than ten hours per day. Most plant growth ceases during the hot summer and resumes only when the first rains arrive, normally about the end of October. Which is not to say that the Mediterranean has a dependable rainy season, like the monsoons of India; there may very well be unexpected summer downpours which can wreak havoc with orchards, terraced gardens and the dry riverbeds known appropriately as *torrentes*. These abnormal downpours can also confuse the seeds that are lying in wait for the autumn; if they deceive the grasses into sprouting in July or August, the sun will soon burn them to a crisp and deprive the farmer of fodder for the winter season.

When the autumn rains come, everything wakes up from the deep summer sleep that is like hibernation in the northern countries. Almost overnight the earth turns green with vegetation and is decorated with bright red poppies. This is the 'second spring' of the Mediterranean. Some species flower during the late autumn and early winter, and some continue active growth throughout the months when it rains. Most perennials flower in the early spring and the flowering period reaches a crescendo towards the end of April, when a great variety of annuals also decks the lowlands and hillsides. By June they have died down in preparation for summer and most have shed

their seeds: only the thistles and members of the mint family are likely to be still in flower.

Withal the Mediterranean shore is renowned for the richness and variety of its plant life, with its remarkable amalgam of the wild and the cultivated, the native species and the exotic. The spiky green paddles of the prickly pear, which are such an atmospheric feature of the landscape, originally came from the New World; Columbus is said to have brought it back from one of his voyages. The century plant, or American agave, another ornamental sentinel in many dry gardens and areas of *maquis*, also came from across the seas. Indeed, palms, cacti, mimosas, eucalypts, oranges and lemons are all foreigners. The all-important olive, too, seems to have made its way westward from Asia. In the classic Mediterranean culture it provides oil for cooking, for putting on to bread and into lamps, and for every kind of medicinal use, as well as being pickled, both green and ripe; its wood is used for the fire and for carving into bowls and spoons. But no one ever cut down a tree – in ancient Greece cutting down an olive tree was a capital crime. The wood for fuel and carving is obtained from the branches and pieces of trunk that are pruned every year.

Many of the truly native plants (some of them were eventually domesticated during centuries of Mediterranean farming) grew here as long ago as Tertiary times, while the myrtle, oleander, vine, and lentisk have all survived the intervening Ice Ages of the Quaternary period. The carob, the sole survivor of some pre-Ice Age family, yields the long brown beans known as St John's bread, as the saint is said to have lived on them in the wilderness. Its fructose-rich filling can, in fact, taste like candy when the bean has ripened to a dark brown, but while green it has an absolutely ghastly taste, and even the sheep won't touch it then.

In valleys such as the Puertos de Beceite the whole brilliant spectrum of Mediterranean plant life can unfold during the spring, autumn and winter: the olives and carobs on the terraced orchards; fruit trees of many varieties; palms rising proudly beside the farmhouses and rustling in the wind; the pine woods in the mountains and holm oak forests; the wild flowers scattered among the rocks. The sheer sensuous pleasure of these fruits and flowers, tastes and odours, is enough to make anyone forget the sandy delights of the beaches that lie just down the road.

GETTING THERE

By air: the airports of the Mediterranean coast are Barcelona, T: (93) 317 01 78, Valencia, T: (96) 370 95 00 and Alicante, T: (965) 28 50 11, all of which have frequent flights to and from the major European cities. There are also regular internal flights.

By sea: the main ports of the region are Barcelona and Valencia, both with regular car-ferry services to the Balearics and sporadic sailing to and from other Spanish ports. International shipping lines are concentrated in Barcelona, whence there are periodic departures and arrivals from Italy, Yugoslavia, Turkey, etc. For information, contact the Puerto de Barcelona, T: (93) 318 87 50; or the Estación Marítima Internacional, T: (93) 301 25 98. The Puerto de Valencia number is (96) 323 09 91; the Alicante number is (965) 20 22 55.

By car: there is easy access to the coast from the French border all the way to Murcia and Cartagena. A superhighway known as the Autopista del Mediterráneo runs parallel to the coast; it constitutes a fast way of getting to the wild places and away from the tourist centre. For road information, T: (93) 204 22 47.

By rail: an excellent service operates along the Mediterranean coast, on RENFE's Barcelona–Valencia–Alicante line. Eight trains a day run from Barcelona (Sants station) to Valencia, with stops at Tarragona, Tortosa and Castellón; about half also make local stops along the line. From Valencia there are 7 trains a day to Alicante: the main stations en route are Játira (Xàtira), Villena and Elda. Only 1 train a day goes from Alicante to Murcia: this is the through train that covers

In Spain, lesser grey shrikes breed only in Aiguamolls de L'Empordà

the distance from Portbou–Cerbère on the French frontier to the Levante, and Murcia is the last stop.

There are frequent trains from Madrid to Valencia and Castellón or Gandía. It is complicated, however, getting from Andalucía to the Mediterranean coastal region, and involves changing from the Madrid–Andalucía line to the Madrid–Alicante line at Alcázar de San Juan. For information and reservations, call Madrid (91) 429 82 28, open every day of the year from 9am–9pm.

By bus: there are regular buses from Barcelona and Gerona (Girona) that cover the entire Mediterranean coast north of Barcelona. There services are mainly provided

by 3 companies: Compañía de Ferrocaril San Felio de Guixols a Girona, T: (972) 20 77 70 (Gerona), and T: (972) 320 05 76 (San Felíu de Guíxols); the 'Línea regular de Viajeros', between Lloret de Mar, Vidreras and Gerona – in Gerona, T: (972) 20 10 18, and Lloret, T: (972) 33 41 42, 33 40 72, and 33 58 32; and the Línea Sarfa, connecting Barcelona, Gerona and the Costa Brava, T: (972) 20 17 96 (Gerona).

Numerous companies cover the coast south of Barcelona; for information, T: (93) 329 06 06 (Barcelona); (965) 22 07 00 (Alicante); (968) 29 22 11 (Murcia); and (96) 349 72 22 (Valencia).

WHEN TO GO
Needless to say, when the coastal resorts are not jammed with tourists they look depressingly deserted. But if you keep away from the coast, there's not much problem of overcrowding.

WHERE TO STAY
Thousands of hotels have been erected on Spain's Mediterranean coast, but the wild places behind the beaches and in the Sierra tend to be in areas where hotels are few and far between. For accommodation near the nature areas, consult the individual entries or ask at tourist offices (see below).

ACTIVITIES
Mountaineering Clubs: Federació d'Entitats Excursionistes de Catalunya, Rambles 61–1°, Barcelona 2, T: (93) 302 64 16; and Federación Valenciana de Montañismo, Castellón 12–4°, 16a, Valencia 4, T: (96) 321 93 58.
Skiing: the closest resort for downhill skiing is in Teruel – Sierra de Gúdar.

FURTHER INFORMATION
Alicante (965): tourist office, Esplanada de España 2, T: 21 22 85. Red Cross, T: 23 07 02. Highway information, Pl. de la Montañeta, T: 21 22 29.
Barcelona (93): tourist office, Gran Vía de las Coertes Catalanas 658, T: 304 74 43. Red Cross, T: 205 14 14. Highway information, Roux 80, T: 205 13 13.
Castellón (964): tourist office, Pl. María Agustina 5, T: 22 74 04. Red Cross, T: 22 48 50. Highway information, Avda del Mar 16, T: 22 05 54.
Gerona (972): tourist office, C. Ciudadanos 12, T: 20 16 94; hotel information, T: 20 45 49; tourist information for the Costa Brava, T: 20 84 03. Red Cross, T: 20 04 15. Highway information, Gran Vía Jaume I 41, T: 20 92 58.
Murcia (986): tourist office, C. Alejandro Seiquier 4, T: 21 37 16. Red Cross, T: 21 88 93. Highway information, Avda de Perea 1, T: 25 45 00.
Valencia (96): tourist office, C. de la Paz 46, T: 352 28 97, 334 56 04 and 334 56 05. Red Cross, T: 360 62 11. Highway information, Blasco Ibáñez 50, T: 360 06 60

FURTHER READING
Rose Macauley, *Fabled Shore* (London, 1949); George Orwell, *Homage to Catalonia* (London, 1938).

Aiguamolls de L'Empordà

One of the last wetland refuges in Mediterranean Spain, 25km (16 miles) south of the French border

From the air, the Golfo de Rosas, enclosed by the foothills of the Pyrenees, looks as though some huge, mythical sea-beast has bitten a chunk from the land. Although it is one of the least spoiled parts of the tourist-ridden Costa Brava, the area is full of high-rise hotels, and the great Perpignan–Barcelona motorway snakes its way across the lowland plain less than ten kilometres (six miles) from the sea. But sandwiched between sea and speeding cars, in the heart of this piecemeal but ever-growing concrete conurbation, lies one of the last wetland refuges in Mediterranean Spain: Aiguamolls de L'Empordà.

The ruins of three great cities built on top of each other, remnants of Greek, Iberian and Roman civilizations, mark the southernmost limit of Aiguamolls de L'Empordà. It was known at various points in its history as Emporion, Empurias, Ampuñas, and today as Ampurías (Empúries); the name derives from the Greek for 'trading station'. All that remains today is a maze of partially excavated foundations.

As recently as the early eighteenth century, most of the coastal lowlands of Empordà were a wilderness of vast fresh-water and salt-water lakes, interspersed with marshlands and riverine forests. At this time Castelló d'Ampurías, lying on the Río Muga, in the north of the bay, was surrounded by low-lying swamps and lagoons. As this town declined in importance, so the marshes have gradually disappeared, being used originally for rice cultivation and limited cattle-rearing, but more recently for intensive farming of arable crops, such as maize, sunflowers and barley. Now only fragmentary lagoons persist, and the remaining wilderness areas are increasingly threatened by tourism.

The Golfo de Rosas is separated from France by the ancient granite and slate spit of the Cadaqués peninsula to the north. The coastal depression curves upwards to the south and west in a series of dissected hills of Tertiary age, before rearing up to meet the nether regions of the Pyrenees beyond; the southerly promontory, on which L'Estartit stands, is composed of limestone and has spectacular underwater caves at its tip.

In response to the obvious threats from agricultural intensification and tourist development, and as a result of a certain amount of environmental lobbying, the Catalan parliament declared a large area of the remaining wetlands a *parc natural* in 1983. There are three 'integral' reserves within the park: one is a salt marsh area – a large pentagonal block lying inland from the beach between the Muga and Fluvià rivers where the existing lagoon system is to be extended to attract more breeding and migrating birds. There are eight such *llaunes*, or lagoons, which are connected with both rivers when the water levels are high, but are also very close to the sea, and thus are inundated several times a year when storms cause the Mediterranean to break over the dunes.

The second reserve lies farther north, on the site of the former lake of Castelló d'Ampurías. It consists of a number of *estanys* and *closes* – water meadows and grazing marshes – which receive freshwater from Alberes and the St Pere de Roda mountains to the north all year round. L'Aigua Clara is the only remaining part of the great lake, and is now covered with reeds and reedmace. Surrounding this central reserve is a large area of similar countryside, including La Rovina, which comprises tiny strips of land, or *peces*, bordered by irrigation channels and tamarisk hedges. This wetland would seem more at home in central France or southern England, with its small fields, bounded by elm and ash hedgerows or by narrow ditches flanked with all manner of water-loving plants. The freshwater marsh overflows with sedges and club-rushes, stands of yellow flag and purple loosestrife, and the huge purple-pink blooms of the marsh mallow.

By far the smallest of the reserves is the Illa de Caramany, on the Río Fluvià, which was isolated in 1979 by dredging work in the riverbed, and consequently has great value as untouched riverine woodland that serves as a refuge for wildlife. As recently as the spring of 1987 a species of iris new to Empordà was discovered here for the first time.

The salt marsh 'steppes' form a complex mosaic of halophytic vegetation, interspersed with the irregular brackish lagoons. Pure mats of a succulent sea plantain, level enough for a football field, are dotted here and there with golden samphire and sea wormwood. Wetter areas support sea rush, sea purslane, several species of glasswort and sea lavender, while to the seaward side, in the summer, the continually shifting dunes are a blaze of pinks and mauves – flowering sea rocket and sea stock, sea holly and sea bindweed. The lagoons are filled with the delicate fronds of horned pondweed, tasselweeds, water milfoils and hornworts, attracting myriad wildfowl during the winter. One of the most memorable sights is of the white-studded sheets of brackish water crowfoot that bloom on the lake at Vilaüt in spring.

More than 20 mammal species frequent the park, although some such as the otter, are now so uncommon that they are feared extinct, despite breeding further upstream in both rivers. Of the smaller creatures, oak dormice, European white-toothed shrews, Etruscan shrews, water voles, long-tailed field mice, short-tailed voles, moles and hedgehogs have all been recorded here, as have rabbits, hares, weasels and foxes. Beech martens are sighted occasionally, and polecats are quite common in the marshes. The 11 bat species help to control the thriving mosquito population; they include three species of horseshoe bat, as well as bent-winged and Daubenton's bats. In the winter, families of wild boar sometimes leave the neighbouring hills to feed in the *closes*.

The sun sets dramatically over the sand dunes, essential to the preservation of the unique salt marsh habitat of Aiguamolls

Amphibians and reptiles are no less diverse. The marshes ring with the calls of painted frogs, and you can observe natterjack and common toads, western and common spadefoots, marbled and palmate newts and stripeless tree frogs; the latter is only about the length of your little finger with disc-shaped climbing pads on its feet. I was lucky enough to see a stripe-necked terrapin slipping silently into a pool; the European pond terrapin has been recorded here, too. The drier, rocky places are the haunt of the spiny-footed and Iberian wall

lizards, as well as both species of psammodromus and Moorish geckos, or you may catch a glimpse of the much larger green-and-yellow ocellated lizard. Montpellier and ladder snakes, the former mildly poisonous, occur here, as do grass snakes, viperine snakes, slow-worms and three-toed skinks.

But the wealth of birds in Aiguamolls de L'Empordà is the main attraction of these important wetlands: it is an ornithological paradise, particularly during the spring and autumn migratory seasons. The presence of the garganey so far south of its normal breeding quarters is one of the fascinating mysteries of this park. Notable breeding birds include stone-curlews, black-winged stilts and marsh harriers. In the more Mediterranean vegetation of the granite outcrops in the northern part of the reserve, it is not unusual to see rollers, bee-eaters and great spotted cuckoos hunting among the nettle trees and fragrant, narrow-leaved cistus.

The beach, although part of the salt marsh integral reserve, is much visited by sun-seekers, and consequently only a few pairs of Kentish plovers manage to nest here successfully. There are hopes that, if access can be restricted during the breeding season, little ringed plovers and little terns will return to rear their young here.

During the winter, black-throated divers are a frequent sight in the bay, and red-throated divers and great northern divers can be seen occasionally. Winter is also the season when cormorants, razorbills, eiderducks and common and velvet scoters use the sheltered waters of the Golfo de Rosas as a resting point, as do goosanders and red-breasted mergansers. If you are lucky, you may see a small flock of greater flamingoes, who drop in on the salt marsh during migration time; lone individuals have been known to stay for the whole winter.

It is during spring and autumn migrations, however, that these marshlands come into their own. Some of the more exotic species that have been known to frequent Aiguamolls de L'Empordà are spoonbills and glossy ibis, red-crested pochard, black-necked and Slavonian grebes, short-eared owls and common cranes. Almost all European members of the heron family have been recorded here, as well as some rare visitors from Africa: great white egret, bittern, squacco heron, little egret and cattle egret. Purple and night herons, little bitterns and grey herons all breed here, and there are hopes that some of the wild egrets will be attracted to an enclosure which contains several breeding pairs, so that these species return to nest here once again.

Small birds are no less exciting than these giants of the marshes; at any time you can hear reed and Cetti's warblers that frequent the denser stands of vegetation. Both penduline and bearded tits are attracted to the relatively pollution-free Fluvià and Muga rivers to breed. Other breeding passerines include moustached Savi's and great reed warblers, as well as nightingales and yellow wagtails. The three or four pairs of lesser grey shrikes that breed in the freshwater marsh represent the only regular pairs in the Iberian peninsula. In all some 300 species of bird have been recorded within the park, of which approximately 90 are known to breed here.

BEFORE YOU GO
Maps: SGE 1:50,000 Nos. 258 and 259; and Michelin No. 443, 1:400,000.
Guidebook: Rose Macaulay, *Fabled Shore* (1949).

GETTING THERE
By air: there is a wide variety of international flights to Barcelona, which is, of course, well served by Iberia's internal network.
By car: approaching from Gerona or from France, leave the Autopista del Mediterraneo at Figueras, then take highway 260 which continues through the area to Rosas.
By rail: from Barcelona, there are some 6 trains daily to Gerona and points north, taking up to 2½hrs to reach Figueras. If you take the Portbou–Barcelona line the closest stations to the park are Camallera, Sant Miguel de Fluvià, Vilamalla, Figueras and Vilajuïga.
By bus: from Barcelona you
116

can take the Lancha Litoral line ('waterbus') which stops at almost every beach. Alternatively, from Figueras, the SAFRA bus company runs some 6 buses daily to Rosas and Cadaqués from the station on C. Méndez Núñez; alight at the turn-off to San Pedro Pescador (Sant Pere Pescador) and walk to the park, which takes about 30min.

WHERE TO STAY
The nearest town is Castelló d'Ampurías where there are several good hotels, including All Ioli, T: (972) 25 03 00. In San Pedro Pescador there is the Hostal Coll-verd, T: (972) 52 00 75.
Outdoor living: 5 campsites are located within the boundaries of Aiguamolls de L'Empordà itself: Camping Almatà, on the road to San Pedro Pescador from Castelló d'Ampurías; Camping Laguna, on the crossroads of the same 2 villages; and Camping Internacional,

Camping Castell Mar and Camping La Estrella, all situated on the road between Figueras and Rosas near Castelló d'Ampurías.

ACTIVITIES
Walking: the best times to visit Aiguamolls de L'Empordà to see birds are between Mar–May, and Aug, when large numbers of waders and wildfowl use the park as a migration route 'stepping stone'. Morning and early evening are the times when you are most likely to be rewarded by sightings from the bird hides. Botanically, the park is at its best in May. Empordà is subject to a battering from the Mistral for up to a week in spring.

FURTHER INFORMATION
Tourist information: Avda de Rhode, Rosas, T: (972) 25 73 31; and Pl. del Sol, Figueras, T: (972) 50 31 55.
The park information centre is at El Cortalet, at the

entrance to the park near Castelló d'Ampurías (on the road to San Pedro Pescador), T: (972) 25 03 22.

When walking in the reserve, take heed of any signposts indicating the route or forbidding entry: these are to protect the most sensitive breeding areas.

Mosquito repellent is strongly recommended.

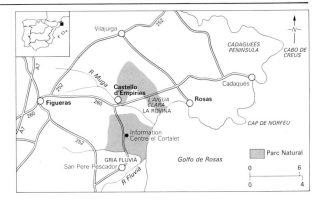

Islas Medes

Small archipelago of uninhabited islands, 2km (1¼ miles) off village of L'Estartit

There are 2 islands (*illes*), Meda Gran and Meda Xica, and 3 islets (*illots*): Magallot, Cavall Bernat and Tascons. Collectively they represent a far-flung spur of the Montgrí massif whose limestone has been deeply eroded by the action of the sea. Important colonies of gulls have existed here for many years as well as breeding pairs of cormorants

Cormorants are the most conspicuous beneficiaries of the ban on fishing in the waters around the Islas Medes

and falcons. A project for turning the Islas (Illes) Medes into a *parque natural* is still under study: meanwhile the Generalitat de Catalunya has issued an order prohibiting fishing in the archipelago and restricting access.

Beneath the waterline some of the islands are honeycombed with caves and tunnels. There is a wide variety of marine life, coral beds, and a small amount of surface vegetation – including sea fennel, or samphire.

The only island that can be visited is Meda Gran, which has a small quay known as the Cos de Guardia, since the island's former military garrison once used it as a landing stage. But the government's intention is to

keep the human presence to a minimum.

Before you go *Maps:* SGE 1:50,000 No. 335; and IGN 1:200,000 Mapa provincial of Gerona.

Getting there *By sea:* during the summer months there is a regular boat service which runs from L'Estartit to the Meda Gran.

Where to stay: L'Estartit is a beach resort; there are more than 20 hotels from which to choose, ranging from the 3-star Bell Aire, T: (972) 75 81 62, to the 1-star Medas II, T: (972) 75 84 80.

Further information *Tourist information:* C. Ciudadanos 12, Gerona, T: (972) 20 16 94. ICONA, Avda San Francisco 29, Gerona, T: (972) 20 09 87.

Montseny

*Protected area of representative
European woodland growing on the
easternmost peaks of the Pyrenees*

The massif of Montseny resembles nothing so much as a geological castle bordered by a moat that acts as a watershed. The castle's four towers are the Turó de l'Home ('the man's peak', 1,714 metres/5,622 feet); Les Agudes ('the sharp ones', 1,707 metres/5,600 feet); Matagalls ('the cock-killer', 1,694 metres/5,556 feet); and Puigdrau (1,350 metres/4,430 feet). Together with the tableland known as El Pla de la Calma ('the plain of tranquility'), they form a clearly defined ecological zone that lies a short distance inland from the Mediterranean coast, roughly midway between Gerona and Barcelona. Montseny – which means 'the mountain of good sense' – was made a *parque natural* in 1978 and declared a Biosphere reserve by UNESCO shortly afterward.

The mountain landscape is gentle rather than dramatic, with rounded hilltops and wooded slopes occasionally interspersed with steep ravines. Just as Catalan culture combines both Spanish and northern Euro-pean influences, the ecosystem of this region unites virtually every tree that grows in Western Europe: the Mediterranean pines and holm oak at the base of the mountains, and the northern beech and fir higher up on the slopes, together with Scots pines, the maple of the Bohemian forests and the chestnut trees of Italy.

One of the higher passes of Montseny, Col Pregón (1,600 metres/5,250 feet), is reached by travelling through some of the most extensive beech woods in this part of Spain. On reaching the summit, the flora changes abruptly to dwarfed high-altitude species, the variety limited somewhat by the acidic granite and gneiss bed-rock. One plant worth a mention is the endemic *Saxifraga vayredana*, an aromatic species with resinous leaves and, like most saxifrages, small white flowers. It grows together with the ubiquitous meadow saxifrage, a plant indicative of acid soils, but also with mountain cornflower (*Centaurea montana*), which usually favours a more calcareous environment. An orchid species typical of southern Spain and the Mediterranean region, the violet bird's-nest orchid (*Limodorum abortivum*) grows in the pine woods that flank the lower slopes of Montseny, its large upright spikes studded with curved, purple-flushed blooms at regular intervals.

Probably the most interesting species at Montseny – and in the immediately adjacent mountain areas – is an endemic race of the spring ringlet butterfly (*Erebia epistygne ribasi*). This rather ordinary-looking brown creature prefers open areas in the mountains, between 1,000–2,400 metres (3,300–7,900 feet), and flies between May and June.

The mountains are full of Romanesque ruins, but among the churches still standing is the thousand-year-old monastery of Sant Marçal near the centre of the massif: from here it takes about two hours to walk to the summit of Matagalls. Because amethysts have been found in this region, the poets have called Montseny 'the mountain of amethysts'. This is something of an exaggeration – but it may be advisable to walk with downcast eyes while rambling through the park.

Trees of many kinds grow on the well watered slopes of Montseny, just inland from Barcelona

BEFORE YOU GO
Maps: SGE 1:50,000 Nos. 332 and 364; and IGN 1:200,000 Mapas provinciales of Barcelona and Gerona.
Guidebooks: *Montseny* (Editorial Alpina, Barcelona); and *El Montseny, parc natural* by A. Jonch (Barcelona).

GETTING THERE
By car: on A17 (Autopista Barcelona–Perpignan) exit towards Vich and then take your choice of the villages of the massif, which itself lies just west of the highway.
By rail: there is a regular service from Barcelona to Sant Celoni on the line to Gerona and to Vich on the Barcelona–Ripoll railway.
By bus: buses run several times a day from Sant Celoni to most of the villages of the massif, T: (93) 867 10 38.

WHERE TO STAY
At Montseny there is a 3-star hotel – the San Bernat, T: (93) 847 30 11 – and 2 1-star hostels. Viladrau, a lovely village to the north, has 6 hostels, including de la Gloria, T: (972) 884 90 34. Tona and Taradell also offer accommodation.

FURTHER INFORMATION
Tourist information:
C. Ciudadanos 12, Gerona, T: (972) 20 16 94. ICONA, Avda San Francisco 29, Gerona, T: (972) 20 09 87.

Montserrat's fantastic crenellations overlook orderly bands of woodland

Montserrat

Area of unusual landscape and rare vegetation 50km (30 miles) from Barcelona

Famous for its religious connotations and its serrated silhouette, Montserrat has drawn millions of visitors to its C9th monastery and shrine of the Black Madonna. The highest point of the mountain is San Jerónimo (Sant Jeroni – 1,238m/4,060ft); the towering pillars, eroded into fantastic, smooth-walled pinnacles, suggest a greater altitude.

The Oligocene conglomerates that make up much of this surreal landscape are responsible also for the acidity of the soil, and the

relatively low botanical diversity. The middle slopes are clothed in forests of pine and evergreen oaks, with a dense understorey of junipers, snow mespilus (*Amelanchier ovalis*), strawberry tree, tree heath, box, shrubby hare's-ear (*Bupleurum fruticosum*) and laurustinus. Among this largely evergreen display stand out the bright yellow flowers of scorpion senna (*Coronilla ermerus*).

On the south-facing slopes there is a more Mediterranean vegetation, characterized by fewer trees and more aromatic shrubs, such as cistus and rosemary, as well as stunted Kermes oaks (*Quercus coccifera*). This latter, also known as the grain tree, is the host plant of the scale insect *Coccus ilicis*, the female of which produces a red dye when dried.

More open patches within this *matorral* are colonized by such herbs as grass-leaved buttercup (*Ranunculus gramineus*), easily distinguished by its linear, glaucous leaves and large golden flowers, and thyme and snapdragons, with trailing stems of the woolly white-leaved *Convolvulus lanuginosus*, studded at intervals with pink, candy-striped, bell-shaped flowers. Broomrapes and grape hyacinths shelter beneath the tall stems of *Thalictrum tuberosum*, topped by its spectacular, shaggy cream-coloured flowers.

Other parts of Montserrat harbour an assemblage of species more typical of north-eastern Spain and the Pyrenees. On the rocky, exposed summit, for instance, bloom Spanish gorse (*Genista hispanica*) and gromwell (*Lithospermum fruticosum*).

Before you go *Maps:* SGE 1:50,000 Nos. 420 and 421.
Getting there *By car:* Montserrat is about 50km (31 miles) from Barcelona on the N-II Barcelona–Lerida highway. Turn right off this road on to either the C1411 to Monistrol or, a little farther north, on to a small road towards Guardiola.
By rail: there is a regular train from Barcelona to Montserrat, the 'Ferrocarriles Catalanes', leaving from below Pl. d'Espanya. The train connects with a cable-car that takes you up the mountain – a popular but splendidly scenic trip.
By bus: from Barcelona, buses for Montserrat leave from the Pl. de la Universitat.
Where to stay: since Montserrat can easily be explored in a day and is so close to Barcelona, you could stay in the city. Montserrat itself has limited accommodation.
Outdoor living: there is a campsite near the monastery of Montserrat.
Further information *Tourist information:* Sant Cugat: Pl. de Barcelona 17, Barcelona, T: (93) 674 09 50. ICONA, Roberto Bassas 22, Barcelona 14, T: (93) 321 13 29.

Delta del Ebro

Tens of thousands of birds are attracted to these vast wetlands at the mouth of the Ebro near Tortosa

The Ebro – the ancient Iberus river that gave its name to the entire peninsula – is the only one of the five great rivers of Spain that flows into the Mediterranean. Draining a vast watershed, it reaches the sea near the southern boundary of Cataluña (Catalunya), where its delta juts out from an otherwise regular coastline: from the air it resembles a giant green-and-brown arrowhead.

It is an area of rice fields and wetlands that attracts birds by the tens of thousands. An ornithological census conducted in 1980–81 determined that the autumn popu-
lation included some 53,000 ducks and 13,000 coots, with, in each case, a little less than half that number wintering in the region. Among the delta's most closely watched and carefully protected species is the red-crested pochard, which is on the endangered list. The drakes are truly spectacular: large birds with bright crimson bill, eyes and legs, contrasting strongly with the vermilion-orange head and black breast. The flamingo gatherings in the Salinas (Salinés) and the Punta de la Banya are one of the major attractions of the Parc Natural del Delta de L'Ebre, as the local park is officially known.

Waders such as sandpipers, plovers, snipe, curlew and lapwing also find this a congenial habitat. Thousands of them migrate here from the Baltic and other northern regions, while others remain throughout the year. At any given time the number of birds in residence varies from

120

50,000 to 100,000, drawn from about 250 species – which is all the more remarkable considering that the delta has an area of only 32,000 hectares (79,075 acres).

The Delta del Ebro reminds me of Holland, not only on account of its wind-swept expanses of flat fields but by virtue of its tidy houses and villages, its canals and river boats. Everything here seems to move as slowly as the water in the ditches and canals. Along the narrow tracks leading past canals and rice fields you still see carts pulled by marsh ponies, bells jingling on their harnesses. The whole landscape has a hand-made look, and indeed, although tractors have taken over much of the heavy work, many farmers still perform stoop labour of the kind more often seen in Asia than in Europe. Often there are patches of cane between the fields and shallow ponds in which stilt-legged birds are busy looking for a mid-day snack.

The rice paddies change dramatically with the seasons. In winter the fields are dry and covered with stubble and weeds; in spring they plough up the fields and the whole delta smells of newly turned earth – once the rice is sown, the fields are flooded and transformed into shallow lagoons.

Whatever it might lack as a wilderness, the birds certainly find the delta a good environment in which to nest and raise their young. And although only a few areas of the delta have been set aside as a *parc natural*, all of it strikes me as an exceedingly restful place to visit when you want to get away from it all. Except during the hunting season, when an average of 34,000 ducks are shot.

The hunting season aside, among the memorable delta experiences, though only for early risers, are the huge flights of ducks that pass noisily overhead just after the sun comes up; often, thousands spend the night in the large lagoons on the right bank of the Ebro – L'Encanyissada and La Tancada. But some of the most interesting birds are difficult to find: the squacco, purple and night herons, the marsh harrier, bittern, pratincole and short-eared owl, as well as the oystercatcher, avocet, slender-billed and Audouin's gull. Several species of tern find a suitable summer home here. Among the rice fields whiskered terns hawk for insects and build their nests. Gull-billed terns, regarded as 'sea' terns, mainly nest on drying islands in the lagoons, and plunge into the sea in search of fish. Sandwich terns have a major Mediterranean colony here.

The Salinas are the preferred breeding ground of terns, avocets and black-winged stilts. Some 500 pairs of little terns have been observed at Punta del Fangar, where there is also a colony of gull-billed terns; at Punta de la Banya there are colonies of little terns, common terns and black-headed gulls. Whiskered terns are particularly common on the Canal Vell lagoon, and purple herons breed in the reeds on Buda Island (which is privately owned but within the park boundaries). This is the easternmost point of the delta, the tip of the arrow as it were.

Otters are to be found in the park, too, along with several other protected species: the Valencian and Iberian toothcarp; the stripeless tree frog; and the stripe-necked and European terrapins.

BEFORE YOU GO
Maps: SGE 1:50,000 Nos. 522, 523 and 547; and IGN 1:200,000 Mapa provincial of Tarragona.

GETTING THERE
By car: on the Autopista Barcelona–Valencia (A7) take the exit for L'Aldea and Amposta. The ordinary highway, N340, from Barcelona to Valencia runs through the villages on the western boundary of the delta. Near Amposta you have to decide whether to drive along the right or the left bank of the Ebro – there are no bridges further downstream. Three small flatboat ferries operate between Deltebre and Sant Jaume d'Enveja, at the centre of the delta, but only during daylight hours. The 2 roads that run parallel to the river both continue to the mouth of the Ebro, about 25km (15 miles) to the east of Amposta, and you may well want to begin your explorations at the far end.

The name Deltebre, incidentally, was recently created when 2 adjoining villages were amalgamated, and some of the road signs have not yet been brought up to date: the signs 'Jesús i

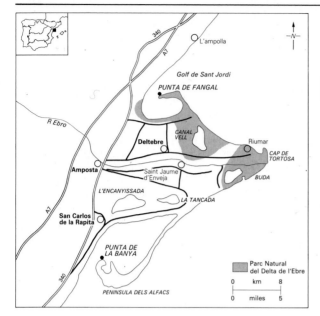

The stripe-necked terrapin starts life with vivid orange stripes which fade to creamy yellow in the adult

María' and 'La Cava' refer to the constituent villages of Deltebre and will get you there.

By rail: the delta can be reached from any of 3 stations on the railway line between Barcelona and Valencia: L'Aldea–Amposta, Camarles and L'Ampolla. There are several local trains a day in each direction, but the schedule varies with the season: make certain that the train you take stops at one of the above stations.

By bus: the long-distance Barcelona–Valencia buses stop at Amposta, from where there is a local bus service to all the villages within the delta. For information, T: (93) 322 78 14 in Barcelona, or T: (977) 44 03 00 in Tortosa.

WHERE TO STAY

It is not difficult to find a place to stay in the delta. Accommodation includes the 3-star Miami Park, T: (977) 74 03 51, and 9 other hotels or hostels in San Carlos de la

Ràpita, at the south-west corner of the delta. Within the delta are hotels and small pensions in every village.

The people of the delta are remarkably friendly and helpful toward the visitors who come pouring into this peaceful corner of the world. Simply by asking around in the smaller villages – notably Sant Jaume d'Enveja – you

Astragalus monspessulanus is a form of vetch adapted to dry, stony soils

can find yourself a guest room in a country house at a very modest price.

Outdoor living: there are also several campsites. In Amposta: Mediterrani Blau, T: (977) 48 62 12; in San Carles de la Ràpita: Alfacs, T: (977) 74 05 61, and Noya, T: (977) 74 17 21. For camping inside the delta, ask the information centre at Deltebre (see below), which can direct you to many possible sites.

FURTHER INFORMATION

Tourist information: Pl. Carles III, Sant Carles de la Ràpita, T: (977) 74 01 00; and Amposta, T: (977) 70 00 57.

The park information centre at Deltebre (Pl. 20 de Maig, T: (977) 48 95 11) has a staff of specially trained guides, organizes group tours, and can provide summer rental lists.

Try not to visit the delta on holiday weekends; even if you can manage to avoid the many holidaymakers who crowd into the area on such occasions, the birds are aware of their presence and go into hiding.

As it nears its mouth, the Ebro flows slowly through reed-fringed channels between a succession of small islands

'Between Tortosa and the sea spreads the marshy, lagoon-strewn delta of the Ebro, and the strange encircling hook, like a parrot's beak, of the Punta del Calacho curls protectingly round the almost enclosed harbour basin that for centuries was fought for by Romans, Carthaginians, Saracens, French and Spaniards. It is indeed a harbour, as Tortosa is a city, and the Ebro a river, worth fighting for.'

Rose Macaulay, *Fabled Shore*

Puertos de Beceite

Land of contrasts encompassing nearly 30,000ha (74,000 acres) of reserva nacional, *and spanning three provinces*

This is another of the half-forgotten corners of Spain, notable for the striking contrasts of its rugged mountain terrain and the neatly tended fields and orchards of its unspoiled valleys. The massif forming the Puertos de Beceite (also called Puertos de Beseit) constitutes a kind of bridge between the Sistema Ibérico and the Prelitoral mountains. The range starts south-west of the Ebro and continues inland in a chain of calcareous peaks that rise from the Tossal d'En Grilló (1,076m/3,530ft) to Encanadé (1,396m/4,579ft). Nearly 30,000ha (74,130 acres) of the Puertos have been designated a *reserva nacional* which abounds in vast numbers of chamois, wild boar and red partridges.

Beceite includes portions of 3 provinces – Tarragona, Castellón and Teruel – and takes its name from the little fruit-growing village of Beceite, the last in the Teruel province. The Tossal dels Tres Reis (1,356m/4,450ft) rises at the meeting point of the 3

regions, near Fredes on the road to Los Puertos. According to legend, the 3 kings of Cataluña, Aragón and Valencia used to arrange meetings here in days of old, each standing on a slice of his own domain.

A range of mountains called Rafelgarí forms a wedge between the provinces of Castellón and Teruel. There is a refuge for hikers in the Rafelgarí, about 12km (7 miles) from Fredes and separated by a steep ravine from a historic hermitage, the Ermita de San Miguel. The bare bones that are always dropping into this ravine are crumbs from the table of the many vultures which have their natural feeding trough high above the gorge, at the edge of an almost sheer cliff. (Rafelgarí boasts yet another

Some of the finest beech trees in Europe grow in the Puertos de Beceite

refuge, this one more centrally placed.)

Fredes is lost among the mountains at 1,090m (3,575ft). It has only a handful of residents in the winter but numerous inhabitants in the summer, when it still manages to live up to its name: *fred* means cold in Catalan. The Barranco del Retaule, in the southern part of the Puertos, near La Sénia, is noted for its remarkable forest of beech trees, pines and box trees (whence its name, for Catalan altar pieces, or *retaules*, used to be made of box wood). Some of these beeches, growing at 1,200m (4,000ft), are not only among the most southerly in Europe but among the largest: 'El faig pare' ('the father of trees') is enormous as beeches go. The same forest also contains the biggest pine tree in Cataluña, El Pi de la Vall Canera, which measures a massive 5m (16½ft) in circumference. It would take four good-sized people standing finger-tip to finger-tip to span its trunk. **Before you go** *Maps:* SGE 1:50,000 Nos. 496, 520, 521, 545, 546; IGN 1:200,000 Mapas provinciales of Tarragona, Castellón and Teruel.

Guidebooks: El Matarrana y la Sierra Turolenses by J. Monclus; and *Los Montes de Tarragona* by Antonio Calero Pico (Alcoy, 1982).

Getting there *By car:* the Puertos de Beceite can be approached from the north or south via the Vinaròs–Zaragoza highway, N232. At Monroyo, take the TE302 side road that takes you to Valderrobres; from there Beceite is at the end of a dramatic 7km (4½ mile) mountain road (TE304). Starting from Tortosa, take highway N230 toward Gandesa and turn west

towards Prat de Compte after some 40km (25 miles) on to the T330, which again leads to Valderrobres. From Tarragona, the most direct route is via highway N420 in the direction of Gandesa.
By bus: there are daily buses from Tarragona and Tortosa to Valderrobres and Alcañiz; they stop at most of the villages in the Puertos. For more detailed bus information, T: (977) 44 03 00 in Tarragona or T: (93) 322 78 14 in Barcelona.
Where to stay: only 3 villages within the Puertos offer accommodation: Ulldecona, Calaceite and Valderrobres.

Nearby Tortosa has a choice of hotels ranging from the 4-star Parador Nacional de Castillo de la Zuda, T: (977) 44 44 50, to 1-star hostels. Morella, a magnificent old walled city, also makes a good base for exploring the region, and has several hotels, including the 2-star Cardenal Ram, T: (964) 16 00 00.
Refuges: there are 2 refuges in the Rafelgarí mountain range. Les Clotes is in the north of the range about 12km (7 miles) from Fredes, while Caseta del Frare is situated more in the central region.
Activities *Walking:* a particularly enjoyable

excursion is that following the track from Embalse de Ulldecona up to the village of Fredes. The trail skirts impressive ravines such as El Mangraners and La Tenalla, and crosses the Portell de l'Infern ('the door to the inferno') to Fredes; it takes about 5 hrs at least at a brisk pace. Though count on spending quite a lot longer, if you want to admire the countryside at leisure.
Further information *Tourist information:* Carrer de Fortuny, Tarragona, T: (977) 23 34 15. ICONA, Avda de Cataluña, Tarragona, T: (977) 21 78 56.

La Albufera de Valencia

One of the largest bodies of freshwater in Spain, located just south of Valencia and attracting birds of passage

This famous *laguna* south of Valencia is an important wetland, and birds of passage love to feed in its surrounding rice fields. People like to eat here, too: the village of El Palmar, more or less surrounded by La Albufera, has been transformed from a collection of reed-thatched fishermen's huts into an agglomeration of restaurants, each trying to outdo the others with the magnificence of its *paella valenciana*. You come here, therefore, to watch birds through binoculars and then, when the sun has set, to study menus with equal intensity. It is sometimes very difficult to move after one of these gargantuan feasts of rice, game birds and seafood. Fortunately for the comatose (although not for resident birds), there is a surfeit of nearby beach hotels along the strip of land between the *laguna* and the sea; in any of these you can sleep off the effects of a too-rich *paella* and be none the worse for it the next day.

The hydrographics of La Albufera are complex. In the winter it fills up with freshwater from the Río Turia and the Acequia de-Rey, but although it is one of the largest

bodies of freshwater in Spain – 2,837 hectares (7,010 acres), of which about a tenth is taken up by reed beds and interior islands called *matas* – it is very shallow, varying from 1–2.5 metres (3–8 feet) in depth. At the southern end of the *laguna* there is a canal, the Perelló, which can be opened and closed at will to allow water to flow into the Mediterranean. It is estimated that the *laguna* receives eight times more water, on average, than it can accommodate without flooding the surrounding area, notably the sandbank separating it from the sea, the Playas del Saler and de la Dehesa. The rise and fall in the level of the *laguna* is thus closely watched. Equally

The shoveler uses its broad bill to sieve the muddy water of L'Albufera

125

important, experts have detected a growing contamination of its waters by industrial effluvia, domestic sewage and agricultural residues that are washed into the *laguna* every year and are threatening its ecological balance. La Albufera is a wetland under 'stress'; it is not only threatened by chemical poisoning but also by a gradual silting process that adds heavy layers of sediment to the bottom with each annual flooding.

La Albufera has already shrunk enormously. In the Middle Ages it was over ten times its present size, but as farmers took over the western marshlands and turned them into rice paddies the *laguna* was gradually reduced. In recent years the conflicting interests of local duck hunters and conservation groups have led to heated controversies concerning the legislation and management of what has become, at the eleventh hour, a *parque natural* with stringent protective measures imposed by the autonomy of Valencia.

The birds, unaware of the battles that have been fought for and against their interests, have continued to flock to La Albufera by the tens of thousands. About

The river which carved this deep ravine in the Puertos de Beceite (opposite) has dried to a trickle, while a little bittern (below) enjoys the plentiful water of L'Albufera

250 species of birds – 90 of whom breed here regularly – have been recorded at the ornithological station of La Albufera, near Mata del Fang. Cattle egrets, little egrets, red-crested pochards, mallards, shovelers and wigeon, all counted in their thousands.

The census of passage birds includes between 1,000–2,000 lapwing, 2,000–14,000 red-crested pochard, more than 6,000 black-tailed godwit and somewhat fewer little ringed plover, as well as snipe, dunlin, sanderling, golden plover and redshank.

Among the species that breed in the reed beds of La Albufera are great crested grebe (about 100 pairs) and black-necked grebe, egrets, night, purple and squacco herons, bittern and little bittern (about 30 or 40 pairs), little ringed plover, Kentish plover, redshank and avocet. Noted for the large number of breeding pairs are black-winged stilt, pratincole, common and gull-billed tern, fan-tailed, reed and great reed warblers, and the penduline tit.

The recent increase in breeding numbers indicates that La Albufera, although threatened on all sides by insecticide pollution and the proximity of urban developments, is all the more important to Europe's birdlife now that so many other natural marshes have been destroyed or are under threat and the number of alternative wetlands is steadily decreasing.

CHAPTER 5: THE MEDITERRANEAN COAST

'As ever in this deep clear water over rock, the sea was a polished inter-weave of sombre but refulgent colours that contained no blue. Past every headland the view opened on a new adventure of riven cliffs and pinnacles, of caves sucking at the water, of rock strata twisted and kneaded like old-fashioned toffee. Boulders of colossal proportions had fallen everywhere from the cliffs and we threaded through a maze of them over water possessed of a surging, muscled vivacity to reach an inlet where the fishing would take place, and where the shallows were of such transparency that the weeds under us showed through, like the fronds, the fanned-out petals and the plumes of a William Morris design . . .

I left him, to explore the deeper water . . . and swimming on I entered a new and wholly extraordinary submarine world, an underwater preserve that might have remained unchanged for thousands of years.

Everything in this sunny scene, every form and colour, was fresh. The panorama was one of the sea-gouged and polished bedrock, splashed all over with scarlet and ochreous algae, with its sierras, its jungles of weed and its teeming population of fish. Apart from the birds, the visible life of our world is largely restricted to surfaces. Here limitless stratification encouraged a dense marine populace with fish of all sizes from darting coloured particles to enormous bull-headed meros stacked at varying depths to feed, to circulate in a slow ruminative way, to rise or sink with a gentle ripple of fin or a flicker of tail . . .

Norman Lewis, *Voices of the Old Sea*

BEFORE YOU GO
Maps: SGE 1:50,000 Nos. 722 and 747; and also IGN 1: 200,000 Mapa provincial of Valencia.

GETTING THERE
By car: 2 highways originating from south Valencia border on to La Albufera: these are the N333 and the autopista to El Saler.
By bus: there is a regular service every ½hr from Valencia to La Albufera. The leaving point is the Pl. El Parterre.

WHERE TO STAY
Valencia is well-equipped with more than 70 hotels and hostels; the 4-star Parador Luis Vives, T: (96) 323 68 50, is at El Saler.
Outdoor living: there are large camping grounds at both El Palmar and El Saler.

ACTIVITIES
Boating: boats can be hired in the town of Sila for sailing on the lagoon.
Diving: for information,

contact the Federación Actividades Subacuáticas Levantina, Arzobispo Mayoral No. 14–20, Valencia, T: (96) 332 86 72.
Fishing: licences can be obtained from the ICONA office in Valencia (see below for address and telephone information).

FURTHER INFORMATION
Tourist information: Cataluña 1, Valencia, T: (96) 369 79 32. ICONA, San Vicente 83, Valencia 7, T: (96) 22 89 95.

Sierra Espuña

13,855ha (35,000 acres) of parque natural – the largest reserve in Murcia province

The sierra occupies part of the eastern end of the Cordillera Bética, just at the point where the mountains meet the coastal plain. The cliffs and crags of the 2 highest peaks – Espuña (1,585m/5,200ft) and Morrón (1,446m/4,750ft) – are used by mountain climbers for training exercises. Lessons learned in the Sierra Espuña can then be applied, with far more spectacular results, in the Sierra Nevada at the western end of the same *cordillera*.

The sierra is home to at least 2 species of rare and endemic butterflies. It is the type locality for the small brown Spanish argus (*Aricia morronensis*). The species is confined to Spain, and occurs in very small colonies, each of which varies slightly, the northern ones, for example, being larger. It flies at middle altitudes in open mountain areas during Jul and early Aug. The other rare butterfly is the Nevada grayling (*Pseudochazara hippolyte*), known from just 4 localities in south-east Spain, but also from southern Russia and parts of Asia. It is a handsome brown and gold butterfly that flies in Jun and Jul between 2,100–2,700m (6,900–8,900ft) on stony slopes often over crystalline bed-rock. The larvae eat various mountain grasses.

The park was originally established in the 1970s as part of a comprehensive programme that introduced herds of African *mouflon* into the game reserves of southern Spain. Since the *mouflon* was accustomed to a very similar habitat in the Atlas mountains, it has done very well in the Sierra Espuña. Wild boar, foxes and wild cats are also on the list of residents, along with eagles, owls and partridges. But for most visitors the park's main attractions are neither its wildlife nor its rockfaces, but rather its vast tracts of untouched Mediterranean pine forest where hiking and camping are an unmitigated pleasure.

The summers are hot and dry – Murcia is one of the

The wild sheep, or *mouflon*, has been introduced to the Sierra de Espuña from Sardinia

driest provinces of Spain – but in winter the sierra normally receives about 15cm (6 inches) of snow. In former days the snow-cutters of the mountains had storage 'wells' of packed snow, or *neveros*, which they would haul down to Murcia during the summer, where it was used for making ice cream. You can still come across some of the *nevero* wells, and also the abandoned coal mines on the southern slope of the Perona (1,185m/ 3,900ft). Nowadays the only modern intrusion in this archetypal forest is a Spanish air force station on top of the highest mountain, which prevents hikers from actually ascending to the summit of Espuña. Still, the views from lower down are sufficiently panoramic, and the summit of the neighbouring Morrón affords absolutely breathtaking views to both the south and east.

Before you go *Maps:* SGE 1:50,000 Nos. 932, 933, 953 and 954; and IGN 1:200,000 Mapa provincial of Murcia.
Getting there *By car:* take highway N340 (Murcia–Almería) to the village of Alhama de Murcia, about 23km (14 miles) south of the capital, then turn north on the well-marked side road, Alhama–Mula, turning west after 5km (3 miles) up a steeply inclined road that leads into the park but is not signposted in any way.
By bus: there is no service to the Sierra Espuña but buses on the Murcia–Almería line stop at Alhama de Murcia, about 10km (6 miles) from the heart of the park as the crow flies.
Where to stay: the 1-star Hostal Tánger is in Alhama de Murcia, T: (968) 63 06 99.
Outdoor living: within the park, no permit is needed for camping only 1 night. If you

The maritime pine can reach heights of more than 30m (100ft)

intend on a longer stay, however, be advised that you should apply for a permit from the Servicio de Montes, Caza y Pesca, C. Juan XXIII, Murcia.
Activities *Walking:* the park's many paths are unmarked, but there is plenty of scope for walks, ranging from the easy to the fairly strenuous; ask the park wardens, who are extremely helpful, for details.
Further information *Tourist information:* C. Alejandro Séiguer 3, Murcia, T: (968) 21 37 16; and in Cartagena, Ayuntamiento, T: (968) 50 64 83, and C. de Castellini 5, T: (968) 50 75 49. ICONA, Avda José Antonio 42–3°, Murcia, T: (968) 23 95 04.

129

CHAPTER 6

Andalucía

Many of the things that the rest of the world considers quintessentially Spanish are native to Andalucía, the glorious south of Spain. This is the home of flamenco music and of such electrifying dances as the *sevillana*. Here you'll find the remarkable mosque of Córdoba and the marble fountains and audience chambers of the Alhambra of Granada; the rolling countryside of Jaén, dotted with olive-tree patterns as far as the eye can see; the perpetual snows of the Sierra Nevada; the processions of *penitentes* who move through the streets of Seville at Easter time; the horse and sherry fairs at Jerez de la Frontera; the gypsy cafés of Triana; the bullfights in Cádiz or Arcos de la Frontera. The excitements and pleasures of Andalucía are as varied as the region itself, for no other part of Spain enjoys greater contrast and variety. Even the snob capital of Spain, Marbella, and the crowded beaches of the Costa del Sol contribute to this extraordinary kaleidoscope of Andalucían images.

I'll never forget my first introduction to Andalucía, years ago, when a friend and I rode there on horseback from La Mancha. In one remote valley that consisted entirely of olive orchards and was still untouched by electricity pylons, we came on a young farmer who was working by himself and singing a nonchalant flamenco melody that floated out over the empty landscape like smoke carried by the breeze. There was not a cloud in the sky and the air was crystal clear; the yellow-ochre earth looked as though it could

Generations of Andalucians have toiled to maintain their neatly terraced olive groves in the shadow of the badlands of Almería

not possibly be fertile (although, in fact, it produces some of the world's finest olives) and off to one side loomed the dark blue mountains of the Sierra Morena. It was an incredibly secluded spot, made all the more haunting by the endless *melismas* of that ancient peasant song, half Arabic, half European.

Although Andalucía is now one of the most important of the autonomous communities of modern Spain, it still has innumerable out-of-the-way corners in which you can feel a very un-European sense of loneliness. It is a vast and often underpopulated land. The forest-covered Sierra Morena forms its northern rampart; in the south it is bounded by the Mediterranean and on the west by the Atlantic – a very different kind of sea – while its tip faces the African continent across the blue waters of the Straits of Gibraltar.

Andalucía covers nearly nine million hectares (2¼ million acres), an area nearly as large as Portugal, although with a population density that is only about 80 per cent of that country's. Essentially it consists of a great plain, the valley of the Río Guadalquivir, hemmed in by mountains on every side except the south west, where it descends to the Atlantic. But before reaching the Gulf of Cádiz the river forms a blocked-up delta, the marshes of Doñana, which were once one of the great hunting preserves of Spain and are now its foremost national park.

The lowlands, known as Andalucía *baja*, contain a number of brackish lakes – often important bird habitats – and salt-impregnated wastelands (*despoblados*) which are partly attributable to the fact that the whole area was covered by the sea in the not very distant geological past. The Guadal-

quivir rises in the mountains of Jaén and is joined by a large number of tributaries on its way to the sea. To the south, its valley is flanked by mountains, notably the immense massif of the Sierra Nevada, which includes the highest peaks of the Iberian peninsula. These highlands, together with the mountains of Almería and Jaén, constitute Andalucía *alta*.

As a result of these dramatic topographical variations, Andalucía possesses a series of ecosystems that have fascinated generations of naturalists. Indeed, vegetation in the most 'typically Spanish' of regions runs the whole gamut from bougainvillea to edelweiss. The lowest belt, from sea level to about 500 metres (1,650 feet), is characteristically Mediterranean, dominated by olive and mastic trees, holly oak and so on, along with the caper bush, the aloe, the cactus, orange and lemon trees, palms and other semi-tropical plants that thrive in the warm climate of the coast. Above this there are the forests of holm oak, up to 1,600 metres (5,250 feet), succeeded by a 300-metre (1,000-foot) zone of thick marescent forests with sporadic stands of Corsican pine and, more rarely, Scots pine.

From 1,900–2,600 metres (6,200–8,500 feet) there is a belt of juniper and savin brushwood, although much deteriorated and fighting to hold its own against a massive invasion by members of the broom family. In the Sierra Nevada are two high-altitude belts that have both received a great deal of botanical attention in recent years. Up to 2,900 metres (9,500 feet) the 'Sierra Nevada tundra' produces peat bogs with mosses and montane pasture plants (such as *Carex fusca* of the sedge family and the grass *Festuca hallieri*); deep-soil areas, or *borreguiles*, where the pastures are always green; and patches known as *cascara-jes*, with cushion-shaped vegetation. The highest belt has been called the 'cold desert' because it contains few plants and only lichens are plentiful, although in some sheltered areas there are pastures of *Festuca clementei* and the bent-grass *Agrostis nevadensis*. The vegetation of these two highest belts includes 40 plants found only in the Sierra Nevada, another 12 species that grow in nearby mountains of Andalucía, about 20 that are also found in the high mountains of Morocco, and a further 70 that are shared with the Alps. One rarity that has been saved from extinction by recent conservation measures is *Artemisia granatensis*, a type of wormwood, which was endangered because of excessive collection by the local people.

Another notable native of Andalucía is the rare Spanish fir, *Abies pinsapo*, whose last major forest lies within the boundaries of the Parque Natural de Grazalema, west of Ronda. Elsewhere in the region this remarkable 20- to 30-metre (65- to 100-foot) tree was threatened by the voracious grazing habits of the local goats, whose appetite for seedlings prevented the *pinsapo* from reproducing naturally. To encourage the regeneration of these forests, the Sierra de las Nieves – part of the Serranía de Ronda – was also declared a *parque natural*, from which hungry goats are rigorously excluded. The cork oak, *Quercus suber*, also thrives in Andalucía, where sherry bottlers regard it as an essential national resource. Unlike the *pinsapo* it holds its own very well in many areas as long as there is sufficient rainfall: in the *reserva nacional* at Cortes de la Frontera, for example, cork oaks cover some 93 per cent of the total area. Cork forests are usually carefully managed so that

layers of the bark that grows around the trunks can be removed every eight to ten years; meanwhile black Iberian hogs are left to shift for themselves among the acorns that fall from the trees, and in due course develop into a *jamón serrano* that is highly prized for its nutty flavour.

The wealth and variety of Andalucía's flora is paralleled by an abundance of birds and beasts. The Coto Doñana is a paradise for birds of Europe and Africa. There are golden eagles and the eagle owl in the sierras of Tejeda and Almijara, and some of the other highlands are inhabited by Bonelli's eagle, the goshawk, the peregrine falcon and Egyptian and griffon vultures. Roe deer thrive in the mountains of Cádiz and western Málaga, and the red deer, reintroduced by ICONA ecologists, has done well in the Doñana and Cortes de la Frontera. Wild boar flourish in the national and regional parks, though they are hunted regularly in the game reserves so numbers there are less.

Yet the old hunting tradition is still stronger than the ecology movement, and while Andalucía has only one national park there are no less than four *reservas nacionales de caza*, which protect big game from the local poachers so that licensed hunters can bag their 'trophies'. The *reserva* of Cortes de la Frontera, previously mentioned, lies furthest to the west; it is famous for roe deer stalking in May and June. The largest and easternmost is the *reserva* of Sierra Nevada, comprising 35,430 hectares (87,550 acres) of the most important massif in the entire region, all of it within the province of Granada. The province of Málaga has the *reserva* of the Sierras de Tejeda and Almijara, and still further to the west is the Serranía de Ronda,

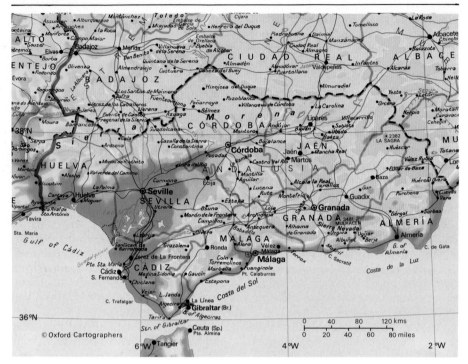

© Oxford Cartographers

comprising 23,663 hectares (58,470 acres) between Ronda and the coast, including the massifs of the Sierra de las Nieves, the Sierra Parada de Tolox, the Sierra Real de Istán and the Sierra Blanca of Ojén and Marbella.

Unlike some of the other autonomous regions of Spain, Andalucía was never a single, independent kingdom. Historically it either formed part of other empires, such as those of Rome or Damascus, or was divided into petty kingdoms that were often at loggerheads. Since 1833, Andalucía has consisted of eight provinces: Almería, Cádiz, Córdoba, Granada, Jaén, Huelva, Málaga and Sevilla. Although now governed by a central body, the Junta de Andalucía, the individual provinces are still fiercely protective of their local traditions and prerogatives – and at the same time concerned about expanding their nature reserves as a

way of safeguarding their ecological patrimony. Hence the provinces are doing more than ever before in the realm of conservation, placing lakes, forests, marshes and other animal habitats under the protection of the local departments of the environment. Not so long ago, travellers would shake their heads over the 'backward' condition of Andalucían agriculture. 'Almost half Andalucía is abandoned to a state of nature,' grumbled Richard Ford in the middle of the nineteenth century, who wondered how they could go on using mule-powered irrigation wheels rather than centrifugal pumps. But now, at the end of the twentieth century, many of us give grateful thanks to the happy circumstance that has preserved so much of the Andalucían landscape from 'progress' and kept so much of it in the once-lamentable state of nature.

134

These dunes at Punta Paloma on the Atlantic coast are being stabilized by the planting of pine trees

GETTING THERE

By air: there are airports at Almería, T: (951) 22 19 54; Córdoba, T: (957) 23 23 00; Granada, T: (958) 44 64 11; Jerez de la Frontera, T: (956) 33 43 00; Málaga, T: (952) 32 20 00; and Seville, T: (954) 51 06 77. With the exception of Málaga and Seville, they handle mainly internal flights, with primary connections to Madrid and Barcelona as well as Alicante, Valencia and Las Palmas de Gran Canaria. Málaga is an important international airport, with scheduled flights to most major European cities as well as New York and Tangier; Seville has fewer international flights (but still a considerable number).

By sea: Andalucía's principal ports are Almería, Motril, Málaga, Algeciras, Cádiz and Huelva. There are regular services to Málaga from Barcelona, the Canaries, Melilla, Tangier, Marseilles, Genoa and Casablanca. Algeciras has services to Cueta, Tangier, Barcelona, Genoa, Palermo, Naples, Cannes, Lisbon, New York and the principal ports of South America. From Cádiz there are regular sailings to the Canaries and South America.

For more detailed information, phone Málaga (952) 22 28 00; and Cádiz (956) 25 65 50.

By car: on a north-south route, N630 links Seville with Mérida, the N-IV Córdoba with Madrid. Jaen and Granada lie due south of Madrid on N323, which hooks up to N-IV near Bailén.

By rail: RENFE's train connections to Andalucía from Madrid are excellent. There are 10 departures per day to Málaga and Algeciras, some of which stop at Fuengirola and Ronda. There are 5 trains a day to Jaén, Granada, Almería, Córdoba, Seville, Cádiz and Huelva. For information, call the RENFE reservation office, open all year 9am–9pm, T: (91) 429 82 28. In Seville, the RENFE number is (954) 231 19 18; in Cádiz (956) 23 43 01 and 23 43 02; and in Málaga (952) 21 00 66, 21 31 22 and 21 43 71.

By bus: the main national bus services connect Seville with Badajoz, Cáceres, Mérida, Salamanca, Valencia and Valladolid; Málaga with Alicante, Barcelona, Castellón de la Plana, Murcia, Tarragona and Valencia; Córdoba with Badajoz, Ciudad Real and Mérida;

Almería with Alicante, Barcelona, Cartagena, Castellón, Murcia, Tarragona and Valencia; all the Cádiz buses go through Seville.

Bus information: Almería, T: (951) 23 90 35; Cádiz, T: (956) 27 39 12; Córdoba, T: (957) 47 26 84, 47 20 18 and 47 00 00; Granada, T: (958) 22 75 14; Huelva, T: (955) 24 50 92; Jaén, T: (953) 25 77 02; Málaga, T: (952) 34 73 00, 34 73 04 and 34 73 08; and Seville, T: (954) 22 89 00.

WHEN TO GO
Some mountain excursions are impossible during the winter months. On the other hand, skiing in the Sierra Nevada during the winter is particularly pleasant because there is so much sunshine at these latitudes and altitudes, even in Jan, when northern Europe has short days and cloudy skies. But the summers may be too hot for some strenuous activities in certain areas.

WHERE TO STAY
The cities and towns of Andalucía have large numbers of hotels in every price range, from the simplest hostels to the most luxurious *paradores*. For information on the best localities for accommodation see the individual entries.

ACTIVITIES
Mountaineering clubs: Federación Andaluza de Montañismo, C. D. Ramiro San Salvador, Melilla 18, Almería, T: (951) 22 48 25.
Excursions: the so-called Ruta de los Pueblos Blancos ('route of the white villages') is a well-established circuit of some of the best-preserved hill towns and villages of Andalucía. One suggested route begins at Arcos de la Frontera, taking in Prado del Rey, El Bosque, 136

Benamahoma, Grazalema, Ubrique and Benaoján (all in Cádiz province) and terminates in Ronda.

Another circuit comprises Ronda, Atajate and Jimera de la Frontera, in the province of Málaga. A further route takes in Arcos, Bornos, Villamartín, Algodonales, Zahara, Torre Alhaquime, Olvera and Setenil de las Bodegas.

There are daily bus connections between all the villages on the routes. Most of them have official campsites and offer fishing in season.

FURTHER INFORMATION
Algeciras (956): tourist office, Avda de la Marina, T: 60 09 11.
Almería (951): tourist offices, Paseo Generalísimo 69, T: 23

67 44; and C. Rodrigo Vilar Téllez, T: 22 21 66. Red Cross, T: 22 09 00. Highway information, Hermanos Machado s/n, T: 23 14 55.
Cádiz (956): tourist offices, Avda Ana de Viya 5, T: 23 60 56; and C. Calderón de la Barca 1, T: 21 13 13. Red Cross, T: 23 42 70. Highway information, Avda de Andalucía 1, T: 23 36 05.
Córdoba (957): tourist office, C. Hermanos González Murga 13, T: 47 12 35. Red Cross, T: 29 34 11. Highway information, Avda Mozárabes 1, T: 23 41 95.
Granada (958): tourist offices, Pl. Isabel la Católica 1, T: 22 17 44; and Pl. del Padre Suárez 19, T: 22 10 22. Red Cross, T: 26 32 77.
Huelva (955): tourist offices,

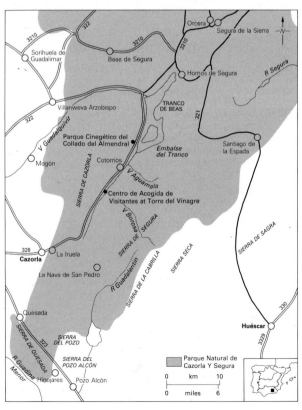

C. Vásquez López 5, T: 25 74
03; and C. Fernando ɪ
Católico 18, T: 25 74 67. Red
Cross, T: 24 12 91. Highway
information, Avda Italia 14,
T: 24 73 99.
Jaén (953): tourist office,
C. Arquitecto Bergés 3, T: 22
27 37. Red Cross, T: 21 15 40.
Highway information,
Arquitecto Bergés 7,

T: 22 03 58.
Málaga (952): tourist offices,
C. Puerta del Mar 12, T: 21 04
77, 21 04 78 and 21 35 41; and
C. Larios 5, T: 21 34 45. Red
Cross, T: 21 13 58. Highway
information, Paseo de la
Farola 23, T: 21 15 70.
Seville (954): tourist office,
Avda de la Constitución 21,
T: 22 14 04. Red Cross, T: 35

01 35. Highway information,
Pl. de España, T: 23 22 25.

FURTHER READING
Gerald Brenan, *South from
Granada* (London, 1957);
Robin Collomb, *Gredos
Mountains and Sierra Nevada*
(Reading, 1987); Washington
Irving, *Tales of the Alhambra*
(Madrid, 1832).

Sierras de Cazorla y Segura

*Limestone reserva natural cut through by
Río Guadalquivir and containing several
peaks over 700m (6,500ft)*

The great Río Guadalquivir (literally, 'big river' in Arabic) rises in the Sierra de Cazorla, amid some of the wildest landscape in Spain, in the Cañada de las Fuentes. For a while the resulting stream flows confidently north and east, as if it were going to make its way to the Mediterranean. But the mountains will not let it pass; it meets the Sierra de Segura head on and is forced to make a dramatic change of course, curving suddenly westward to begin its long run down to the Atlantic and the *marismas* of the Coto Doñana.

At the start of its long march to the sea, the Guadalquivir gives its name to a valley bounded by the sierras of Cazorla, Segura, del Pozo and de la Cabrilla: it goes on widening its V-shape toward the south east, confined by a series of peaks that are over 2,000 metres (6,500 feet) in altitude. The highest peak in this immense *reserva nacional* is Cerros de las Empanadas (2,107 metres/6,910 feet), and virtually everything within the boundaries of the reserve is higher than 700 metres (2,300 feet), except the land located on the shores of the artificial lake occupying its heartland, the Embalse del Tranco, which is fed by the infant Guadalquivir and its first tributaries.

Innumerable brooks and rivulets pour from the sides of this mountain enclave, and virtually all rush to join the Guadalquivir (except the waters of the nascent Río Guadalentín, which eventually flows into the Guadiana Menor). The area has more than 20 rivers and brooks important enough to have names of their own. Besides the main valley of the Guadalquivir, the reserve comprises several adjacent valleys, such as that of Guadalentín and the canyons (*barrancos*) of Borosa and Aguamala: dramatic narrow cuts in the landscape, with steep slopes covered in bushes and pine trees, and high mountain meadows full of succulent grasses and wild flowers – rich pasturelands for herds of sheep.

Geologically, the sierra is composed of hard limestone, beneath which lies a softer layer of clays and red sands; they can be seen in section in some of the larger gorges. Its sheltered position between the Montes Universales and the Sierra Nevada means that it was ideally situated to provide a refuge for high-altitude plants during the tremendous climatic changes in the Ice Ages. Consequently, these mountains contain a number of Tertiary relict species not found anywhere else in the world. *Viola cazorlensis*, a shrubby violet with unusual deep crimson or carmine flowers and very long slender spurs, is one of the most interesting. It flowers in May, from the depths of shady rock crevices; its nearest living relatives are found as far away as Mount Olympus in Greece, and in Montenegro. Another of these relict species is the butterwort *Pinguicula vallisneriifolia*. This carniv-

137

orous plant is found in a highly specialized habitat under towering limestone cliffs drenched in continually dripping water, and totally out of reach of the rays of the sun.

Two endemic species of daffodil also thrive in these mountains – *Narcissus longispathus* and *N. hedraeanthus*. The latter is a tiny hoop-petticoat daffodil found in early May in snow-melt areas high in the mountains. A further endemic to this range is the columbine *Aquilegia cazorlensis*, which is known only from the shady limestone slopes around the summit of Pico de Cabañas and flowers in early June.

All told, the reserve contains over 1,100 species of plants, but you needn't be a specialist to enjoy the forests of tall pines that reach 20 metres (65 feet) in height, and the sweet profusion of thyme, rosemary, sweet marjoram and lavender. Along the

banks of the streams are 'tunnels' of flowers, grasses, ferns and shrubs; the minor rivers are lined with poplars, ash trees and willows. On the lower slopes the pine forests are made up of aleppo pine (*Pinus halepensis*), while above about 1,300 metres (4,260 feet) maritime pine (*P. pinaster*) dominates. Here, too, snowy mespilus (*Amelanchier ovalis*), *Sorbus domestica*, Montpellier maple (*Acer monspessulanum*) and *A. granatense* flourish along with such bushes as *Lavandula latifolia* and *Helianthemum croceum*. Oaks are also frequent. The high valleys, called *navas*, are covered with grasses and wild flowers – ideal fodder for the moufflon, red deer and ibex. Some of the mountain tops are treeless; sometimes this is due to natural causes but more usually it is because overgrazing has tipped the ecological balance in favour of low-growing shrubs rather than trees.

This is a fine camping and hiking area as

The Guadalquivir is already impressively wide as it leaves the Sierra de Cazorla

well as one of Spain's great nature reserves. You can wake up in the middle of the night to the sound (and smell) of boars snuffling around outside. This is the spot where you are most likely to happen upon a herd of red deer in the underbrush. They're not tame, and will turn tail at your approach, but encounters are frequent and help give Cazorla a sense of being part of the 'peaceable kingdom' where the camper can, as it were, lie down with the ibex.

The Spanish ibex, an almost mythical member of the goat family, once lived throughout the Iberian peninsula, but was hunted for its splendid scimitar-shaped horns. Today only small isolated populations exist, each with slightly different characteristics, and there are thought to be distinct sub-species. The last ibex was seen in the Pyrenees in 1907; the few that persist in central Spain today are now highly protected by law. They are known in Spanish as the *cabra hispánica* and are very much more difficult to observe than the fallow and red deer that inhabit the lower regions of the reserve.

By contrast, deer-watching is easy. If you happen to be on hand in September or the beginning of October you can observe the extraordinary spectacle of the *berrea*, when the stags stake out both their territorial claims and their harems. Tilting back their heads so that their antlers rest on their backs, they bay to the winds to attract any females within earshot. Sometimes their cry is answered by a challenge and there then follows fierce butting and crashing of antlers until the weaker male gives way.

The animals to be culled are picked very carefully, and the effect is virtually that of an integral protected zone. The red deer and roe deer are not easily intimidated by the presence of human intruders. Their visibility varies, however, according to the season. During the summer, when the days get very hot, especially in the rocky and treeless areas, the animals come out only at night, so you may catch a glimpse of them in the evening or in the early dawn. In winter their habits change, however, and with a reasonable amount of discretion you can come close to them before they run off.

Water is often a rarity in Spanish wild places, especially in the south. Here, there is more than enough of it, thanks to a weather pattern that provides an abundance of rainfall, particularly during the summer thunderstorms that hurl banks of dark clouds against the perpendicular walls of the high sierras. The mountains catch the moisture from the Atlantic and the Mediterranean, and their effectiveness as a natural barrier is enforced by the thermal masses of warm air from the Levant which usually prevent the Atlantic clouds from moving further east: rain falls in sheets when warm air meets cold air above Cazorla. These periodic inundations are irregular and unpredictable. During the summer, the woods turn to tinder and there are frequent dramatic electrical storms that have often led to major forest fires.

Because of the high rainfall and despite the southerly location of these mountains several birds occur here which you would normally expect to see further north. There is an isolated population of alpine accentor (and another in the Sierra Nevada), and alpine choughs have also been recorded here, despite a distribution that does not normally extend into the southern half of Spain. Other species include rock thrush, blue rock thrush and ortolan bunting. The Embalse del Tranco attracts mallard and teal; woodpigeons and turtledoves inhabit the pine forests in spring and summer, when quail (and to a lesser extent, red-legged partridge) abound in the high meadows. Birds of prey include Egyptian vultures, eagles, kites, sparrowhawks and kestrels. Cazorla is now the only region of Spain outside the Pyrenees where the magnificent lammergeier can still be found, but the numbers may be down to a single pair. Their Spanish name, *quebrantahuesos* ('bone-breaker'), refers to their habit of dropping bones on to rocks to smash them so they can extract the marrow easily. The modernization of Spain and the decline in numbers of horse, donkey and goat has seriously reduced the quantity of carrion on which the scavengers depend. Thus all four European vultures, are in serious decline and in need of conservation measures.

Viola cazorlensis is a cherished rarity of the Sierra de Cazorla

BEFORE YOU GO
Maps: SGE 1:50,000 Nos. 790, 816, 841, 842, 865, 866, 886, 887, 906 and 907; IGN 1:200,000 Mapas provinciales of Albacete, Jaén and Granada.
Guidebooks: *Cazorla y Segura* (C. E. Cajas de Ahorro, 1976); and *Coto Nacional de Cazorla* by F. Rueda (Editorial Everest, 1976).

GETTING THERE
By car: if you are driving from Jaén or Granada, the best access is through Jódar; an alternative is the scenic drive through Guadix, Pozo Alcón and Quesada, which takes in the valley of the Guadiana Menor. From Madrid, the best road is N-IV to Guadix; at La Carolina, turn east on C3217 toward Ubeda and Cazorla – or you may want to turn off at Arquillos towards Beas de Segura and the northern end of the range.

Entering the Sierra from the north is often the preferred route during the winter, since the southern approach is
140

sometimes blocked by heavy snowfalls. The road from the north, which is clear the year round, proceeds from Puente de Génave to Hornos de Segura or, alternatively, to Siles on the northern edge of the reserve.
By bus: services from village to village are infrequent: usually there is 1 daily bus from one community to the next. For information, consult Transportes Alsina Graells Sur in Granada, T: (958) 25 13 54; and Córdoba, T: (957) 23 64 00.

A daily bus covers the 170km (105 miles) between Jaén and Cazorla via Ubeda and Baeza. From Cazorla northwards you'll need your own means of transport. Albacete is the nearest provincial capital to the northern end of the Sierra and offers a daily bus to Orcera which is operated by Juan Manuel Córcoles Rodríguez, Pl. Mateo Villa 17, Albacete, T: (967) 21 26 70. This bus also represents the only practical connection between a major railway station and one

The butterwort *Pinguicula vallisneriifolia* traps insects on its strap-shaped leaves

of the villages of the *reserva nacional*.

WHERE TO STAY
There is a wide range of hotels and inns along the Carretera del Tranco and in almost all the small villages of the Sierra. For example, in Cazorla is the Parador Nacional el Adelantado, T: (953) 72 10 75; in La Iruela a 1-star pension, Arroya de la Teja, T: (953) 72 02 11; and in Quesada, the 1-star hostel, Mari-Mer, T: (953) 73 31 25.
Outdoor living: an ideal area for camping; many spots are marked *zona de acampada* and are under the supervision of forest wardens. For stays of longer than 1 night, you should obtain a permit from the Agencia del Medio Ambiente de Andalucía, C. Laraña 4, Seville, T: (954) 22 27 81. The *zonas de acampada* are: Linarejos in Cazorla; Los Rasos in Peal de Becerro; Cañada de las Fuentes in Quesada; El Tobón in Beas de Segura; Campamento de los Negros in Orcera; El Llano de Arance, Puente Baden de Cotorrios and La Toba in Santiago de la Espada; El Cerezuelo, Baden de la Piscifactoria, Fuente Sepura and Fuente de la Pascuala in Pontones; and Acebeas in Siles.

ACTIVITIES
Walking: there are innumerable possibilities for walks and excursions, including 3 well-marked hiking trails. Detailed information is available at the *reserva* information centre (see below).
Bathing: the village of Cotorios (Coto Rios) has a small artificial lake that is open to bathers.
Deer-watching: Cabeza de la Viña, an island in the Embalse de Tranco, for which deer

have a special *penchant*.
Gardens/collections: the Parque Cinegético del Collado del Almendral on the shores of the Tranco contains representatives of the Sierra's main animal species. There are botanical gardens at Siles and Torre del Vinagre; at Río Borosa you can visit the fish hatcheries that provide trout for all of Andalucía's rivers.

FURTHER INFORMATION
Tourist information: Avda de la Constitución 21, Seville, T: (954) 22 14 04. ICONA, Avda Ramón y Cajal 1, Seville, T: (954) 63 96 50.
The *reserva* information centre is at Torre del Vinagre, on the paved road that skirts the river and Tranco de Beas. Enough snow falls during the winter months and sometimes as late as Apr and May to close the highway from Cazorla to the valley and, quite often, the road to La Nava de San Pedro.

Sierra Nevada & Las Alpujarras

Highest mountains in mainland Spain, reaching 3,482m (11,420ft); diversity of flora is guaranteed by the proximity of the Mediterranean

The highest road in Europe is the highway 'de la Sierra' which leads from Granada to the ski resort known as Solynieve (literally, 'sun-and-snow') in the Sierra Nevada. It is a pleasant, scenic highway that gently wafts you up 2,500 metres (8,000 feet) or so, and almost before you realize it you will have arrived at airline cruising altitudes.

Indeed, most of the year the highest part of the road is snowed in, so that the only way to proceed to the famous lookout point on the Pico Veleta ('the weathercock') at 3,398 metres (11,148 feet) is on foot, on skis or by means of the *telecabine* recently installed there for the convenience of skiers. The road and the *telecabine* have made it almost too easy to ascend to the top of what are the highest, and were once the most remote, mountains in mainland Spain. But there are still countless ways of proceeding from the modern conveniences of La Veleta to the untrodden wilderness of its even higher neighbour, Mulhacén (3,482 metres/11,420 feet) and the rest of the Sierra Nevada – literally the 'snowy mountains', since the higher peaks are snow-covered the year round.

This is the main mountain chain of the Cordillera Penibética, a mighty barrier some 70 kilometres (45 miles) long which runs parallel to the Mediterranean coast about 48 kilometres (30 miles) inland. Altogether the range has 14 major peaks that are higher than 3,000 metres (4,850 feet), where the perpetual snow contrasts with black schists. Up until recently one of the highest valleys contained a small glacier, Corral de Veleta, which was the southernmost such formation in Europe, but it is no longer permanently covered with ice. In general, however, the deep *barrancas* show little evidence of past glacial activity – except the well-formed cirques high up at their heads.

Structurally, the Sierra Nevada resembles the alpine system, composed of nappes (rock-sheets) which have been thrust from the south northwards. These folded strata are rich in zinc, copper, lead, mercury and iron. The central dome of the range (the mica schists) has weathered to form rounded, smooth contours at high altitudes, but the Triassic limestones and sandstones of the flanks have been deeply dissected by powerful rivers to form gorges.

Just to the south of the Sierra Nevada lies

FLORA AND FAUNA OF THE SIERRA NEVADA

Its closeness to the Mediterranean and the extreme altitude mean there is an incredible diversity of life-forms in the Sierra Nevada. Most of the endemic species are concentrated in the alpine zone, over 2,600m (8,500ft). The unique community here boasts some 200 snow-tolerant herbs, of which approximately 40 are endemic to these mountains. One feature that many of the plants share is the dense hairs, usually whitish, on their leaves. This is characteristic of high-altitude species, a means of coping with the high levels of ultra-violet radiation that exist in these habitats. And many of the typical species here bear spines as a defence against the large number of herbivores, both wild and domestic, that inhabit these middle-mountain zones.

The endemic daffodil *Narcissus nevadensis* is one of the first flowers to appear in the spring, in boggy areas especially around melting snow patches. Its golden-yellow trumpets are often accompanied by the slender-stemmed pink flowers of the crocus *Colchicum triphyllum*, a mountain species of southern and central Spain. On the stony slopes above, thousands of blue, white and mauve Nevada crocuses (*Crocus nevadensis*) spring from apparently barren ground; despite the apparent exclusiveness of its name this species is also found in various other sierras of southern Spain.

Another feature of the vegetation of the Sierra Nevada is the band of dome-shaped, spiny, xeromorphic shrubs that lies between 1,700–2,000m (5,575–6,500ft), appropriately known as the 'hedgehog' zone. A major component of the flora here is the hedgehog broom (*Erinacea anthyllis*) with blue-violet flowers in clusters at the ends of stems bearing vicious spines. It grows with a number of other leguminous shrubs such as the Nevada race of the mountain tragacanth (*Astragalus sempervirens* ssp *nevadensis*), *A. granatensis*, and *Echinospartum boissieri*.

The Sierra Nevada shares several of its butterfly species with the Pyrenees – often the Pyrenean colonies differ slightly from those here; the *Agriades glandon*, the Glandon blue, is an example. In the Sierra Nevada this lycaenid, more brown than

blue, is of the sub-species *zullichi*; in the Pyrenees it is much more blue-flushed, especially the male, and of the type race *glandon*. Within the Sierra Nevada, the Glandon blue is restricted solely to altitudes above 3,000 metres (9,800 feet) in the east of the range (Granada). The larvae are thought to feed off various plants of the primrose family, but as with many of these highly restricted butterflies, little is really known of its ecology, except that it flies in July and August.

A species with an almost identical range within the Sierra, but this time found nowhere else in the world, is the Nevada blue (*Plebicula golgus*).

Another Pyrenean/Sierra Nevada butterfly is the Spanish brassy ringlet (*Erebia hispania*), again flying in the Granadan part of the Nevada mountains. It is a species with a world distribution confined to Spain and the French Pyrenees, feeding on mountain grasses such as poas and fescues at altitudes in excess of 1,800 metres (5,900 feet). The Sierra Nevada contains the type race of the Spanish brassy ringlet with the Pyrenean sub-species being *rondoui*, from the central part of this mountain range.

Although the valleys and lowlands surrounding the Sierra Nevada offer a fine cross-section of birds typical of Andalucía and the Mediterranean coast, it is sheer altitude that gives the range its special character. Birds typical of more northerly latitudes find a final European outpost here – it is strange for a visitor from northern Europe to be suddenly confronted with greenfinch, crossbill, great tit and blackbird that have been left behind hundreds of kilometres to the north. Here too are those typically montane birds, alpine accentors, which gather around the ski resorts like sparrows. Choughs wheel in great flocks over the gorges and golden eagles soar effortlessly across their huge territories. At first, the Sierra Nevada may seem birdless, but searching the lusher valleys rather than the bare mountain tops is always more productive. Rock buntings feed among the rocky walls and where a scree runs down to some isolated farmstead the black wheatear may be found.

The Sierra Nevada owes its name to the perpetual snow of its highest peaks

the range of Las Alpujarras, which consists mainly of valleys descending at right angles from the crest of the Sierra Nevada; midway down the slope white villages cling precariously to the terraced mountainside. The name Alpujarras derives from the Moorish *Al-Busherat*, 'the grassland', and it was the Moors who terraced and irrigated these valleys, cultivating semi-tropical fruits on the slopes of the white-capped mountains. 'Ever faithful to the precepts of the Koran,' writes Pedro Antonio de Alarcón, they 'introduced every such species of exotic fruit or herb as was calculated to flourish and enrich the land.' As a result, these are some of the most fertile valleys in Spain, noted for their grapes, oranges, lemons and figs. About 80 villages, 40 hamlets and countless farms and *cortijos* (manor houses) make up the nucleus of Las Alpujarras. They form two parallel strips that are quite different in altitude and climate: L'Alpujarra Alta lies just south of the great peaks, and L'Alpujarra Baja is in the Sierra de la Contraviesa, which borders the Mediterranean. The latter are less than half as high as the Sierra Nevada, and are covered with grapes, almonds and figs.

Between these two mountain ranges lies the Valle de Lecrin, at whose entrance the last Moorish ruler of Granada, Boabdil, is said to have paused in his flight to cast a

143

final glance at his lost kingdom: the spot is known as El Ultimo Suspiro del Moro ('the Moor's last sigh'). Between Orgiva and Trevélez the vegetation changes dramatically as the altitude increases: pines, chestnuts, almonds, olives, palmettos, poplars, holm and cork oaks grow in the carefully tended woods and orchards. At the far eastern end of the Sierra Nevada, to the north of Almería, lies the desert-like gorge of Tabernas. Best known as the scene of several 'paella-westerns', this is also the only European habitat of the African trumpeter finch.

The way to the heart of Las Alpujarras leads up the Valle de Poqueira, a Cyclopean incision in the landscape that provides space for three perfect villages – Capileira, Bubión and Pampaneira, with their houses jutting out over the cliff. The flat roofs are covered with heavy stones known as launas, and often serve as terraces for the houses situated above them.

The massive Mulhacén, the very roof of the Iberian peninsula, was named for the penultimate of the Caliphs of Granada, Mujley-Hacen, who is said to be buried in some glacial niche of this great peak. There is a road up the mountain but as it approaches the summit, at the 3,000-metre (9,850-foot) level, drifts of snow up to two metres (6½ feet) deep impede progress. Climbers trying to reach the summit from the road have often been forced to turn back by winds that threaten to hurl them off the ridge. Where the snow has melted there is a riotous assembly of tiny wild flowers attended by swarms of brilliant butterflies that somehow manage to continue their dance without being blown away.

This is a landscape that reveals its greatest beauties only to the traveller on foot or on cross-country skis. In the 1920s the writer Gerald Brenan used to cover the distances between his home in Yegen and the other villages of Las Alpujarras on foot; he would even walk to Málaga. 'The path from Yegen to Orgiva was always an adventure,' he told a reporter in the 1970s. 'There were always many ravines, and the extremely cold weather in the winter carried with it the added risk of dangerous storms finding you away from the shelter of an inn or a cave. But the feeling of pleasure and well-being provided by this way of travelling cannot be matched by modern methods of travel.' It would be doing the Sierras an injustice – and showing the white feather – to drive through them by car without getting out to walk.

BEFORE YOU GO

Maps: SGE 1:50,000 Nos. 1,011, 1,026, 1,028, 1,041 and 1,042; SGE 1:200,000 Nos. 5–11 and 6–11; IGN 1:200,000 Mapa provincial de Granada; Michelin No. 446; and Firestone T–29.

Guidebooks: Pablo Bueno Porcel's *Sierra Nevada, Guía Montañera* (Editorial Mont Blanc, 1963); though some of its practical information may be outdated, it describes more than 25 itineraries throughout the range, from easy hikes to the routes to the highest peaks. Also P. A. de Alarcón, *La Alpujarra*, and Gerald Brenan's *South from Granada.*

GETTING THERE

By car: access to the Sierra Nevada ski resort, Solynieve, and the adjoining Parador Nacional de Sierra Nevada is via the 35-km (21-mile) highway 'de la Sierra'. The unpaved road that leads from the *parador* and La Veleta across Mulhacén and down into Las Alpujarras is open to traffic only in Aug. When it is closed by snowdrifts the only way to reach Las Alpujarras from Solynieve by car is to retrace the route to Granada, then head south along highway E103/N323 and east to Lanjarón.

By bus: schedules vary according to season, but at least 1 bus a day runs from Granada to the *parador* and back. For information, contact Empresa Bonal, Avda Calvo Sotelo 19, Granada.

From Lanjarón there is a bus to Orgiva and Motril (from where there are excellent connections to Málaga). But bus connections among the various villages are sporadic; walking is still considered a standard means of local transportation.

WHERE TO STAY

In the Sierra Nevada, the 3-star Parador Nacional de Sierra Nevada, Granada, T: (958) 48 03 00, has 30 rooms, but reservations are hard to come by. The Solynieve resort, just below it on the same road, has several hotels open only during the ski season, usually Dec–late May. There is also the 2-star Hotel

El Nogal, T: (958) 136, at Güéjar-Sierra, near km21 of the Sierra Nevada highway. Another possibility is to stay at one of the more than 60 hotels in Granada, 35km (21 miles) away.

In Las Alpujarras: At Lanjarón, the gateway to Las Alpujarras, there are 24 hotels and hostels, for the town is well-known for its mineral springs. The Pensión Mirador, km10 on the road to Orgiva, caters for simple tastes, T: (958) 77 01 81.

Orgiva, at the junction of

Ranunculus acetosellifolius is a rare buttercup of the Sierra Nevada

the roads to Alpujarra Alta and Alpujarra Baja, has the 1-star Hostal Mirasol, T: (958) 78 51 59. Elsewhere in Las Alpujarras, most villages also have a *fonda*, hostel or private accommodation.
Outdoor living: the Sierra Nevada campsite in Granada is open from 15 Mar–15 Oct, T: (958) 27 09 56.
Refuges: there are various refuges in the Sierra Nevada; contact Federación Andaluza de Montañismo (see below).

ACTIVITIES
Walking/climbing: the map shows a white (unpaved) road that snakes its way from Capileira across the spine of Mulhacén to the yellow (paved) road that goes to Solynieve and the Veleta. For practical purposes, this road does not exist for cars except

in Aug, the 1 month of the year when it is not blocked by snowdrifts. It does, however, afford an uncomplicated route for high-mountain hiking and for back-packers.

The walk from Capileira to the ski resort below the Veleta is possible in late spring and during the summer and early autumn. It requires sturdy boots, a sleeping bag and covers and a 2-day supply of food. As a mountain adventure it is not quite the same as scaling the Eiger North Wall, but for the average, fit person it offers an exciting way to become acquainted with Las Alpujarras and the Sierra Nevada. The road leaves the village of Capileira as a fairly wide stony track that winds uphill through an afforestation zone of neatly planted pines. El Chorillo is the midway point and a favourite overnight stopping place. The road continues toward the massive bulk of Mulhacén, skirting it and curving westward, past the Puntal and Lagunas de la Caldera beneath it: the lakes are partly iced over and there is snow on all the surrounding faces. The track sweeps southward along the Loma Pela and then turns northward again toward the Veleta, where it crosses yet another ridge and finally descends toward the *parador nacional*.
Cross-country skiing: the area offers good opportunities for cross-country skiing; check with the tourist offices for details.
Tours: there is a weekly coach tour into Las Alpujarras leaving at 8am each Sun from the Acera del Darro, Granada.

FURTHER INFORMATION
Tourist information: Casa de los Teiros, Granada, T: (958)

22 10 22. ICONA, Gran Vía 48, Granada, T: (958) 27 84 37.

Comité de Refugios de la Federación Andaluza de Montañismo, Reyes Católicos 1, Granada, is responsible for maintaining the mountain refuges and will provide you with detailed information about them, plus local climbing clubs.

For information on road conditions in the area, T: (958) 48 01 53.

El Torcal de Antequera

15km (9 miles) south of Antequera, a limestone landscape overrun by ivy, hawthorn and wild roses

Geologists call El Torcal de Antequera the most important karstic phenomenon in southern Europe; laypeople tend to think of it as a fantastic city in stone.

Here are vast limestone blocks and outcrops, sinks and ravines that have been gradually eroded into an endless series of Henry Moore sculptures to which whimsical imaginations have given such titles as La Muela ('the molar'), El Aguilucho ('the eaglet'), La Copa ('the wine glass'), El Lagarto ('the lizard'), La Loba ('the she-wolf') and Los Dos Iguales ('two the same'). From the rock called Peña de las Siete Mesas, the whole of the madly inventive surface of El Torcal can be contemplated at leisure: the high walls, towers, spires, alleys and temples, with their air of ruined grandeur, suggest a petrified city that once had sacrificial altars at every street corner.

Fortunately, there is rarely anyone else to share the

ruminations engendered by these bizarre effects of rain, wind and geological eons. The whole thing is what the psychologists call a projective technique, akin to a giant Rorschach test, and one woman's molar may well be another's butterfly. Quite apart from its scientific and sculptural interest, however, El Torcal is a wonderfully windswept spot, overgrown with ivy, hawthorn and wild roses. The only animals are small reptiles, common birds and occasional vultures. The highest point, about 1,600m (5,250ft), is the rock called Camorro de las Villas.

Although vegetation is sparse, there is considerable botanical diversity, due to the absence of highly competitive dominant species. Most of those that grow well in these mountains are low, cushion-forming species, or ones that sprout from crevices. You'll find the tiny, violet-flowered spring rock-cress (*Arabis verna*), *Viola demetria*, an annual with bright yellow blooms, and the endemic *Saxifraga biternata*, whose delicate ferny foliage and white, bell-shaped flowers grace no other locality in the world. Other species typical of these dry limestone rocks are the Spanish bluebell (*Endymion hispanicus*) and shining cranesbill (*Geranium lucidum*). The most spectacular feature of this flora is the colour combination in May of carmine peonies and the tall elegant stems of *Iris subbiflora* bearing velvety blooms of deep purple; this iris is found nowhere else in Spain, but occurs in parts of Portugal.

El Torcal de Antequera is especially renowned for its assemblage of orchids. Some 30 species have been recorded, including the 146

evocatively named brown bee orchid (*Ophrys fusca* ssp *atlantica*) and mirror orchid (*O. speculum*), both of which bear flowers of an iridescent blue with borders of chocolate-coloured fur, as well as woodcock and sawfly orchids (*O. scolopax* and *O. tenthredinifera*). Green-winged, bog and Jersey orchids (*Orchis morio*, *O. palustris* and *O. laxiflora*) flower in wetter seasons in the damp shady valleys beneath the towering pillars and peaks, while the lovely pink butterfly orchid (*O. papilionacea*) blooms on the sun-baked rock surfaces above. Three species of tongue orchid have been recorded here, as has the unhealthy looking and unpleasantly scented bug orchid (*Orchis coriophora*). The cooler grassland habitats and woodland glades are decorated with the summer spikes of the dark red and broad-leaved helleborines (*Epipactis atrorubens* and *E. helleborine*). The intricate, trailing flowers of the lizard orchid (*Himantoglossum hircinum*) grow along the sides of the road in summer, where earlier in the year are found the huge, robust spikes of the closely related giant orchid (*H. longibracteatum*). Other notable examples are the dense-flowered orchid (*Neotinea intacta*), a characteristic plant of limestone soils, and the rose-pink frilly *Orchis italica*, a plant more typical of acid environments. Both summer and autumn lady's tresses (*Spiranthes aestivalis* and *S. spiralis*) can be seen here, too.

Whether or not you join in the El Torcal game of name-that-rock or spot-the-orchid, this particularly rugged bit of scenery should not be missed. Spring and autumn are the best seasons for undertaking

the journey; in winter El Torcal is blasted by icy winds and in summer the rocks radiate heat like a Bessemer furnace.

Before you go *Maps:* SGE 1:50,000 Nos. 1,023, 1,024, 1,037 and 1,038; and IGN 1:200,000 Mapa provincial of Málaga.

Guidebook: Sierra del Torcal by R. Cadanás (1968).

Getting there *By car:* El Torcal is situated 15km (9 miles) south of Antequera. Follow the 3310 road on the way to Villaneuva de la Concepción, taking the first main turning on the right to El Torcal.

By rail: the once-Roman town of Antequera, 50km (31 miles) from Málaga and 161km (100 miles) from Seville, is one of the main stops on the railway line from Granada to Algeciras. There are 3 trains a day in each direction and the journey from Granada lasts about 2hrs.

By bus: there is a direct bus, Málaga–Antequera, that runs 5 times a day on week days but only once on Sun, T: (952) 32 33 63. The Málaga–Seville bus line also stops at Antequera, with service 3 times a day in each direction. The trip takes a little more than 1hr from Málaga (Antequera is the first stop) and 3¼ hrs from Seville, T: (952) 31 04 00 and (954) 41 88 11. There is also a bus running from Almería to Málaga and Seville.

From Antequera, however, there is no bus from the city to El Torcal. Still, if you don't have your own vehicle, the 13km (8 miles) from town are not impossible to negotiate on foot.

Where to stay: the 3-star Parador del Torcal, T: (952) 84 00 61, is located just outside Antequera. Try also the 2-star hostels, La Yedra,

Few landscapes in the world can boast forms as bizarre as the limestone 'sculptures' of El Torcal

T: (952) 84 22 87, and Las Pedrizas, T: (952) 71 43 76.
Activities *Walking:* from Llanos de los Polvillares, the end of the paved road and site of the mountain refuge, follow the trail marked by yellow arrows through the Vereda de la Losa ('path of the flagstone') to La Maceta ('the flowerpot'). Then, via 3 *callejones*, or alleys, the Oscuro, Tabaco and Ancho, it arrives at Los Arregladeros, whereupon it ascends to the Mirador de las Ventanillas and returns to the refuge.

A more ambitious itinerary is the one marked on the rocks with red arrows. It starts at the refuge, passes Sima del Chaparro and takes in the Camorro de las Siete Mesas, with its panoramic view of El Torcal. The path skirts past the Peñón de Pizarro, then leads you through the Callejón de la Maceta, Callejón Oscuro and the Vereda de los Topaderos to a spot called El Asa ('the handle') before turning back to the refuge. Hiking time, about 6hrs.
Caves: 3 dolmen caves just outside Antequera, on the left off the Granada road; open Sat–Mon and Wed 10am–1pm and 4–7pm.
Further information *Tourist information:* Pl. Coso Viejo, Antequera, T: (952) 84 18 27.

'What had really brought me here were the famous dolmens, the prehistoric burial caves which form a curious, ancient link between Spain and Britain. The people we call Picts ("painted ones") appear to have been Iberians who had populated Britain and Ireland by the beginning of the Bronze Age. So it is not surprising that the British Isles (and Brittany) are the main places outside Spain where anything really comparable with the megalithic tombs of Antequera is to be found.
The Cueva de Menga, the finest of the Antequera dolmens, is only a few minutes' walk across the fields. As I stood outside the tumulus, gazing at the giant rock that formed the roof, the guardian brought me the visitors' book . . . someone had written: "Stonehenge underground". And indeed, the same question poses itself here as it does at Stonehenge. How did these primitive people, whose main tools were deers' antlers, shift such enormous stones?'

Alban Allee,
Andalusia – Two Steps to Paradise

Fuente de Piedra

Andalucía's largest lake (2.5km, 1½ miles wide) with a large flamingo population and 75 other species of bird

The Laguna de Fuente de Piedra is the largest lake in Andalucía, and fla-mingoes have long made it their favourite stop in southern Spain. Every spring thou-sands of the big birds swoop in for a landing in this shallow lake, which is nearly 15 kilometres (nine miles) in circumference (2.5 kilometres/1½ miles wide; 6.5 kilo-metres/four miles long) and contains an islet known as La Colonia which, in springtime, is one of the most densely populated bird habitats in the world.

This elliptical lake is the only place in Europe where the greater flamingo breeds inland, as it does in the African lakes. (Indeed, there are only three other breeding sites in the whole of Europe – the Coto Doñana, Las Marismas del Odiel and France's Camargue.) They come here to breed almost every year; in 1984, for example, ornithologists counted more than 3,000 breeding pairs. They are very easy to observe from the path that circles the lake, which is just beyond the village, on the road toward the Sierra de Yeguas. At a spot called the Cerro del Palo, with the aid of a pair of binoculars, you can undertake your own bird census.

The stars of the show stalk through the water, grunting and trumpeting their incessant comments while rummaging the lake bottom for microscopic bits of food. On the crowded islet they build their conical nests with mud dredged up from the bottom. These are built so close together the effect is that of a flamingo tenement, with scarcely enough room for them to spread their wings on takeoff: it's an astonishing sight to see their glides, dives and splashdowns. Throughout the spring, water is continually evaporating and by mid-summer the lake is often bone dry. For the flamingoes, breeding is a race against time – the young must leave their nests before the island can be reached by preda-tors: dogs, cats and foxes. Some years they make it and in others the adults desert their nests. The birds do not need to breed each and every year to maintain their numbers – fortunately!

They have to share the premises, how-ever, with a lot of smaller birds, notably mallards, red-crested pochards, marsh harriers, water rails, moorhens, black-winged stilts, avocets, black-headed gulls, the rare slender-billed gulls and gull-billed terns. Sometimes the *laguna* is visited by storks, who seem to be walking on water, and frequently there are large delegations of Kentish plover looking for their place in the sun.

Seventy-six species of birds directly connected with this *laguna* have been iden-tified and a further 77 take advantage of the surrounding environment for feeding, breeding and, as it were, refuelling stops during north-south migrations. In winter there is no question but that coots are particularly happy in this habitat: the greatest concentration of the species ever observed in Spain took place here in January 1972, when 51,300 coots were counted in the *laguna*! Fuente de Piedra is now protected by ICONA.

The *laguna* is surrounded by the remains of a canal designed to control the inflow of freshwater and so prevent the flooding lake from inundating adjoining fields with its salty water. But the streams that once fed the lake have since been absorbed by agricultural irrigation projects, and nowadays it is fed only by rainwater – a seasonal and highly undependable source in this part of Andalucía.

The flora bordering the *laguna* consists mainly of *Arthrocnemum glaucum*, *Halo-peplis amplexicaulis*, *Suaeda vera*, *Salicornia fruticosa* and *Pholiurus incurvus* – a typical salt marsh community. The erstwhile canal is overgrown with tamarisk and reeds, and there are areas of scrubland abounding in *Genista umbellata*, French lavender, *Micromeria graeca* and *Ulex parviflorus*. Amphibians and reptiles make the most of their opportunities at Fuente de Piedra too, especially in the remnants of the freshwater canal. Look for marsh frogs, parsley frogs, western spadefoots and common toads as well as viperine snakes, grass snakes, stripe-necked terrapins, Montpellier snakes, ladder snakes and the horse-shoe whip snake. The ocellated lizard is the most common reptile in the zone, along with the large psammodromus and the Iberian wall lizard.

BEFORE YOU GO
Maps: SGE 1:50,000 Nos. 1,005 and 1,056; IGN 1:500,000 Nos. 1,006 and 1,023.

GETTING THERE
By car: the village of Fuente de Piedra, just 1km (½ mile) from the *laguna*, is located on highway N334, from Málaga to Granada and Seville.
By rail: not all trains on the Córdoba–Granada, Córdoba–Málaga lines stop at Fuente de Piedra. Take a *tranvía*, or local train, which run twice a day in both directions. Also Fuente de Piedra is just 24km (15 miles) north of Antequera, which is a main station on the Granada–Algeciras and Málaga–Córdoba–Seville lines.
By bus: from Antequera there are buses to Seville that stop at Fuente de Piedra and Osuna. Buses from Málaga – Seville that stop at Fuente de Piedra leave Pl. de Toros Vieja 2 in Málaga and from the main bus station in Seville (Pl. de San Sebastián). There are 4 buses a day between Antequera and Fuente de Piedra; they take about ½hr to cover the 23km (14 miles); T: (952) 32 33 62 and 31 04 46.

WHERE TO STAY
There is a 1-star hostel in Fuente de Piedra on the Seville–Málaga highway, km135 – Málaga, T: (952) 52. There is also accommodation available at Antequera.

FURTHER INFORMATION
Tourist information: Pl. Coso Viejo, Antequera, T: (952) 84 18 27.

Lagunas de Córdoba

Six inland salt lakes

Along the southern flank of the province of Córdoba there are six little-known inland salt lakes that play more or less the same ecological role as the Laguna de la Fuente de Piedra: these are the Lagunas de Zóñar, Rincon, Amarga, Tiscar, Los Jarales and El Conde. In winter they are visited by large numbers of migrating waterfowl: a recent census recorded 13 different species. At the head of the list is the white-headed duck, which was on the brink of disappearing altogether but has made a remarkable comeback, thanks largely to the efforts of the society known as the Asociación Amigos de la Malvasía ('friends of the white-headed duck').

This handsome, short-necked duck, with a bright blue bill, is the only representative of the 'stiff-tail' family in the whole of the Palaearctic region. It is scarce and decreasing in Western Europe, the only known breeding sites being located here in southern Spain; the closest to these lie in North Africa and Turkey.

The Laguna de Zóñar near Aguilar de la Frontera is the largest lake with permanent water: it occupies 38 hectares (94 acres) and has a maximum depth of 16 metres (52 feet). The lake is surrounded by vineyards, olive groves and wheatfields; reeds and marsh grasses along the edge provide the birds with a measure of concealment. This is a favourite winter resort for the white-headed duck, and in some years almost the entire Spanish population can be found here; there were 100 pairs at the last count. Other species found here include red-crested pochard, mallard, great crested grebe, tufted duck, shoveler, coot and marsh harrier.

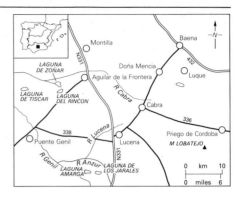

The small kidney-shaped Laguna Amarga ('bitter lake') derives its name salt and magnesium sulphate. It occupies 4.5 hectares (11 acres) near the village of Jauja but within the town limits of Lucena. The water is about four metres (13 feet) deep and is protected by a wide belt of vegetation in which white-headed ducks and purple gallinules breed every year.

Surrounded by vineyards and measuring less than four hectares (ten acres), the Laguna del Rincón ('corner'), near Aguilar de la Frontera, is the smallest of the three permanent lakes. The lake shrinks in the summer months, and was once on the brink of drying up, but is now regarded as the optimum breeding ground for the white-headed duck.

The seasonal lakes disappear during the summer, leaving behind a layer of salt, but once the rains have come and flooded them, they abound with birds. Laguna del Conde, alias Laguna del Salobral, near Luque, is the largest of all the six lakes, covering an area of 47.5 hectares (117 acres) but has a depth of only 70 centimetres (27 inches). Here you will see greater flamingo and shelduck. The salty waters of the Laguna de Tiscar, near Puente Genil, are only 50 centimetres (20 inches) deep, but that is enough to make it a breeding ground for plovers, black-winged stilts, avocets and mallards; sometimes young flamingoes fly in from Fuente de Piedra on reconnaissance missions. The sixth lake, the Laguna de Los Jarales, with 2.6 hectares (6½ acres) and only 40 centimetres (15 inches) of water after the rains, is a favoured spot for many ducks and plovers. It is a stone's throw from the Laguna Amarga, near Lucena.

BEFORE YOU GO
Maps: the *lagunas* are not shown on most road maps: you need SGE 1:50,000 Nos. 966, 967, 988 and 989; or IGN 1:200,000 Mapa provincial of Córdoba.

GETTING THERE
The town of Aguilar makes the most convenient base for seeing the *lagunas*.
By car: highway N331, Córdoba–Antequera, takes you to Aguilar; from there C329 leads west to Puente Genil or east to Lucena. Luque, near Baena, is further

north, near highway C327.
By rail: there is a daily train service to Puente Genil, on the Córdoba–Granada and Córdoba–Jaén lines. For current schedules and other information, telephone the RENFE station in Córdoba, T: (957) 47 93 02.
By bus: regular buses run from Seville to Cabra via Puente Genil and Lucena; for information, T: (954) 41 52 58 in Seville. Buses on the Córdoba–Estepa line stop at Puente Genil and Aguilar; for further information, call Lucena (957) 500 03 02, or

Córdoba (957) 23 14 01.

WHERE TO STAY
Four villages in the *lagunas* region offer accommodation: Lucena, Baena, Aguilar and Puente Genil. For example, in Lucena is the 1-star hostel Muñoz, T: (957) 50 10 52; and in Aguilar, the 2-star hotel, Las Viñas, T: (957) 66 08 97.

FURTHER INFORMATION
Tourist information:
C. González Murga, Córdoba, T: (957) 47 12 35. ICONA, Tomás de Aquino, Córdoba, T: (957) 23 94 00.

Parque Natural de Grazalema

From its source in the Serrania de Ronda the young Rio Guadalete loops round north of the Parque Natural de Grazalema

47,200ha (166,000 acres) of parque natural, *largely consisting of mountain wilderness, with 3 kinds of eagle and many other bird species*

When you get to Grazalema, whatever the time of year, it will probably be raining as the local mountains have a knack of catching all the clouds drifting in from the Atlantic. As a result this vast, stony area furnishes an ideal environment for a very full complement of birds, mammals and reptiles. The main feature for which Grazalema is renowned is the Spanish fir forest on the north-eastern slopes of El Pinar (1,654 metres/5,425 feet), the second-highest peak in the Serranía de Ronda. This tree species (*Abies pinsapo*) is restricted to just four localities in these mountains around Ronda, all occurring between altitudes of 1,000 and 1,700 metres (3,300 and 5,600 feet).

Of course these rare trees, remnants of the last Ice Age, occupy only a small part of the *parque natural*: some 300 hectares (740 acres) out of a total of 47,200 (116,635 acres). This forest of *pinsapos*, as they are known in Spanish, owes its existence to the fact that it has a microclimate all its own: 210 centimetres (82 inches) of rainfall during the average year, plus northern exposure, which means that the forest is wet and cool all summer long. To keep this

151

arboreal jewel intact, the Andalucían environmental agency requires visitors to obtain a permit (see below) and mounts guard over the trees themselves, to make certain no one attempts to use them as Christmas trees.

The greater part of the *parque natural* consists of mountain wilderness lands belonging to 13 villages in Cádiz province and five in Málaga. The grey limestone of these slopes is so friable that hiking is often a chore. One day, as I bent over to take a close-up photo of some wild flowers near the pass, I slid down a scree for about 15 metres (50 feet) before my frantic braking efforts – with heels and elbows – finally brought me to a stop. It was my longest-ever impromptu descent of a mountain.

The bowl shape of the adjoining valley allows it to collect a significant quantity of water and to produce a rich flora noted for ferns and other plants that thrive in wet climates. Birds do well here, and the park is famed for the large number of griffon vultures that nest among the high stone cliffs (both parents share the chore of sitting on the eggs, during an incubation period lasting 59 days). The tiny chicks grow into very large birds indeed, with a wingspread of about 2.5 metres (eight feet). They share their carrion meals with a number of other resident scavengers, including the Egyptian vulture.

Other members of the park's bird population include golden, booted and short-toed eagles, tawny, barn and Scops owls, kestrel, peregrine, buzzard, hoopoe, bee-eater, short-toed tree creeper, redstart, willow and Sardinian warblers, white-throat, wren, cuckoo, jackdaw, goldfinch, spotted flycatcher, golden oriole, chaffinch, green and great spotted woodpeckers, nightingale, stonechat, wryneck, wood lark, Alpine swift, serin, and red-legged partridge.

The ancient village of Grazalema makes an ideal jumping-off point for birdwatching or botanical tours of the park. Among the village fields you'll find blue rock thrush, black wheatear, rock and cirl buntings, while eagles, vultures and goshawk patrol regularly overhead.

BEFORE YOU GO

Maps: SGE 1:50,000 Nos. 1,049, 1,050 and 1,051; IGN 1:200,000 Mapas provinciales of Cádiz and Málaga; and Firestone T-29 and C-9, La Sierra de Cádiz; and Información general y mapa, a useful schematic hiker's map of the mountains of Cádiz province.

Guidebooks: *Grazalema*, an anthology (Diputación de Cádiz, 1981); and *El Bosque*, an anthology (Diputación de Cádiz, 1982).

GETTING THERE

By car: the highway from El Bosque to Grazalema takes you directly through the park, to the imposing Puerto del Boyar at 1,103m (3,620ft).
By bus: the only way to reach Grazalema on public transport is on the Ronda–Ubrique bus. El Bosque can be reached by

means of the Jerez de la Frontera–Ubrique bus and the Seville–Ubrique bus. All these buses run twice daily each way and are operated by Los Amarillos, C. Navarros 22, Seville, T: (954) 41 93 62; in Cádiz their telephone number is (956) 28 85 52.

WHERE TO STAY

El Bosque has a 2-star hotel – Las Truchas, T: (956) 72 30 86 – and accommodation is also available in Grazalema, Ubrique and Ronda.
Outdoor living: there are no official camping grounds, but camping is permitted in the *parque natural*. Check regulations at the ICONA office when collecting your entry permit.

ACTIVITIES

Walking: a series of basic itineraries for hikers has been laid out by the park authorities. The basic route begins at a point on the highway between Puerto del Boyar and Grazalema, proceeds to the Llano del Revés, ascends to the Puerto de los Cumbres and thence to the Pinsapar – the forest of Spanish fir – before circling back by way of the Arroyo del Pinar. It offers the best opportunities for studying the *pinsapo* and other endemic plants of the region.

A second itinerary begins at the Puerto de los Acebuches ('the pass of the wild olives') on the road between Grazalema and Zahara de la Sierra; it leads to the Puerto del Sabinarejo via the Cañada de Cornicabra. This is undoubtedly the best route for studying varied vegetation of a typical area of *maquis* and scrub forest.

A third hiking route also departs from the Puerto de los Acebuches and goes to the Ermita de la Garganta (872m/2,860ft), and the steep slope of the Garganta Verde ('green gorge').
Driving: if you haven't the time or inclination to study the park on foot or horseback there remains the far less exciting alternative of driving through the sierra. The recommended route starts at Zahara de la Sierra, goes to Puerto de los Acebuches, from where you can look across to the Pinsapar, and takes in the Puerto de las Palomas (1,260m/4,130ft),

which affords a superb view of the Sierra del Endrinal. You can continue via the Puerto del Boyar to Benamahoma and then through El Bosque to Ubrique, another of the beautiful *pueblos blancos* (white villages) of the sierra; the road leads past important stands of wild olive and large tracts of wild Andalucían forest.
Riding: horseback tours of the park are available. One trail leads from Zahara to Sierra Margarita, another starts at the Puerto de los Acebuches and ends at the Pinsapar, while a third takes 2 days to make the circuit of Sierra

Margarita. Benamahoma (source of the Río El Bosque) and the Pinsapar. For details, ask at the tourist office at Ronda (see below for address, etc.).

FURTHER INFORMATION
Tourist information:
C. Calderón de la Barca 1, Cádiz, T: (956) 22 48 00; and Pl. de España, Ronda, T: (952) 87 12 72. ICONA, Avda Ana de Viga 3, Cádiz, T: (956) 27 45 94.
    Excursions to El Pinar and the Ermita de la Garganta require a permit from the tourist office in Cádiz (see above).

THE FLORA OF GRAZALEMA

The sierras of Grazalema are geologically very similar to those of El Torcal de Antequera, but Grazalema is by far the most famous locality for its botanical rarities. Two spectacular species growing in the rocks above the village were described by Dwight Ripley in his paper 'A Journey through Spain' (1944): the crucifer *Biscutella frutescens*, 'with its showers of gold and thick rosettes of scalloped velvet', and the endemic 'delicate brick[-red]' poppy *Papaver rupifragum*, which is confined to the mountains of the Serranía de Ronda. Another interesting species which he mentions, albeit in less emotive terms, is the handsome, white-woolly *Centaurea clementei*, a yellow-flowered knapweed that is known only from Grazalema and the Sierra de Yunquera in southern Spain.
    Growing in rock crevices, you can find three saxifrage species that are confined to the southern Spanish sierras: *Saxifraga haenseleri*, *S. globulifera* and *S. boissieri*. All have small, whitish flowers and the latter two are particularly frequent in the Serranía de Ronda. On

the high ridge of the Serranía de Grazalema grows an almost alpine fissure and scree community, including such species as Spanish whitlow-grass (*Draba hispanica*), large-flowered treacle-mustard (*Erysium grandiflorum*) and another crucifer species with lilac flowers, *Ionopsidium prolongoi*.
    In the fir forest of El Pinar, the trees cast a good deal of shade and a specialized shrub flora has evolved beneath the canopy, including such evergreen species as small-flowered gorse (*Ulex parviflorus* ssp *funkii*), spurge laurel and laurustinus (*Viburnum tinus*); the berries of this latter plant are highly poisonous. More colourful species, such as Spanish barberry (*Berberis hispanica*) and the hedgehog broom, can be found in clearings in the fir wood. Stony areas support the dwarf woody crucifer *Ptilotrichum spinosum*. At lower altitudes, the resinous smell of the firs is enhanced by the presence of two aromatic cistus species – grey-leaved and poplar-leaved (*Cistus albidus* and *C. populifolius*) – which also attract myriads of flying insects when they are in full bloom.

Laguna de Medina

Small lake (500ha/1,250 acres) – a stopping place for migratory birds going to and from Africa

This small freshwater lake in the wheat-growing, horse-rearing country around Jerez de la Frontera takes its name from the ducal house of Medina Sidonia, whose ancestral seat – the hilltop town of the same name – lies some distance to the south. Normally this is an insignificant body of water, covering about 500ha (1,235 acres) and ringed with reeds and marsh grasses. But it is important at times for birds of passage, situated as it is close to the point where Europe and Africa almost meet. From the end of Aug, birds migrating from central and northern Europe make it their last stopover before flying on to Africa. Waders, terns and birds of prey all stop to find refuge here.

In times of drought, the lake also attracts birds, but for another reason: just across the Río Guadalquivir lies the Coto Doñana, and if the *marismas* are drier than usual at the end of the summer, some of the Doñana birds come looking for food and water east of the river. In Nov 1973 ornithologists counted 22,626 birds on this 1 lake. Altogether about 47 species have been recorded here, including spoonbills, the white-headed duck, and the greater flamingo.
Before you go *Maps:* SGE 1:50,000 Nos. 1,048 and 1,062; IGN 1:20,000 Mapa provincial of Cádiz.
Getting there *By car:* the *laguna* is in the open country, on highway C440 (Jerez–Medina Sidonia).

By rail: Jerez, 10km (6 miles) to the west, has train and bus connections to Seville and Cádiz.
By bus: there are daily buses from Jerez to Medina Sidonia: for more detailed information, T: (956) 22 78 11 in Jerez, or T: (956) 21 17 63 in Cádiz. Buses also run from Seville to Algeciras by way of Jerez and Medina Sidonia; T: (954) 22 93 65.
Where to stay: the cities nearest the *laguna* offering accommodation are Jerez de la Frontera and Puerto Real. In Jerez there are more than 20 hotels, ranging from the 5-star Hotel Jerez, T: (956) 30 06 00, to the 1-star hostel, San Martín, T: (956) 33 70 40.
Further information *Tourist information:* C. Calderón de la Barca 1, Cádiz, T: (956) 22 48 00; and C. Guadalete, Puerto Real, T: (956) 86 31 45. ICONA, Avda Ana de Viga 3, Cádiz, T: (956) 27 45 94.

Parque Nacional de Doñana

Wetlands, sand dune and pine forest, in lowland parque nacional *at the delta of the Río Guadalquivir*

The first time I visited the Doñana national park I was impressed mainly by the landscape – the vast dunes engulfing the forests behind them, the sandy woodlands inhabited by red and fallow deer, and the teeming marshes adjoining the estuary of the Guadalquivir, where there seemed to be no end to the ducks and herons feeding noisily among the reeds and bullrushes. What stayed with me was a sense of almost limitless space, a wilderness of wetlands, sand dune and pine forest that was bounded on one side by a river as blue as the sky and on another by as lonely a beach as it is still possible to find.

But it was not until my second visit that I began to grasp the real significance of the last great lowland wilderness sanctuary in southern Europe. This time I made the trip in a Landrover that was filled with professional birdwatchers – mostly editors and writers of nature magazines. The leader of the group was one of the grand old men of British ornithology, who had an uncanny way of raising his binoculars to the sky and announcing, about some pinpoint in the far distance: 'There's a marsh harrier just rising to the left of that oak.' Or he would deliver short impromptu lectures such as, 'Here's a short-toed eagle, a snake hunter and nature's killing machine. It's armoured with a helmet of feathers against snakebites and with short, powerful talons to grasp its prey. The feathers on its wing tips splay out aerodynamically so as to prevent drag and turbulence . . .'

These spoonbills return from Africa to breed in the same colony in the Doñana year after year

In the marshlands known as the *marismas* we watched a group of excited shrikes mob a booted eagle that had made the mistake of invading their territory – and our mentor spotted the eagle even before the shrikes did. Not long afterwards he had the satisfaction of telling us, in his matter-of-fact voice: 'Here's the rarest bird we're going to see today, the imperial eagle.'

Its proximity to Africa is one of the principal reasons for the wealth and variety of the Doñana's birdlife. Birds with large wingspans, such as the eagles and kites that abound here, cannot fly across water for long distances because they require thermal updrafts for the long glides that allow them to rest their wings during migrations. Hence they cross the Mediterranean at the three points – the Dardanelles, Gibraltar and Tarifa – where the intervening straits are at their narrowest. For those making the journey from west Africa, the *marismas* of the Doñana are a logical, indeed essential, resting place and hunting ground.

Here, if all goes well, the flamingoes will find the shrimps that play such an important part in their life cycle; if they find no shrimp to eat they will not turn a contented pink, and if they do not turn pink they will not go on to breed (in locations such as Fuente de Piedra and, more recently, Las Marismas de Odiel), but will merely wait out the season and return home without having reproduced.

The Parque Nacional de Doñana – or as it used to be known, the Coto ('hunting estate') Doñana – thus plays a critical role in the reproductive cycle of several species, the more so since other Andalucían wetlands have dried up or been 'reclaimed'. Yet sometimes things go catastrophically wrong – when not enough rain falls to flood the *marismas* to a sufficient depth, or when pesticides infiltrate the region from the neighbouring agricultural areas as happened in 1986, when an estimated 30,000 birds died in or around the park.

The Doñana is, essentially, the delta of the Guadalquivir, the 'big river', or Wada-l-Kebir, of the Moors. But it is a delta with a difference. Unlike most, the river has only one outlet to the sea, just below Sanlúcar de Barrameda. The rest of what used to be its delta has gradually been blocked off by a huge sandbar that stretches from the mouth of the Río Tinto, near Palos, to the riverbank opposite Sanlúcar, and which the sea winds have gradually formed into high dunes. Behind this natural barrier stretch the *marismas*.

The effect of this extraordinary *mélange* of land and water was to create an environment shunned by people but ideal for wildlife. As early as the thirteenth century, the kings of Castile set aside a portion of the Doñana as a royal hunting estate; later the dukes of Medina Sidonia made it their private *coto*. One of the duchesses of Medina Sidonia, Doña Ana de Silva y Mendoza, indulged her antisocial instincts by building a residence there that was more hermitage than palace. As a result the entire region came to be known as the 'forest of Doña Ana', or Doñana. In the eighteenth century, Goya is known to have visited the Duchess of Alba at the Palacio de Doñana when she was its proprietress. Subsequently, the land passed through many hands before the official creation of the *parque nacional* in 1969.

Meanwhile, adjoining areas of wetland were being dramatically reduced. Across the Guadalquivir vast marshes were drained and converted to farmland, until only the protected lands of the Doñana remained intact. For centuries there had been only a vacant spot on the map between Lebrija in the east and Almonte in the north west, but in recent years whole towns and villages have sprung up west of the Guadalquivir, and the resort town of Matalascañas has brought urban sprawl to the south-western edge of the Doñana, a place once occupied by reed-thatched fishermen's huts.

The proximity of these settlements has further complicated the work of the park's wildlife guardians. Two of the Doñana's precious lynxes, for example, have been run over by cars on the highway to Matalascañas; cats and dogs straying out of the nearest town have killed animals in the park, and birds that have overflown the

fences have been gunned down by trigger-happy hunters despite stringent conservation laws. A more permanent threat to the Doñana's ecosystems are the new ricefields and other agricultural projects north of El Rocío, whose run-off waters sluice pesticides into the *marismas*, and the sulphur mines upstream at Aznalcóllar, which wash effluvium into the river.

What you see here depends on the time of the year and the luck of the draw. November, December and January constitute the off-season for human visitors but it is an ideal time for waterfowl, since the autumn rains have brought life back to the *marismas* and filled the *lagunas*. Gradually the water attains a uniform depth of 30–60 centimetres (12–24 inches) over vast areas, and the resulting marshes attract vast flocks of wildfowl, ducks, geese and other water birds of the most varied kind. These are freshwater marshes, incidentally, although there are traces of sea salt in the underlying clay. Here and there small islands known as *vetas* rise above the water; these remain dry throughout the year, creating an ideal breeding ground for waders and terns.

Towards the end of February the geese who have migrated here from northern Europe commence their return journey, but at the same time the spoonbills arrive from North Africa to nest in the cork oaks. In March the waters begin to recede and spring begins in earnest. This is also the time when the imperial eagle hatches its eggs; 15 breeding pairs of these formidable hunters were counted recently in the park – about a third of all the imperial eagles known to survive in Spain. Each pair requires nearly 2,600 hectares (6,425 acres) of land to hunt over in summer, and even more in winter. This is a far from perfect environment for these great birds and Doñana pairs seldom raise as many young as those elsewhere in Spain.

In spring the *marismas* are alive with birds – some settling down to breed, others *en route* for more northern climes. Huge numbers of kites hang in the air, harriers send the duck scurrying skywards in fear of their lives. There are black-tailed godwit and ruff on their way to Holland and beyond, greenshank and wood sandpiper bound for Scandinavia, little stint and curlew sandpiper heading for northern Siberia and usually a marsh sandpiper that should be a thousand kilometres (620 miles) or more further east. Overhead vast flocks of whiskered terns wheel and circle along with a few gull-billed terns and racy pratincoles. There are swallows galore, some of them red-rumped, and bee-eaters and rollers perch on post and wire. All of these and more can be seen from the bridge at El Rocío – perhaps the best free bird-watching in Europe.

From bird hides at the reserve centre just south of the bridge you will hear Cetti's and Savi's warblers and watch egrets, herons and little bitterns come and go. Marsh harriers and kites are continually on view and sometimes a majestic imperial eagle will soar from the woods of Doñana over El Rocío to the Coto del Rey.

In mid-summer the temperature in the parched *marismas* easily exceeds 40°C (110°F). Aquatic birds that remain in the stagnant pools die of botulism, and each year thousands more die during the advancing drought in the Doñana. In August there is almost nothing left of the marsh's aquatic fauna, but it is a good time for observing dozens of summer residents, which include griffon vulture, booted eagle, red and black kites, short-toed eagle, Baillon's crake, purple gallinule, great spotted cuckoo, Scops owl, red-necked nightjar, bee-eater, hoopoe, calandra, short-toed and thekla larks, golden oriole, azure-winged magpie, Cetti's and Savi's warblers, tawny pipit, great grey shrike, woodchat shrike and serin. There is, in fact, no end to the life cycle of this wilderness, where 125 species of bird are known to breed, as well as 28 mammal species, 17 reptiles, nine amphibians and eight species of fish.

The park as a whole comprises three distinct kinds of ecosystem: the *marismas*, the *matorral* and the dunes. A typical motorized visit to Doñana will take in a sampling of all three, but the amount of exposure to each environment varies with the seasons. No two visits will be alike.

The last time I toured the park was during the month of May. It is a bright, sunny morning with unseasonally high temperatures as we enter the park just south of El Rocío, a village that resembles a set for a Hollywood western. We are driven along a rutted dirt track that leads through a forest of eucalyptus trees, planted many years ago for sale to a nearby pulp mill. After a time the eucalyptus give way to a landscape of native scrubland: *Halium* thicket with scattered cork oaks. This is the favourite abode of the park's lynxes, which currently number about 25 pairs and represent the last survivors of their species in southern Europe. Of course they stay out of sight, but the movements of about a quarter of their number are monitored by means of electronic collars. Kites seem to fill the sky, and a herd of red deer peer out from behind the bushes; nearby we see some marsh cattle grazing in a densely overgrown meadow.

A small permanent stream flows to our left: it is the Caño de la Madre de las Marismas del Rocío, one of the two main arteries through which the upland waters reach the marshes. Beyond it stretches an endless plain, part water, part mud, and everywhere clogged with marsh grasses. It

The purple gallinule, an exotic tropical relative of the coot, leads a retiring life among the reeds

Flamingoes congregate in the shallows of the salt-water lagoons of Las Marismas del Odiel

seems incredible that during Roman times this bog was a broad gulf, and ships could bring their cargoes into Lebrija, a town now seven kilometres (4½ miles) from the nearest stream, on the other side of the Guadalquivir.

The Landrover makes another stop to enable us to observe some of the *pajareras*. These venerable cork oaks are located within the park's special biological reserve, the Reserva Científica, which is off limits. On this occasion the area seems occupied by an Afro-European parliament of birds, and the treetops are alive with some of the greatest herons in Europe: little egret, cattle egret, night heron, spoonbill and grey heron.

A man on horseback comes riding past. He is one of the park wardens, for at this time of the year a horse is the only satisfactory means of transport through the *marismas*. Soon our Landrover is taking us over trails of loose beach sand where even a horse might have found the going difficult. We look in on the Palacio de Doñana,

where there are storks and peacocks as well as a stable full of horses. Beyond it lie rolling sand dunes and open places overgrown with brambles, with an occasional stone pine holding down the sand. We bounce along the ruts until we come to a more humid environment – a brilliantly coloured quagmire.

Further on are the dunes, which the Landrover negotiates only with the greatest difficulty. There are flamingoes in a small *laguna* to our left, obviously in the very pink of condition.

It was was first proved here in Doñana that flamingoes do not hatch their eggs sitting astride high conical mounds of mud, as was believed for 200 years. In 1883, Abel Chapman found a colony of greater flamingoes sitting on a mass of nests that were raised just above the mud, deep in the *marismas*: 'We approached within some seventy yards [65 metres] before their sentries showed signs of alarm, and at that distance, with the glass, observed the sitting birds as distinctly as one need wish. The

In Andalucía cork oaks grow on poor acid soils, providing an invaluable commodity

long red legs doubled under their bodies, the knees projecting as far as, or beyond the tail, and their graceful necks neatly curled among their back-feathers like a sitting swan, with the heads resting on their breasts – all these points are unmistakable.'

The dune barrier responsible for creating this paradise is still on the move, creeping inland at the rate of three to six metres (10–20 feet) a year. Wandering among the dunes we see that some of them have half swallowed the stone pines growing in the hollows behind them. This strip of coastal territory is a breeding ground for the stone curlew and the thekla lark, and a favourite hunting zone for short-toed and imperial eagles.

Eventually we reach the seashore, where the long Atlantic rollers beat against the coast. The beach is covered with terns; in fact I have never seen so many black terns in my life. At the edge of the dunes stand old coastal watchtowers, now deserted except for breeding peregrines. Kentish plovers also rear their young in this environment.

A little further on we see Audouin's gull, one of the world's rarest gulls: it is so specialized that it only knows how to fish from the surface of the sea. While other gulls have become inland scavengers, taking advantage of rubbish tips and ripe olives, Audouin's gulls are more discerning and feed themselves the hard way, by dipping in after fish in a similar manner to terns. We also see a flock of flamingoes on the beach, presumably just arrived from Africa and waiting for the sundown to show them the direction of the marshes; not surprisingly, they seem very tired after their long journey.

And so are we, after a day of watching, learning and being astonished and delighted by the immensity of this wilderness.

BEFORE YOU GO
Maps: SGE 1:50,000 Nos. 1,001, 1,018, 1,033 and 1,047; SGE 1:200,000 Nos. 3-10 and 3-11; and Firestone C-9 and T-30.
Guidebooks: *Guía del P. N. Doñana* by J. A. Fernández (Omega, 1982); *Doñana, manual práctico* by J. Vozmediano (Pentathlon, 1983); *El mito de Doñana* by A. Duque (MEC, 1977); and *Torres de almenara de la costa de Huelva* by L. Mora (Diputación de Huelva, 1981).

GETTING THERE
By air: the usual way to reach Coto Doñana is via Seville, which has excellent train and plane connections. Cheap charter flights to Málaga international airport also offer a convenient means of flying to within striking distance of the park.
By car: from Seville, take the A49, turn east at Bollullos par del Condado and follow the N445 from Almonte to

Matalascañas, the modern but ugly beach resort which is the customary jumping-off point for visits to the *parque nacional*. Alternatively, from

---

The red-crested pochard commonly breeds and winters in southern Spain and along the coast

Huelva follow the coastal road to Matalascañas through the little-known dune country.
By bus: buses from Seville to Matalascañas are operated by Empresa Damas and leave from C. Segura, near the Pl. de Armas.

WHERE TO STAY

Matalascañas is a recently-built oceanside resort with 5 large hotels open May–Sep. There are also a number of small hostels. Near Mazagón is the Parador Nacional Cristóbal Colón, T: (955) 37 60 00, as well as the 1-star Hostal Hilaria, T: (955) 37 62 06. If you are in the mood for an inland village that looks like a set from *High Noon*, try the 1-star Hostal Vélez, T: (955) 40 61 17, at El Rocío. **Outdoor living:** there are 3 official camping areas, all vast – Rocío Playa on the Huelva–Matalascañas highway (at km45.2), T: (955) 43 02 38; Doñana Playa (km48.8 on the above highway) in Mazagón, T: (955) 37 62 81; and Playa de Mazagón, situated in Moguer about 20km (12½ miles) from Huelva, T: (955) 37 62 08.

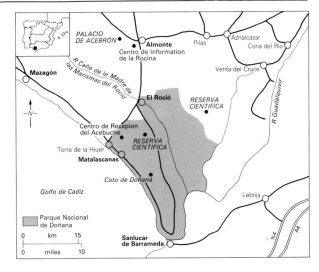

ACTIVITIES

You cannot visit the park on your own. There are organized jeep tours, usually lasting about 4hrs, along 5 standard routes through the park, each a circuit of about 70km (43 miles). The starting point, and the only place to book them, is Matalascañas; ask for details at the Centro de Recepción del Acebuche (see below). It is a good idea to reserve places in advance,

for during the height of the season there is often a waiting list, and Matalascañas, although fine for suntans, holds few other charms for people with a *penchant* for wildlife rather than for *discoteca*.

Birdwatching: also possible outside the confines of the *parque nacional*. Ask at the tourist office about the bird hides that ICONA has erected outside the park, which may be available.

Riding: the park authority is introducing a special riding trail – a 20-km (12½-mile) route; ask at the tourist centre for details.

FURTHER INFORMATION

Tourist information: Centro de Recepción del Acebuche is near Matalascañas, just off the main road, T: (955) 43 04 32; this centre provides extensive information about the park's various ecosystems and their flora and fauna. Also C. Plus Ultra 10, Huelva; T: (955) 24 50 92; and Avda de la Constitución 21, Seville, T: (954) 22 14 40. ICONA, Gran Vía 26, Huelva, T: (955) 21 34 71; and Avda Ramón y Cajal 1, Seville, T: (954) 63 96 50.

The park's tourist office is located at El Rocina, T: (955) 40 61 40.

Las Marismas del Odiel

Paraje natural covering 6,791ha (16,780 acres) within Huelva's city boundaries Breeding ground of flamingoes

The first time I visited the Marismas del Odiel I happened to be present at an historic moment. Accompanied by Juan

Carlos Rubio, the young naturalist who had just been appointed director of the recently created *paraje natural* of the Odiel marshes, we made a jeep journey into the very centre of these wetlands, to the *lagunas* and salt pans of the Salinas de Bacuta. It was a clear, sunny spring day, and there was a large flock of flamingoes in the middle of the principal *laguna*. They were not at all disturbed by our arrival at the embankment that formed its eastern edge, but went on holding what seemed to be a rather noisy family reunion of about 400 birds. Some of

161

them were walking up and down in their restless, peripatetic way, and they were making the goose-like sounds that have been compared to the grumblings of a discontented crowd at a football match. Others were holding their heads under water and sifting mud through their bills to screeen out molluscs, crayfish and algae.

My guide, who had spent many hours of his life watching these gregarious birds, suddenly grew very excited; he had just realized that the flamingoes were building nests and getting ready to raise their young here in the Laguna de Aljaraque. It was the first time flamingoes had been known to breed in Las Marismas del Odiel, and their settling-in represented a triumphant vindication of a conservation programme to which Señor Rubio had devoted several years of intensive effort.

Sometimes as many as 2,000 flamingoes migrate from Africa to the wetlands of the Odiel. The fact that some of them now stay here to breed, rather than go to the *marismas* of the Doñana, may be due to the fact that this *laguna* does not dry up during the summer months, like most of those in the Doñana; they may also prefer the greater salinity of the Laguna de Aljaraque. For Las Marismas del Odiel differ from the freshwater wetlands of the Doñana, 120 kilometres (75 miles) to the east, in that

they consist of tidal marshes and the large salt pans of the local *salinas*, which have long been a feature of the Huelva region. The Atlantic tides that irrigate these salt marshes sometimes run as high as four metres (13 feet). But the reserve itself is also far smaller – 6,791 hectares (16,780 acres) – and much closer to civilization than the Coto Doñana. The *paraje natural*, indeed, is just across the water from the port facilities and industrial installations that line the navigable main channel of the Río Odiel for its last 15 kilometres (nine miles) to the sea.

The Río Tinto, of course, is the industrial artery from which the greatest copper and manganese mines in Europe derive their name (at its confluence with the Odiel stands the Monasterio de La Rábida, where Columbus planned his voyage to the Indies in 1492 – which permits the residents of Huelva to regard their city as 'the cradle of the New World'). Las Marismas del Odiel have thus had to vie for space, air and government funds with a modern port authority, agricultural reclamation projects and the commercial requirements of the *salinas*. Even so the *paraje natural* has managed to hold its own as a wildlife reserve of international importance, thanks to its colonies of flamingoes, spoonbills, purple herons and other wintering and breeding visitors.

BEFORE YOU GO
Maps: SGE 1:50,000 No. 999; and IGN 1:200,000 Mapa provincial of Huelva.

GETTING THERE
By bus: Las Marismas del Odiel lie within the city boundaries of Huelva and are served by regular buses.

WHERE TO STAY
In Punta Umbría, a summer resort placed between the river and the sea, there are more than 10 hotels and hostels, including the 3-star Pato Amarillo, T: (955) 31 12 50, and the 2-star El Ayamontina, T: (955) 31 14 50. There is a 1-star hostel, La

Galera, T: (955) 39 02 76, in El Rompido on the sea near Huelva.
Outdoor living: 4 camping grounds are located within the Huelva area – in Punta Umbría is Pinos del Mar; Catapum in El Rompido; the Fontanilla Playa in Mazagón; and the Playa de Mazagón in Moguer.

ACTIVITIES
Birdwatching: the best areas are within the confines of the Salinas de Bacuta, the gates of which are kept firmly locked against uninvited human visitors. Make prior arrangements with the management of the *paraje*,

which is under the jurisdiction of the Agencia de Medio Ambiente of the Junta de Andalucía: Pl. del Punto 6, Huelva 3, T: (955) 24 57 67, 24 57 68.

FURTHER INFORMATION
Tourist information: C. Plus Ultra 10, Huelva, T: (955) 24 50 92. ICONA. Gran Vía 26, Huelva, T: (955) 21 34 71.
Mosquito repellent is essential.

A patchwork of gold and green fields, a flourishing olive grove, bare-ribbed mountains: this is the elemental landscape characteristic of Andalucía, and much of inland Spain

Sierra de Aracena

Low range of mountains up to 1,000m (3,300ft) where Spanish lynx, black vulture and imperial eagle are found

Huelva, home of Spain's best-known national park, the Coto Doñana, also has an immense upland region that is virtually unknown to the outside world. The Sierra de Aracena forms the western edge of the Sierra Morena.

The Sierra Morena, formerly known as the Cordillera Mariánica or Montes Mariani, extends over some 500 kilometres (300 miles) from the mountains of southern Portugal to the steppe region of Albacete in the east. This mountain chain represents the eroded edge of the Meseta. While its maximum height is only 1,323m/(4,340ft), its breadth (over 65km/40 miles) is responsible for the historic and continuing economic and cultural separation of Andalucía and northern Spain.

The main ridge is composed of slates and greywacke, largely covered with an evergreen mantle of cistus scrub: if you stand on the east you see an extensive area of *matorral*, with its full complement of holm, cork and Lusitanian oaks.

The only important break in this formidable wall is the pass of Despeñaperros. The easternmost, and highest, ridge is that of the Sierra de Alcaraz, while the less lofty collection of ridges on the borders of Portugal is the Sierra de Aracena. These convoluted and irregular

FLORA IN THE SIERRA MORENA

In May, the hillsides of Despeñaperros are covered with gum cistus, and you have to search for the blue-purple spikes of the Spanish iris (*Iris xiphium*) that lurk beneath the foliage of these aromatic shrubs. Also to be seen here is the endemic foxglove *Digitalis purpurea* ssp *mariana*, which differs from the common European race by having leaves covered in long, silky white hairs.

Within the oak woods of the more sheltered areas of the *matorral* grow a number of highly attractive herbs, including the nodding yellow spring flowers of the palmate anemone (*Anemone palmata*), replaced slightly later in the year by the wild tulip *Tulipa australis*. Larger plants include a striking red-flowered peony *Paeonia broteri*, which grows amid bushes of *Genista tournefortii*, a typical south-west Mediterranean shrub bearing clusters of golden-yellow flowers.

One strange feature of the Sierra is that, despite its considerable distance from the sea, it is home to 2 monocotyledonous plants normally found in coastal areas: the Barbary nut (*Iris sisyrinchium*) and the sea squill (*Urginea maritima*), both of which also occur in Gibraltar.

ridges of the Sierra Morena are rich in metals and minerals, including the famous copper mines of Tharsis and the Río Tinto, as well as deposits of iron, pyrites,

Dense sands of the sea club-rush grow in the salt marshes and ditches of Las Marismas de Doñana

manganese, tin, tungsten, nickel and coal.

Although 40 per cent of all the villages in Huelva are located in the sierra, it is also the province's most thinly populated *comarca* – just as well, really, for the region's wolves, lynxes, imperial eagles and black vultures.

The Spanish lynx, also known as the pardel lynx, is thought to be a different species from the bulk of the European population; it is smaller and has more distinct spots than its northern counterparts. The lynx was once widely distributed in southern Europe but is found today only in the mountains of Greece, and in 2 main populations in Spain – the other is in Doñana. Each of the locations in Spain has about 30 individuals. Their numbers have declined drastically owing to the cutting down of much of the primeval forest cover which is essential to their lifestyle and also to hunting.

The sierra is also the home

of the tiny blue butterfly called Lorquin's blue (*Cupido lorquini*). This species, very similar to the ubiquitous small blue, is confined to just 3 mountain localities in Spain and occurs sporadically in Portugal and North Africa. Little is known about its ecology but it is usually seen in areas of short grassland during May and Jun, its violet-blue upper wings distinguishing it from the dark brown of the small blue butterfly.

As mountains go, the Sierra de Aracena is hardly more than a range of rugged hills, with median altitudes betweeen 500–600m (1,650–2,000ft) and the highest peaks not over 1,000m (3,300ft). The *comarca* as a whole encompasses nearly 300,000ha (741,315 acres), only a fraction of which are protected. What is fascinating about hiking through these mountains is the contrast between half-forgotten villages with orange and lemon orchards and the superb oak forests – silent woods in which you can, at your peril, find the hallucinogenic mushroom *Amanita muscaria*, the fly agaric, whose juice gave the shaman-priests of ancient Europe their second sight.

From the summit of the Peña Arias Montano you can look down on the whole of the sierra. This was a sacred peak in pagan times; the Christians built a shrine to the Madonna de los Angeles on the spot – perhaps because the view from here is nothing short of angelic.

Approaching Aracena from either Seville or Huelva, you pass through a very different region, the Andévalo, once famous for its pyrite fields and now the summer retreat of *sevillanos*. Once arrived in Aracena you will hardly be able to escape the local attraction known as the Gruta de la Maravillas ('grotto of the wonders'), which was discovered by chance by one of the thousands of black pigs rooting hereabouts, while snuffling about for a stray acorn.

Before you go *Maps:* SGE 1:50,000 Nos. 917, 918, 938 and 939; and IGN 1:200,000 Mapa provincial of Huelva.
Getting there *By car:* from Huelva, take highway N43S north to Jabugo, then east via N433 to Aracena. From Seville, drive due west on highway N630 and turn off at km35, taking N433 to Aracena.
By bus: there are 2 buses a day from Seville to Aracena; for information, T: (954) 41 27 60 or 41 05 19. A daily bus runs from Huelva, but only on weekdays; it takes 3 hrs 20min to reach Aracena, T: (955) 25 62 24 and T: (955) 25 05 63.
Where to stay: Aracena has 2 2-star hostels – Sierra de Aracena, T: (955) 11 07 75, and Sierpes, T: (955) 11 01 47 – and in nearby Almonaster la.

Real there are 2 1-star hostels – Casa Gracia, T: (955) 13 04 09, and La Cruz, T: (955) 13 04 35.
Activities: the Gruta de las Maravillas in Aracena is Spain's largest cave and is well-supplied with stalactites, *lagunas* and underground waterways. A fascinating spot (though definitely not for the claustrophobic), it is open daily except Mon, from 10am–7pm.
Further information *Tourist information:* Avda de la Constitución 21, Seville, T: (954) 22 14 04. ICONA, Avda Ramón y Cajal 1, Seville, T: (954) 63 96 50.
Within the area the public transport system between villages is very poor and hiking/hitch-hiking is often resorted to by those without cars.

The deadly fly agaric was used by ancient Iberians as a hallucinogen

CHAPTER 7

The Balearic Islands

The Balearic Islands – Mallorca, Menorca, Ibiza, Formentera and Cabrera – are neatly positioned in the navel of the western Mediterranean, a little closer to Europe than to Africa. They were pushed up from the sea bed when the African continent squeezed against Europe in one of those great shifts known as plate tectonics, which explains why there are marine fossils on top of the highest mountains.

Robert Bourrouilh, the French geologist, has demonstrated that the Balearics were not, as it might appear on the map, simply a continuation of the mountains of Andalucía. Indeed, there is this significant difference: that while Ibiza, Formentera and Mallorca are an extension of the Cordillera Penibética of southern Spain, Menorca is a 'displaced' piece of central Mediterranean geology.

People and nature have worked together in harmony for many centuries in these beautiful islands, producing such extraordinary landscapes as the terraced mountainsides of northern Mallorca and the rolling hills of Menorca, neatly outlined with fieldstone walls whose tops are regularly whitewashed – as though a titanic Mondrian had decided to carve up the meadows. I know of few more striking views in all Europe than the one from Las Salinas of Formentera across the intervening strait to Ibiza with its shining white citadel.

Unfortunately, during the last 30 years or so, the tourist trade has made

The sun rises over Cabo de Formentor, the long, narrow promontory that forms the rugged northernmost tip of Mallorca

tremendous inroads on the natural beauty of the Balearics. In a sense, the islands have become the Miami Beach of Europe. Yet highways, hotels and apartment blocks have affected the three main islands very differently, and travellers should take care to disregard hearsay and judge each on its particular merits.

There are important climatic differences among the islands. On the two northern ones, Menorca and Mallorca, the prevailing winds are from the north, and they have what amounts to 'Catalan' weather. Statistically, Mahón (Maó) and Ciudadela (Ciutadella), on Menorca, have approximately 35 very windy days per year, and Pollença, in north-eastern Mallorca, has 75; but Palma, sheltered by Mallorca'a mountain range, has only 19 days of high wind, while Campos del Puerto has only four such days a year. The islands all average around 2,500 annual hours of sunlight. The wettest place is Lluc, high in the Mallorcan mountains, with 115 centimetres (47 inches) of rain per year, almost three times more than Palma, Mahón and Ibiza. Which means, in broad terms, that Menorca and the plains of Mallorca have a dry season that lasts for four months, while mountainous Mallorca can count on only a three-month dry season and Ibiza is without rain fully half the year. Yet it is the wettest, wildest part of Mallorca that holds the greatest attraction for hikers, birdwatchers and botanists.

Time of year is important in the Balearics, whose seasons are very different from those of northern Europe. January usually brings some wet and windy days but is also famous for the *calmos de enero* – the calm, sunny fortnight known to the ancient Greeks as halcyon days – when many people are found sunning on the beaches. February, the month when the vulture and peregrine falcon lay their eggs, usually brings cold weather and sometimes snow on the highest peaks; people from the north are often surprised that there is a real winter here when the *tramuntana*, the north wind, howls and the local residents huddle around their stoves and fireplaces.

But late in February the first signs of the Mediterranean spring appear, along with the first asphodels: hiking in the mountains on cold days but under clear blue skies is an unmitigated pleasure. At the same time the island's almond trees burst into bloom, frosting the landscape with a layer of white or pink blossoms until one day a strong wind puffs them all to the ground in a flurry of floating petals. (Something like three-quarters of all the almonds consumed in Europe are produced in these islands.)

In March and April the Balearic spring begins in earnest. Migrating birds arrive on the islands and begin to breed. The hoot of Scops owl and hoopoe and the shriek of the stone-curlew are heard. March is the best month for seeing wild orchids in bloom; from now until the end of May the myrtle, spurge, lentisk, strawberry tree and a lot of other plants with magical and mythological associations put out their strongest scents to encourage the bees to do their thing. There is something about this springtime effusion that arouses your senses without drowning them in odours, as the tropics do.

May is virtually a summer month. Nightingales sing by moonlight near open springs. Occasional migrants still arrive, and this is the breeding season for summer visitors such as the black-winged stilt and the bee-eater. In June the dry season starts: the ants take flight and swarm in the mountains. The summer's dryness turns green fields a dusty beige and brings much of nature to a standstill. When the *sirocco* – known locally as the *xeloc* – blows up from the Sahara for more than two or three days at a time, the whole of creation seems prostrated by the heat. This is definitely not the moment to go hiking over the bare, broiling rock of the high sierra.

In September the weather cools; shore birds begin their autumn migration. Lentisk and other wild berries ripen, providing the basic diet for some wintering birds. The rains begin in October and revive the greenery of Mallorca and Menorca – in Ibiza it takes a little longer – and the *Charaxes jarus* butterfly makes its appearance amid the ripe fruit of the strawberry tree. When the olives ripen in November vast flocks of starlings and gulls wheel out of the sky to rob the farmers of their crop, and the migratory painted lady butterfly (*Vanessa atalanta*) arrives in the islands. December brings more rain, even to Ibiza; in Mallorca the black vulture's mating season is in full swing. In spite of what you may have thought, there is wildlife in the Balearics.

GETTING THERE
By air: the islands are well served by international and internal flights. Son San Joán airport, Palma de Mallorca, T: (971) 26 46 24 and 26 08 03; Es Codola airport, Ibiza, T: (971) 30 03 00; and Mahón airport, Menorca, T: (971) 36 01 50.
By sea: there are regular ferry services from the mainland – Barcelona and Valencia – to Mallorca, Menorca and Ibiza. Also services linking Mallorca with the 2 other main islands (but no service between Ibiza and Menorca). In addition, ferries run to the Balearics from France, Italy and the Canary islands.

For more detailed information, contact Compañía Trasmediterránea, Muelle Viejo 5, Palma, T: (971) 22 67 40; Vía Layetana 2, Barcelona, T: (93) 319 82 12; and Avda Manuel Soto 15, Valencia, T: (96) 367 65 12.

There is also a regular service that goes between Denia (Alicante) and Ibiza; it is run by Compañía Flebasa, T: (965) 78 40 11.

Please note: some inter-island flights are much cheaper than the ferry equivalent, so it is wise to check out this option before deciding to travel to the Balearics by sea. On the other hand, the ferry trip can be very pleasant and the blue Mediterranean waters are a much more attractive backdrop than the interior of an aircraft cabin!

WHERE TO STAY
From mid-Jun to mid-Sep accommodation can be in rather short supply and therefore advance booking is highly advisable (particularly for those wilderness explorers who take no pleasure in sleeping out under the stars). For a detailed list contact the Foment del Turisme de Mallorca, C. Constitución 1, Palma, T: (971) 72 45 37 and 71 53 10.

The whole range of accommodation is available, ranging from 5-star hotels to small pensions and hostels. But be warned: prices tend to be considerably higher than those you will encounter on mainland Spain.

ACTIVITIES
Mountaineering club: Federación Española de Montañismo, Delegación en Baleares, Pedro Alcántara Peña 13, Palma de Mallorca. It has no telephone.

FURTHER INFORMATION
For all islands (971): tourist offices, Jaime III 8, Palma, T: 21 22 16; Pl. de la Constitución 13, Mahón, T: 36 37 90; and Paseo Vara del Rey 13, Ibiza, T: 30 19 00. Red Cross, T: 29 50 00. Highway information, Miguel Santandreu 1, Palma, T: 46 34 50.
Language: outside of the main towns, you are more likely to hear a local dialect than Castilian Spanish. *Mallorquín*, *Menorquín* and *Ibizenc* are all closely related to the Catalan spoken on the Spanish mainland.

FURTHER READING
Arthur Foss, *Ibiza and Minorca* (London, 1978), and *Majorca* (London, 1972); and Hazel Thurston, *The Travellers' Guide to the Balearics* (London, 1979).

The Island of Mallorca

A lone pine stands sentinel among rocks overlooking the peaceful Mediterranean

111,400-ha (275,000-acre) island, rich in plant and birdlife, with good trekking routes and a bird sanctuary at S'Albufera

For more than 20 years I have lived at the edge of one of the last great wilderness regions of Europe, the Sierra (in Mallorquín, Serra) de Tramuntana that

runs the full length of the north-west coast of Mallorca. The olive farm where I live turns its back on a range of mountains that rises by giant steps to the Puig Mayor (Major), which is a kilometre and a half (one mile) high but plunges abruptly into the sea: you could almost toss a stone into the Mediterranean from its summit.

In times past the lower slopes of the Sierra were tilled by olive farmers while the holm oak forests higher up were tended by

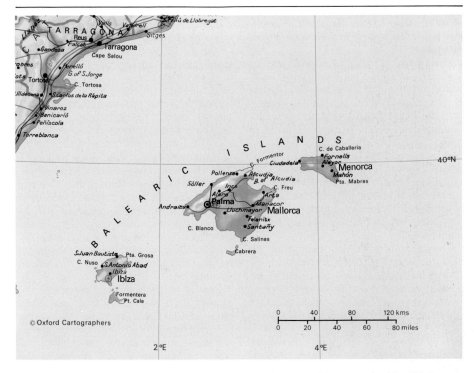

© Oxford Cartographers

charcoal burners. The former built the countless fieldstone terraces that enabled olive trees to take root on these precipitous mountainsides. They terraced the coast wherever the lay of the land permitted, from sea level to altitudes of one thousand metres (3,300 feet) or more, and the result is a feat of landscape engineering comparable to the Cyclopean walls of the Peruvian Andes.

Nowadays there is no money to be made from olives in the Sierra and the orchards are virtually deserted: you can walk for hours through the terraced groves at whatever level you choose. Follow some of the old footpaths that lead from village to village, which skirt the sheer rock faces of the high Sierra but afford magnificent views of the rocky shore that lies beneath your feet. If you climb higher you are, literally, on the roof of the island – the windswept peaks and high plateaux that scarcely any tourist has ever seen. Here, the limestone surface has been scarred and potholed by wind and weather, but wherever there is

soil the ground is covered with wild flowers such as orchids, foxgloves and hellebore. In some areas, between 60 and 70 per cent of the ground cover consists of endemics – species unique to the island. In the 1960s the Belgian botanist Jacques Duvigneaud stretched out for a summer *siesta* on a mossy clifftop overlooking the sea and found himself gazing at a small plant he had never seen before and was unable to identify. It turned out to be not just a new species but a hitherto unknown genus, which received the name *Naufraga balearica*.

If you hike through the mountains of the Sierra you will have the world to yourself, for there is nothing for 50 kilometres (30 miles) or more, except the ruins of erstwhile charcoal-burners' huts and a few half-wild sheep. A single road meanders along the corniche, but except for the small port of Sóller there are no tourist resorts, only a few villages perched precariously on the lower slopes of the mountains – a sort of Switzerland set down in the middle of the

Mediterranean. Along most of the north-west coast you have to be a mountaineer to get down to the sea.

This sense of solitude is what makes Mallorca – and the other Balearics as well – a kind of Jekyll and Hyde among Mediterranean islands. On the one hand it is everybody's package holiday destination: every summer about four million tourists arrive in Palma, which means that there are seven tourists to every resident. The island is not large – about 111,400 hectares (275,275 acres) – and yet it has found ways of absorbing this annual influx of sun-seekers, most of whom head for concrete-block hotels on or near the sandy beaches and proceed to acquire suntans.

From the Sierra peaks, the rest of the island slopes toward the south like the back of a giant hand, though here and there isolated hilltops provide a better view. Many of them are the sites of ancient sanctuaries, hermitages or shrines to the Virgin. One favourite hike through the southern half of the island, the Midjorn, takes in the Monasterio de Nuestra Señora de Cura on Randa (the mountain where the mystic poet Ramon Llull is said to have meditated during the thirteenth century), the Santuario de Montesión ('Mount Zion') and the hilltop castle of Santueri, a Roman and medieval fortress used by both Moorish and Aragonese kings as a base for defending the south-east corner of Mallorca.

But the wildest parts of the island all lie in the north, where there are great trekking routes that begin and end in one or another part of the Sierra de Tramuntana. Curiously enough, although conservationists have been agitating for it for many years, there is no national park in the Balearics, and only one major reserve, the recently opened bird sanctuary of S'Albufera along the north-eastern coast of the island. However, the authorities have acquired a number of publicly owned estates and forest areas, so that at least some of the hiking routes traverse public rather than private property. For the moment there is no great danger to the Sierra, but it would be reassuring to see all of it become a

parque natural, to prevent further commercial exploitation of the region.

Among the special glories of this landscape are the ancient olive trees, which time and the north wind have twisted into an astounding variety of shapes. There are some trunks that fan out like a prehistoric theatre curtain; others spiral upwards, leaving a hollow core that has been worn away by centuries of weathering; still others resemble giant gargoyles. 'When walking in their shade at dusk,' George Sand noted, 'you have to remind yourself that they are trees, because if you accept the evidence of your eyes and imagination, you will be terror-stricken by these fairytale monsters, looming over you like enormous dragons.' Some of the more corpulent veterans are up to an astounding six metres (20 feet) in circumference.

Few farmers now keep up the practice of pruning their trees every year, and many have ceased ploughing up the earth between them. As a result, oleaster shoots are taking over from the sweet olive, and pine seedlings are moving in among the olive groves, undoing the work of centuries. Eventually the pines crowd out the olives and destroy the terraces; torrential downpours wash away the earth no longer held in check by the terrace walls, and sooner or later the whole hillside crumbles away.

THE FLORA OF MALLORCA

Large areas of the island are covered in *matorral*. Herbs are restricted to the edges or sunny glades where there is sufficient light for them to flourish. White asphodels, both *Asphodelus albus* and *A. aestivus*, produce their towering spikes in summer.

The greatest number of endemics occur in the mist-swept heights of the north-western mountain range, especialy in the vicinity of Puig Mayor. A few of the more attractive or unusual species are the birthwort *Aristolochia bianiorii*, occurring especially at Faro de Puerto Pollença; a huge species of parsnip with unpleasant smelling leaves (*Pastinaca lucida*); a Balearic species of shrubby hare's ear, *Bupleurum barceloi*; and *Hippocrepis balearica*.

Ornithologically, Mallorca is one of the most interesting islands in the Mediterranean. A local birdwatchers' guide lists 270 species, including the rare Eleonora's falcon. This gregarious bird migrates to Madagascar in the winter, but returns to the Mediterranean each summer to rear its young. The population of this dark, long-tailed falcon is always very small, and thus vulnerable to any adverse outside influences. They nest on rocky cliffs along the northern coast as far as Cabo Formentor, and have the remarkable habit of breeding in late-summer when the flood of south-bound migrant birds provide a plentiful food supply with which to feed their young. The bird is named after a fourteenth-century Sardinian princess who introduced what was probably the first law protecting nesting hawks and falcons.

The Sierra is also one of the last haunts of the black vulture, the largest bird in Europe, whose wingspan has been known to reach three metres (ten feet). It likes these mountains because it needs updrafts for its long glides, and it feeds on the carcasses of dead sheep.

At Las Salinas, an area of salt pans on the south-west tip of the island, you can see little egrets and black-winged stilts, as well as black, white-winged black and whiskered terns. Mediterranean and Audouin's gulls also use this area, the latter species being endemic to the Mediterranean and easily identified by its green legs and red bill with a black-and-yellow tip. It is closely related to the herring gull, but unlike this ubiquitous bird, it is the rarest breeding gull in Europe.

Other interesting elements of the bird fauna of Mallorca include the Balearic race of the Manx shearwater and the yellow-billed Cory's shearwater, both of which breed on the off-shore islets and marine cliffs of the island. The latter is the largest of the tube-nose family (*Procellariidae*) breeding in Europe. Marsh harriers and booted eagles also rest here, the former wintering in the islands, as well. Birds on migration which drop in from time to time include flamingoes, whiskered terns, pratincoles and the spectacular glossy ibis.

The attractive bee-eater has chestnut, blue-green and yellow plumage and a flute-like call

S'Albufera (also known as La Albufera), just south of Alcudia, derives its name from the Arabic Al-Buhayra, a lake or lagoon. The large lake at one end of it has now been taken over by a housing project, unfortunately, but the rest of S'Albufera remains an untouched basin of reed-covered marshes fed by the waters that descend from the eastern Sierra de Tramuntana and the low hills of the central plain.

It is a short walk or drive from the main road to the reception centre, Sa Roca, where park wardens issue the necessary permit – gratis – to visitors, who must leave their cars at the centre and proceed through the marshes on foot. With its whispering reeds and croaking frogs as a sort of continuo accompaniment, S'Albufera is alive with bird songs, for this is a garden of Eden for the birds whose flyways cross the Mediterranean, as well as a year-round residence for many other species. The purple gallinules and night herons that were sent from Mallorca to Rome for gastronomic purposes in the days of the Empire were probably caught in S'Albufera.

173

During their periods of migration it harbours red-footed falcons, grey plover, whiskered tern, collared pratincole, ringed plover, nightjar, sand martin and many other species. Winter visitors who stay for the season include shelducks and the greylag goose, red-crested pochard, teal, shoveler and pintail, wigeon, Montagu's harrier, golden plover, kingfisher, lapwing, little stint, meadow and water pipit, bluethroat, black redstart, chiffchaff and others. The summer census is headed by Eleonora's falcon, little bittern, purple heron, woodchat shrike, little ringed plover, tawny pipit, turtle dove, cuckoo, swift, bee-eater, swallow, house martin, yellow wagtail, nightingale, Sardinian and reed warblers, black-winged stilt and the spotted flycatcher. And there are large numbers of other species that live here the year round, among them the marsh harrier,

peregrine falcon, moorhen, barn and long-eared owls, to say nothing of the mallard, stonechat, crag martin, fan-tailed, Cetti's and moustached warblers, corn bunting and many more: altogether more than 200 species have been recorded here. The authorities have made things easy for birdwatchers by building a hide not far from the reception centre: the way to it leads over a rickety pontoon bridge and a path of stepping stones made of second-hand building blocks.

Aficionados return from the hide with tales of superb views of moustached and great reed warblers, of osprey fishing before their eyes and Eleonora's falcons deftly catching and devouring birds in flight.

Most birdwatchers base themselves at Puerto Pollença and in May they are sufficiently numerous to hold weekly meetings at one of the local hotels in order to exchange news.

Spring arrives at the end of February, as Mallorca's almond trees burst into blossom

Even at extreme heights snow is rare in the mountains of Mallorca

BEFORE YOU GO
Maps: SGE 1:50,000 Nos. 671, 672, 699, 724 and 725.
Guidebooks: *Rutas Escondidas de Mallorca*, detailing hiking routes available from the author, Jesús García Pastor, C. Baron de Santa Maria del Sepulcro 12, Palma de Mallorca 12; and Herbert Heinrich's *12 Classic Hikes through Mallorca* (Palma, 1987). Heinrich has also published 3 companion volumes in German: *Wanderführer durch Mallorca's Südwest-Region*, volumes 1 and 2, and *Das Mallorca's Ludwig Salvators heute erlebt*.

GETTING THERE
By air: Mallorca's airport, Son San Joán, is one of the busiest in Europe during the summer months, with more than 500 flight arrivals and departures on an average day. Iberia's Barcelona–Palma flights operate so frequently as to constitute what amounts to a shuttle service. Three other Spanish companies also fly to Palma – Aviaco, Spantax and Hispania.
By sea: 2 main ferry connections are maintained by the Compañía Transmediterránea: the Barcelona–Palma ferry runs at least once a day throughout the year, more in the summer months, and carries vehicles as well as passengers; the car-carrying ferry from Valencia to Palma runs 6 days a week. From Nov–May there is a weekly service from Palma to Genoa and another to the Canary Islands, via Málaga and Cádiz. There are also various connections between Palma and Ibiza, one of which goes on to Valencia and another to Sète, France.
ON THE ISLAND
By car: the most convenient

way to see the island and to approach its wilder areas is by car. To see the whole island, drive along the corniche road on the north-west coast from Andratx to Sóller and then to Lluc and Cabo Formentor, completing the circuit by way of Alcudia, Artá and the south coast. Rented cars are quite cheap; a leaflet available from tourist offices lists 70 car-rental firms in Palma and more than 100 elsewhere.

By rail: a regular service between Palma and Inca. The Palma–Sóller train, which runs 5 times a day, is a lovely ride with spectacular views from the heights of the Sóller Pass; built by Swiss engineers, it behaves just like a Swiss narrow-gauge mountain train, running through tunnels and dizzying switchbacks before finally descending into the valley of Sóller.

By bus: the island is covered by an excellent network of buses, which take you to the best starting points for hikes and excursions. Current schedules are always available from the tourist office at C. Constitució 1, Palma.

WHERE TO STAY

Mallorca has hundreds of hotels; during the summer most of them are crowded with tourists. Still, accommodation is plentiful and varied even in the most remote towns and villages adjoining the Sierra de Tramuntana. Hotels range from the sumptuous 4-star La Residencia in Deyá (Deià), T: (971) 63 90 11, to the modest, traditional Baronia, a 1-star hostel in Banyalbufar, T: (971) 61 01 21. Good bases include Puerto de Andratx near Mallorca's northern Cordillera; Estellencs, which clings to the mountainside beneath the 1,025-m (3,360-ft) Puig de Galatzó; and Valldemossa, where Chopin and George Sand spent 2 rainy months during the winter of 1838 and where some of the most enjoyable mountain routes start. Deyá and Sóller on the west coast and Pollença, at the eastern end of the Cordillera, are small towns with accommodation available. Finally, Alcudia, not far from S'Albufera bird-marshes, has 3 modest hotels: Panoramic, T: (971) 54 54 84; More, T: (971) 54 55 05; and Posada Verano, T: (971) 54 62 23.

Outdoor living: there is 1 official camping ground, Platja Blava, and several privately owned sites, including 1 at Ermita de la Victoria; for information, contact the tourist office at Palma.

Monasteries: most of the mountain monasteries will accommodate visitors for short stays; except in Lluc, facilities are of the simplest and prices correspondingly low. To make reservations at Lluc, T: (971) 51 70 25. Other monasteries welcoming visitors are Santuario La Victoria, about a 1-hr walk from Alcudia to Cabo Pinar; San Salvador, near Felanitx, T: (971) 58 06 56; and Nuestra Señora del Cura (between Algaida and Llucmajor in the centre of the island).

ACTIVITIES

Walking: there are innumerable footpaths through the wilder parts of Mallorca. It is easy to get lost in these mountains because the resident sheep have made their own paths which look exactly like footpaths – but turn out to end suddenly at the edge of some 60-m (200-ft) drop.

One of my favourite walks is the all-day hike along what used to be the bridle path of the Austrian archduke Ludwig Salvator (1847–1915), from Valldemossa to the Teix (1,062m/3,483ft). The archduke must have been utterly fearless, for part of the path skirts a really breathtaking bluff: clearly this is not a route for people suffering from vertigo. You can enjoy some of the same views from a less spectacular altitude by taking the old footpath that led from Deyá to Sóller before a road was laid. The track is narrow, paved with fieldstones, and winds high above the coast, through abandoned olive groves and

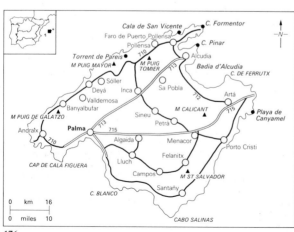

Eleonora's falcon breeds on coastal cliffs in late summer, preying on birds migrating south to Africa

stands of pine.

Some other notable treks in this area are the descent from Son Marroig to the rocky peninsula known as Sa Foradada ('the perforated one'); the 'hike of the thousand bends' from Sóller through the Biniaraix Gorge via the Mirador de Xim Quesada (1,009m/3,300ft); and the ascent of the slopes of Puig Mayor and the Migdia massif to the Comellar de l'Infern ('valley of hell'), all of which are described in Heinrich's guide (see above).

The Sierra de Llevante, in the Artá area, is worth visiting and many long walks can be enjoyed from the town itself – for example, taking the northernmost road out of the village, you can follow the narrow country lane up to the Ermita de Betlem. From there a marked trail leads to a viewpoint giving a panoramic view of the Bay of Alcudia.

Climbing: the monastery of Lluc, with its famous image of La Morenita (the Black Madonna), is 'the heart of Mallorca' and has been a centre for mountain pilgrimages since the Middle Ages. Modern highways and the gentrification of the monastery have converted Lluc into something rather more touristic than medieval, but it remains a starting point for many exciting mountain tours.

The limestone mountains are honeycombed with caves, some of them of great interest to speleologists who have been studying the magnetic orientation of their bottom sediments. Thousands of bats make their homes here, and the region's remoteness favours birds of prey – osprey and booted eagle, Eleonora's falcon and Scops owl. Also in the Lluc area are black vultures, and it is one of the few reliable places on the island to see rock thrush.

The mountain hike from Lluc to the Puig Tomir by way of Binifaldó is fairly strenuous. Another easier walk circles the Puig Roig (1,002m/3,285ft). Farther to the north there is the descent from the *finca* (estate) of Mortitx via the Rafal d'Ariant valley to a seaside cave known as the Cova de les Bruixes ('of the witches'); the route is known as the Cami del Ratal and can also be used as an approach to the lunar landscapes of the hidden plateau known as La Malé.

The walk to Castell del Rei, which begins at Pollença, is now open Mon only; it traverses a privately owned *finca*. The Castell itself is an ancient fortress-observation post.

Far more demanding is the ascent to the Puig de Massanella (1,348m/4,420ft) from the Coll de Sa Batalla ('battle pass') on the road between Inca and Lluc. Since the top of the Puig Major is closed to hikers, the Massanella is the highest accessible mountain on Mallorca. Inexperienced climbers are advised that the going is rough, and the excursion is best made with a guide.

Mountain reserves: in addition to S'Albufera, Mallorca has 16 mountain and forest reserves that are publicly owned. they vary considerably in size, but each is a self-contained bird sanctuary and nature reserve. Ask at tourist office (see below) for details.

Caves: the Cuevas de Campanet, situated 8km (5 miles) off the C713, about 50km (30 miles) from Palma, are full of well-lit stalagmites and stalactites. Las Cuevas de Artà are on the PM 404-2 above the Playa de Canyamel; a long stone stairwell takes you up into a vast dark hole in the rockface and the entrance to the caves, which were pirate hideouts. The Cuevas del Drac are situated off the PM 404-4, just outside Porto Cristi.

Gardens: the gardens at Alfabia have elegant arbours, pavilions and lily ponds; situated on the C711 Palma–Sóller road, 17km (10 miles) out of Palma.

Mopeds: this is a convenient way of seeing the island. When hiring, make sure that the insurance policy covers theft as well as accident.

FURTHER INFORMATION
Tourist information: C Constitucío 1, Palma, T: (971) 72 95 37 and 71 53 10; Avda Jaime III 8 (972) 72 36 41. ICONA, Guillermo Torrellá 1, Palma, T: (971) 21 74 40.

There is a small tourist office at Palma airport with hotel, car and moped hire information.

The Island of Cabrera

*Small island, whose
sparse population makes
it a refuge for birds,
reptiles and marine life*

Naturalists are agreed that
Cabrera is potentially a great
parque nacional. At the
moment, however, the island
and its neighbouring islets
(notably Conejera) are a
military zone, inhabited by a
lighthouse keeper and a
garrison of about a dozen
soldiers who maintain what is
essentially an artillery firing
range. A conservation group
has been trying to persuade
the government to turn it into
a wildlife reserve instead, but
the issue still hangs in the
balance.

Cabrera lies about 18km (11
miles) from the nearest point
on Mallorca – Cabo Salinas –
and 50km (31 miles) from the
Bay of Palma. It measures
about 7 by 5km (4½ by 3
miles) and has a 22-km (13½-
mile) coastline dominated by 2
hills, the Puig de Picomosques
and the Puig de la Guardia.
On the north side a narrow
channel guarded by a ruined
castle leads into a horseshoe-
shaped natural harbour that is
completely protected from
winds. The island's vegetation
resembles that of southern
Mallorca, but its isolation and
sparse population have made
it a refuge of last resort for
several species of plants,
birds, reptiles and marine life.
The Cabrera sub-species of
Lilford's wall lizard are

The quality of the sunlight
changes the face of Mallorcan
landscapes from one minute to the
next

underfoot everywhere, and so fearless they will eat a sandwich out of your hand. Whales, seals and dolphins often visit this coast, for artillery practice takes place so infrequently they have nothing to fear. It is one of the ironies of the modern world that some of the most undisturbed areas for wildlife are those where military installations keep the rest of the human population at bay.

Getting there *By sea:* there is a boat to the island from Colonia Sant Jordi, in the south of Mallorca; bookings can be made at the Restaurante Miramar, T: (971) 64 90 34. It is

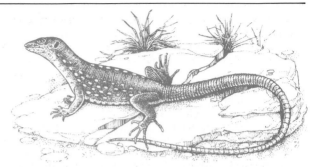

Lilford's wall lizard has died out on the main Balearic Islands, but this dark sub-species survives on Cabrera

sometimes possible to 'hitch' a ride with fishermen.

Further information: there are

no tourist facilities on Cabrera and visitors are not permitted to stay overnight.

Permits: if you want to do more than the harbour and ruined castle, you need a special permit, issued in Palma: enquire at the tourist office.

The Island of Menorca

Second largest of the Balearics, at 49km by 19km (30 miles by 12 miles) with numerous coves and golden beaches

The windiest and most mysterious of the Balearics, Menorca has managed to preserve something of its ancient splendid isolation. It is the second largest and north-ernmost of the islands.

It has unique advantages as a summer holiday destination, thanks to the 120 sandy beaches and coves that form the greater part of its coastline: no other Mediterra-nean island has so many beaches. Most of them have long since capitulated to the tourist invasion, but a few are still deserted and undeveloped – for the simple reason that they can only be approached on foot, along difficult paths. The best of these forgotten beaches lie in the north of the island, between Cala Pregonda (now menaced by urbanization) and Cabo Gros, where there are no access roads and where some of the local caves can only be reached by boat.

Apart from the bird sanctuary at El Grao, however, Menorca has no parks or wildlife reserves. Much of the interior remains untouched by the fell hand of the

twentieth century, and no other spot in the world is as thickly strewn with relics of the Bronze Age. In scores of places you come across some of the earliest buildings in Europe, the so-called *talayots*, which resemble stone igloos built by a race of giants. Here and there a side road leads to a miniature Stonehenge: a circle of huge limestone slabs surmounted by a giant T-shaped *taula*, usually interpreted as having been a sacrificial table, although I suspect nothing like as sinister, but rather that they were merely meant to be schematic repre-sentations of a bull's head.

Although boasting fewer endemic plant species than Mallorca, the island is the only known habitat of the dwarf shrub *Daphne rodriguezii*. This attractive, purple-flow-ered evergreen grows on the siliceous cliffs of the north-east coast. Another extremely localized species that is restricted to Menorca is the loosestrife, *Lysimachia minoricensis*. The coastal limestone cliffs of the southern shores have a unique flora: a community comprising species adapted to lime-rich and saline soils. They include an aromatic spikenard (*Inula viscosa*), the Balearic speciality *Bellium belloides*, the caper (*Capparis spinosa*) and *Astericus maritimus*.

But it is the island's cast of reptiles that

really attracts attention. There are only four species of lizard found in the Balearics – and Menorca boasts populations of three. Lilford's wall lizard is a beautiful creature, sometimes green and brown, but also with several melanic populations, black with blue underbellies; it has a distinctive 'turnip-shaped' tail. The Moroccan rock lizard is, as its name suggests, a native of North Africa; it was introduced to this island. It is a small, rather flattened rather flattened creature, usually with a bronzed, olive skin, and a completely transparent 'window' in the lower eyelid.

The third lacertid is the Italian wall lizard, for which this island is the only Spanish locality. It is vivid olive green with a black dorsal pattern of stripes, and has a long head. It is larger and more robust than the other lizard species of the Balearics, preferring not to climb to hunt down its food.

By picking your route carefully, you can back-pack across the island, although asphalt is hard to avoid. The lanes lead past Menorca's spick-and-span dairy farms whose Holstein cattle look strangely out of place in this arch-Mediterranean landscape of rolling hills and whitewashed villages. (Not so long ago Menorcan farmers were in the habit of whitewashing their houses once a week; now, as a concession to the twentieth century, they refrain from doing it more than once a month.)

In winter the island is lush and green, and virtually deserted by tourists; in summer the fields turn a predictable beige, brown and ocre. June and September/October are ideal times for a visit that might focus on the island's natural history.

BEFORE YOU GO
Maps: SGE 1:50,000 Nos. 618, 619 and 649.

GETTING THERE
By air: Iberia and Aviaco run frequent flights to Mahón from both Barcelona and Palma de Mallorca. Numerous charter flights from the capitals of northern Europe also serve Mahón airport, T: (971) 36 01 50 during the tourist season.
By sea: the principal sea link to the mainland is provided by car-carrying ferries of the Compañía Transmediterránea, T: (971) 36 29 50, which runs 6 times a week in each direction during the tourist season, less frequently at other times of the year. There is 1 boat a week each way between Palma and Mahón.
ON THE ISLAND
By car: the main route crosses the centre of the island, linking Mahón and Ciudadela and branching off to Cala'n Porter, Cala Santa Galdana, Fornells and other small coastal towns. There are few coastal roads (and no railway).

By bus: The bus routes are very limited and are mostly confined to the main central road between Mahón and the port of Ciudadela. Routes branch off it to the coast.

WHERE TO STAY
Like the neighbouring islands, Menorca has a surfeit of tourist and beach hotels in every price range, from the 4-star Port Mahón, T: (971) 36 26 00, to the 1-star Roca, T: (971) 36 47 63, in Mahón. In Ciudadela examples are the 3-star Cala Blanca, T: (971) 38 04 50, and the 2-star Ses Voltes, T: (971) 38 04 00.
Outdoor living: at Cala Tirant there is a cheap and rough campsite, with cold showers and a bar.

ACTIVITIES
Walking: in the centre of the island, Mercadal is the starting point for the hike of Monte Toro (358m/1,175ft) – the highest point. This is a steep hike of about 4km (2½ miles) but the view from the top is certainly worth the effort. Some other suggestions: the cliffs around the Playa de Binimel'la offer some good walking routes and there are streams flowing down the beach to the sea; the road from Ferreries to Cala Santa Galdana is lovely, although it does lead, in the end, to the inevitable tourist development; heading south from Ciudadela the rough road leading to Playa son Saura, Cala d'es Talaier and Cala Turqueta makes for a good day's outing through green countryside to sunny beaches.
Driving: La Albufera d'es Grao: north of Mahón, on the road to Fornells; the second fork in the road will take you to El Grao and the salt marshes of La Albufera.
Caves: the Cuevas d'en Xoroi, near Cala'n Porter in the south, have been somewhat commercialized but further round the cliff face you will find more caves. The best way to see these is from the water; boat trips are available from the town.
Mopeds: available for hire. Ask for a list of rental

181

Like Mallorca, Menorca (left) has its forgotten beaches of rocky coastline and the remote south west of Ibiza commands a fine prospect of the islet of Es Vedrà (above)

companies at the tourist office in Mahón. Ensure that your insurance covers theft of the machine. Remember also that gas stations are few and far between.

Museum: the Ateneo Científico, Literario y Artístico on C. Conde de Cifuentes, Mahón, is a small museum which has the biggest collection of dried seaweeds in southern Europe.

FURTHER INFORMATION
Tourist information: Pl. Explanada and Pl. de la Conquista, Mahón, T: (971) 36 37 90 and 36 23 77.

In Ciudadela the office is at the Ayuntamiento, Pl. d'es Born, T: (971) 38 07 87.

The Island of Ibiza

Crowded with pines and in the summer with tourists Wall lizard and oleander flourish here

In ancient time the whole Balearic archipelago was known as Gymnasiae, as it was believed that the

inhabitants ran naked even during the winter; whether through ignorance or extreme hardiness is an intriguing mystery. Ibiza (Elvissa or Eivissa) was then the most important of the 'Pityussae' – pine-clad islands – of this group, which comprised Formentera and Espalmador to the south, Tagomago to the east, and Vedrá and Conejera to the west. Sadly, it has become the most over-touristed island of all the Balearics, especially in recent years.

By exercising a great deal of care, it is still possible to get away from the madding crowds who overrun the

183

resorts to search out the island's curiosities. One way to do this is to confine your visits to the autumn and winter. There are dense forests, with aleppo pine (*Pinus halepensis*) in the higher areas, in sharp contrast to the arid environment elsewhere.

The dwarf fan palm (*Chamaerops humilis*), the only palm native to Europe, is found in dry sandy areas here and along the Mediterranean coast, and its ½-m (18-in) fronds provide cover for a number of reptile and bird species. Another plant to look out for is the spectacular orchid, *Ophrys bertolonii*, known only from the Balearics and France; its furry orange-brown flowers are crowned by 3 slender, pale pink perianth segments.

The most characteristic plant of Ibiza is the oleander, which can be seen overflowing from the dried river beds of the plains in summer. Its grey, leathery leaves are arranged around the stem in whorls of 3, and the whole plant is topped with huge pink blooms over 5cm (2in) in diameter. It is often found growing with myrtle, and the sight and smell of these beautiful, fragrant plants in full bloom is quite dizzying.

Ibiza's most important animal is the Ibiza wall lizard. It is endemic to the Balearics, particularly here, as the name suggests, and also to Formentera and some small adjacent islets. The lizard lives in barren, shrubby areas; it is robust and short-headed, sometimes a vivid green on the back, and may have a spotted throat and belly. Equally interesting is the archetypal hunting dog found on the island, known locally as *ca ervissenc*. Reputedly, this tall, loose-limbed, fawn-

coloured beast was introduced by the Egyptians or Carthaginians, and it is still entirely possible to find animals of almost pure bloodline.

Before you go *Maps:* SGE 1:50,000 Nos. 772, 773, 798 and 799.

Getting there *By air:* as well as direct flights from various European cities, there are regular flights to Ibiza from Palma; Ibiza airport, T: (971) 30 03 00.

By sea: there are regular sailings to Ibiza from Barcelona, Valencia and Sète, France. There are also regular ferries from/to Palma and Formentera. Phone Compañía Transmediterránea, T: (971) 31 34 13 and 31 36 63 for details.

ON THE ISLAND
By sea: there is a regular ferry service between Ibiza Town and Playa Talamanca, between San Antonio Abad and Portinatx, and also ferry trips from Santa Eulalia del Río.

By car: the main route connects Ibiza Town, San José, San Antonio Abad, San Rafael and Santa Eulalia del Río. There is also a good network of minor roads connecting the smaller villages, but no coastal route right round the island. Be careful about parking: wheel clamps are used on offending cars!

By bus: the service is fairly comprehensive with regular buses to San Antonio, Santa Eulalia, San Carlos, Es Caná, San Juan, Cala San Vicente, Portinatx, Las Salinas, San José, San Miguel, San Mateo and Santa Inés.

Where to stay: there is a vast array of hotels and hostels to choose from; for example, the 3-star Argos, T: (971) 31 21 62, and the 1-star Mare Nostrum, T: (971) 30 26 62 in

Ibiza Town; and the 2-star Pacific, T: (971) 34 11 62, in San Antonio Abad.

Outdoor living: there are several campsites on the island. The one closest to the city of Ibiza is Garbi, on the road to Playa d'en Bossa, 2km (1 mile) out of town. At Casla Llonga, on the coastal road to Santa Eulalia, the camping ground is close to the sea and has its own swimming pool. North of Santa Eulalia, betweeen Es Caná and Punta Arabia, is the Flórida campsite. Further up the coast are sites at Playa Cala Nova, Cala Portinax, and Cala Bassa.

Activities *Walking:* the road from Ibiza Town to San Miguel takes you through the most attractive parts of the island where you can readily stop for walks in the hills and through picturesque villages with their groves of almond, carob and olive trees. There is a steepish trail from the port of San Miguel which goes over hilly coastal land to Cala Benirras.

Caves: Cova Santa ('the holy cave') lies just off the San José–Ibiza road. There is a trail just to the south, from the caves to Cala Yondal.

Museums: the Museu Arte Contemporáneo is situated in Ibiza Town above the arch of the Portal de las Tablas. The Museu Archaeologica and the Museu Puig des Molins with finds from the Necropolis, are in the vicinity of the Pl. de España.

Sailing: contact Club Punta Arabí at Es Caná, T: (971) 33 00 85 for further details regarding this most Mediterranean of pastimes.

Further information *Tourist information:* Vara del Rey 13, Ibiza Town, T: (971) 30 19 00; there is also an office at the airport.

'The landscape was of the purest Mediterranean kind – pines and junipers and fig trees growing out of red earth. Looking down from the hill-top, the plain spread between the sea and the hills was daubed and patched henna, iron rust and stale blood – the fields curried more darkly where newly irrigated, the threshing-floors paler with their encircling beehives of straw, the roads smoking with orange dust where the farm-carts passed . . .

The course of Ibiza's only river was marked across this plain by a curling snake of pink-flowered oleanders. Oleanders, too, frothed at most of the well-heads. A firm red line had been drawn enclosing the land at the sea's edge. Here the narrow movements of the Mediterranean tides seemed to submit the earth to a fresh oxidation each day, and after each of the brief, frenzied storms of midsummer, a bloody lake would spread slowly into the blue of the sea, all along the coast.'

Norman Lewis, *A View of the World*

The Island of Formentera

Just south of Ibiza; barren for the most part, but boasting empty, sandy beaches

Of all the islands of the Balearic archipelago, Formentera is closest to the coast of Africa, just 115km (71 miles) away. The name comes from the island's days as a Roman granary (*frumentaria*). The landscape is quite barren and the highest point rises only 197m (645ft) above sea level. Like Ibiza, its near neighbour, it has its fair share of pine woods, as well as a healthy population of the Ibiza wall lizard, which is larger than the Ibiza race and often a brighter green. The lizards living on the off-shore islets are almost independent of any vegetation cover, and tend to be melanistic, or with brightly coloured flanks of blue or orange.

Before you go *Maps:* SGE 1:50,000 Nos. 824 and 825.

Getting there *By sea:* daily ferry crossings from Ibiza to Puerto de la Sabina; for information, T: (971) 32 01 57. The crossing can be rough, and if your stomach is likely to be affected, remember to take some seasickness pills along with you.

ON THE ISLAND

By car: a car is by far the best means of getting around the island. There are several car hire companies in La Sabina and 1 in San Francisco Javier. The tourist office will be able to provide you with a list of companies.

By bus: infrequent buses service the towns of San Francisco Javier, La Mola, La Sabina, El Pilar and San Fernando. There is no bus service on Sat, Sun, public holidays or during the winter months.

Where to stay: there is a wide variety of hotels and hostels in La Sabina, San Francisco Javier, San Fernando and El Caló. Try the 2-star hostel, Casbah, T: (971) 32 00 34, or the 1-star Pin-Por, T: (971) 32 02 93, in San Francisco Javier.

Outdoor living: there are no official camping grounds, but many isolated areas are suitable for camping: check with tourist office (see below).

Activities *Birdwatching:* Las Salinas – salt pans in the north of the island between La Sabina and San Francisco – and the nearby lakes are a haven for birdwatchers, being an important migratory port of call for many birds each year.

Boat trips: there are daily (summer) boat trips from La Sabina to Illetas and Espalmador. Be sure to check schedules at the hostal Bahía in La Sabina, T: (971) 32 01 06.

Caves: some small caves, Cuevas d'en Xeroni, are situated near San Fernando.

Diving: tuition can be arranged at the Hotel Club La Mola, Playa Mitjorn.

Mopeds and bicycles: these are available for hire in La Sabina and Es Pujols.

Viewpoints: on the Mola plateau, on the eastern edge of the island, is the Mola lighthouse, which is easily reached by car. It provides wide and spectacular views both of the island and of the sea.

Further information *Tourist information:* Casa Consistorial, San Francisco Javier, T: (971) 32 00 32.

CHAPTER 8

The Canary Islands

From the air, the Canaries look like beached shells when the tide has gone out. Strong north winds that blow for most of the year are responsible for the current and the trail of foam that extends southward from the islands, and these same winds are responsible for the prevailing climate of the group.

Yet the initial impression of uniformity is misleading. At sea level the seven main islands of the archipelago are very different from one another, and these differences are exemplified by the four national parks – on Lanzarote, Tenerife, Gomera and La Palma – which are the most important of the more than 60 nature reserves that have been created in the Canaries.

The possession by Spain of this archipelago, which is ten times closer to Africa than to the Iberian peninsula, is a curious leftover of empire. The islands were long a stopping-off point for explorers, at least as far back as the time of the ancient Greeks: Pliny the Elder described them in some detail. But it wasn't until the fifteenth century that they were claimed for Spain, who found it inhabited by a native population of unknown origin, known as Guanches. The islands have never been of great strategic or economic importance, which is perhaps why they have remained, unchallenged, in Spanish hands for so long.

The origin of these remarkable islands has always been the subject of controversy: one ancient theory was that they were the peaks of the

Of native trees, the one which most successfully exploits the fertility of La Palma is the magnificent Canary pine

legendary lost continent of Atlantis. Now there are two conflicting, but rather more scientific, explanations. One suggests that the origin of the islands is purely volcanic and that they rose from the sea bed independently; the other insists that they were once part of Africa and split off to drift westwards to their present position, 100 kilometres (65 miles) off the western coast of Morocco. It is likely that the truth lies somewhere between the two: the eastern islands – Lanzarote and Fuerteventura – are derived from the same land plate as Africa, while the western islands – Tenerife, La Palma, Hierro, Gomera and Gran Canaria – have volcanic origins.

Whatever the roots of the Canary Islands, the flora has undoubtedly been evolving for millions of years, as is indicated by the large number of species found nowhere else in the world. Fossil evidence has shown that the legendary dragon tree (*Dracaena draco*), the Canary laurels and indigenous fern species may be up to 20 million years old, with their nearest living relatives found today in South America and Africa.

The total flora numbers some two thousand species. Many of these are relics of a previously much more widespread type of vegetation, which has gradually shrunk, due to the drying out of the area now occupied by the Sahara Desert and the southwards movement of the glacial climate caused by the Ice Ages. The islands were protected from these climatic extremes by the mediating influence of the sea and thus an element of this sub-tropical flora managed to survive. In addition, the extreme altitude of some of the islands provided a climatic gradient for species sensitive to temperature variation and, as the world climates fluctuated, these species were able to migrate up and down the mountain slopes.

Lanzarote, closest to Africa, has the *parque nacional* that is most interesting geologically, especially to vulcanologists – but by the same token it is virtually devoid of vegetation. The impression that the *parque* makes on its visitors is of a bleak, harsh landscape – windy, dusty and unwelcoming.

Tenerife presents a completely different profile, from the rocky shore up through a layer of cloud that lies like a collar around the magnificent peak of Monte Teide, the Atlantic equivalent of Fujiyama. The park known as the Cañadas del Teide is by far the highest of the four, and its remarkable ecosystem is famous for its unique alpine flora.

You can only approach Gomera from the sea – by ferry from Tenerife, less than one and a half hours away. A steady stream of clouds pours over the island's peaks like a silent Niagara, shifting continually, but always hiding the heights from view. This crown of moisture-laden clouds gives the Parque Nacional de Garajonay some of Spain's most luxurious vegetation.

Moving a bit farther north west you arrive at La Palma, again with a wholly idiosyncratic landscape. From the sea the island appears less remarkable than the others. Only from the highest points – or from the air – can you gaze down into the vertiginous depths of the deepest crater in the world, La Caldera de Taburiente. It is hardly surprising that this extraordinary phenomenon – an extinct volcano that has streams running within its crater – has been a protected zone and national park for more than 30 years. It is like a milestone set in the sea; from here there is no land westwards until you reach America.

GETTING THERE

By air: there are numerous flights to Las Palmas and Tenerife from all over Europe, as well as from Morocco, Casablanca, Agadir and Layoune. Iberia airlines has flights connecting with the main islands except Gomera, which does not have an airport.

Iberia offices: Tenerife – Avda de Anaga, Santa Cruz de Tenerife, T: (922) 28 11 50; Gran Canaria – Avda Ramírez Bethencourt, Las Palmas, T: (928) 37 21 11; Lanzarote – Arrecife, T: (928) 81 03 50; Fuerteventura – 23 de Mayo 7, Puerto del Rosario, T: (928) 85 12 50.

By sea: Compañía Transmediterránea runs ferries from Cádiz, Valencia, Barcelona and the Balearic Islands to the Canary Islands. There is also a ferry service from Casablanca, provided by Paquet Africa and several lines have sailings originating at Tangier.

Transméditerranéenne Aucona offers the inter-island ferry link and there is also a jet-foil linking Tenerife and Gran Canaria. For information on departure times you should contact the Transméditerranéenne offices at: Tenerife – La Marina 59, Santaz Cruz de Tenerife, T: (922) 28 78 50; La Palma – General Mola 2, Santa Cruz de la Palma, T: (922) 41 11 21; Gomera – San Sebastián de la Gomera, T: (928) 87 13 00; and Hierro – Valverde del Hierro, T: (922) 55 01 29.

For full information about the Gomera Ferry Company: Tenerife – Avda 3 de Mayo, Santa Cruz de Tenerife, T: (922) 21 90 33, and on the dock of Puerto de los Cristianos, T: (922) 79 05 56; Gomera – Avda Fred Olsen, San Sebastián de la Gomera, T: (928) 87 10 07.

WHEN TO GO

The main tourist season is from Jan–Mar; hotels are generally pretty full during these months, and advance booking is strongly recommended.

The summer months are hot, Aug's mean temperature being 25°C (76°F), but still comfortable enough for hiking. Swimming is possible all year round, though the beaches can get very crowded with sun-seekers during the high season. Spring is unquestioningly the best time for walking in the mountains and exploring the surrounding countryside.

WHERE TO STAY

All the islands have a very wide choice of accommodation available. This can range from 3-star hotels to very simple pensions and hostels. Comprehensive lists are available from tourist offices (see below for addresses and telephone numbers).

ACTIVITIES

Mountaineering clubs: Federación Canaria de Montañismo, La Naval 32, Las Palmas de Gran Canaria; and Federación Tinefeña de Montañismo, San Sebastián 76, Santa Cruz de Tenerife, T: (922) 24 20 44.

FURTHER INFORMATION

Gran Canaria (928): tourist office, Parque Santa Catalina, Las Palmas, T: 26 46 23 and 27 07 90. Red Cross, T: 24 59 21. Search and rescue, T: 21 58 17.
Fuerteventura (928): search and rescue, T: 85 05 03.
Lanzarote (928): tourist office, Parque Municipal, Arrecife, T: 81 18 60. Search and rescue, T: 81 09 46.
Tenerife (922): tourist offices, C. Marina, Santa Cruz de Tenerife, T: 28 21 54 and 28 21 58; and Pl. de la Iglesia 3, Puerto de la Cruz, T: 38 60 00. Red Cross, T: 28 29 24. Search and rescue, T: 22 31 00.
La Palma (922): tourist office, Pl. de España, Santa Cruz de la Palma, T: 41 16 41. Search and rescue, T: 41 11 84.
Gomera (928): tourist information, T: 80 54 80. Search and rescue, T: 87 02 55.
Hierro (922): search and rescue, T: 55 01 05.
Highway information: for details concerning the state of the roads on the Canary Islands contact La Marina 26, Santa Cruz de Tenerife, T: (922) 27 81 00.
Clothing: tough footwear is a must if you are planning to hike in rocky terrain. From Nov–Apr be prepared for snow at high altitudes.
Drinking water: this can be in short supply, particularly on Lanzarote, and you are recommended to drink bottled water which is widely available with and without gas.
Telephones: all four islands have telephone booths from which you can make international calls; be prepared to pay an advance deposit.
Weather forecasts for the islands: Centro Meteorológico de Canarias Occidentale will provide you with up-to-the-minute information, T: (922) 21 17 18.

FURTHER READING

Noel Rochford, *Landscapes of Gran Canaria* (London, 1986) and *Landscapes of Tenerife* (London, 1984); and Olivia M. Stone, *Tenerife and its Six Satellites* (London, 1889).

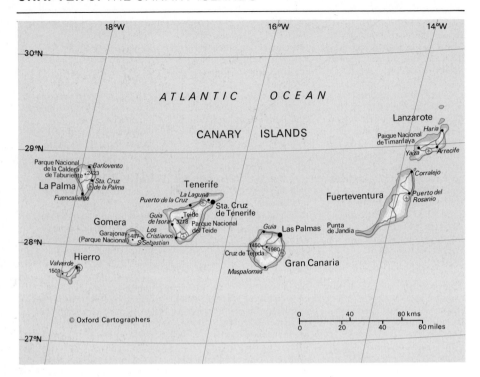

The Island of Lanzarote

Largely unspoiled island, with several interesting endemic plant species Including the Parque National de Timanfaya

The north of Lanzarote through the vine-growing areas of Uga and La Geria is a startling contrast to the arid 'badlands' of Timanfaya, the volcanic area that dominates the island. On sloping ground, every vine is protected from the wind by a semicircular wall of volcanic rock. The geometrical pattern of the semi-circles on the hills above the straight lines of the walls in the valleys covers the countryside in a strange grid pattern.

From the vineyards to Teguise, I drove through the mountains to the Peñas de Chache at 668 metres (2,200 feet): from here the road drops down into the valley of Haria, known as the valley of ten thousand palm trees. Suddenly I notice the landscape is looking decidedly Moroccan. The closely
190

shuttered, single-storey houses between the palm trees, an occasional camel to carry heavy loads, the view – all speak of the proximity of the Sahara.

The highest point on this part of the island is the ridge of Famara, rising to some 700 metres (2,300 feet) above sea level. It is the sea cliffs at the northern face of the ridge that house the majority of the island's rare or endemic species, especially the highly restricted *Echium decaisnei* ssp *purpuriense* and the composite *Argyranthemum ochroleucum* which, though endemic to Lanzarote, resembles a rather untidy ragwort.

At sea level you can find two yellow-flowered members of the daisy family which are confined to the two eastern Canary Islands: the fleabane *Pulicaria canariensis* and *Astericus schultzii*. The cliff tops, known as Peñitas de Chache, are no less important, harbouring the umbellifer *Ferula lancerottensis*, found only in this locality, and the more widespread lavender species *Lavandula pinnata*.

The pounding action of Atlantic waves on Lanzarote's lava cliffs (here seen at Los Herrideros) produces the island's famous black sand beaches

Farther north is the Mirador del Río, looking across from the island, over the straits (El Río) to the two islets of Graciosa and Monte Clara. The viewing gallery was designed by the local artist César Manrique to blend into the landscape: the dome above the gallery is already acquiring a patina of lichen and the signs are all on wood, so unobtrusive that it is possible to overlook them. Far below at sea level are the salt pans, adding a brilliant splash of pink and white to the view.

Return through Ye to the little fishing hamlet of Orzola, where brightly painted boats bob at anchor in the shelter of a few rocky islets, and eat some freshly caught fish – you will never taste better! Then drive past the Malpaís de la Corona, where there are a few tiny beaches with the only white sand on the island, from the Sahara, contrasting with the black rocks. The caves at Jameos del Agua and the Cueva de los Verdes are worth visiting. The entrances are again designed by the ubiquitous Manrique; the juxtaposition of large green plants and wooden seats by the pools of water is far more imaginative than cave entrances elsewhere. As at Timanfaya, the recorded commentary through the galleries is accompanied by music, which echoes round the central cavern, 50 metres (164 feet) deep. The level of lighting (and of some galleries) is low, and signposting is poor or non-existent; by refusing to sit and listen to a guide, I took a wrong turning in the gloom and found myself sometime later at a dead end. I was glad finally to find the sunlight again. A little further along the east coast road, around the village of Mala, there are still extensive plantations of prickly pears, grown for their fruit but more particularly for the beetle that lives on them – the *cuchinillo* – from which the dye cochineal is produced.

Much of the coast is being spoiled by indiscriminate tourist developments.

Freshwater is in short supply: turn on the tap and malodorous, slightly yellowish water comes out. The rapid growth of tourism has overtaken the infrastructure to support it. But seek out the wild parts; the protection of the Parque Nacional de Timanfaya, created in 1974, ensures that the stark beauty of the volcanoes cannot be destroyed.

It's no small wonder the symbol of Timanfaya is a menacing devil! The feeling, even the smell, of the whole island is redolent of sulphur, and the landscape is so hostile it requires an effort of the imagination to conjure up the picture of a fertile agricultural plain, with small streams flowing to the sea – as it was in 1730 before the succession of violent eruptions that lasted for six years and left the burned-out husks of volcanoes that dot the plain to this day.

The entrance to the *parque nacional* is eight kilometres (five miles) from Yaiza, one of the small villages hastily evacuated at the start of the eruptions; the volcanoes rained down not only rocks and small stones (lapilli), but steam and boiling water from the sea. An exciting way to travel up to the scene of desolation is by camel: caravans wait halfway along the road from Yaiza for visitors to take a leisurely ride. Africa seems very close when the *sirocco* blows from the Sahara, and the camels plod slowly through the soft, black sand.

The park information centre is called the Islote de Hilario, after a hermit who lived there with a camel for 50 years; legend says that he planted a fig tree which never bore fruit. Since meals for the tourists are cooked on a geothermal barbecue, it is surprising that the fig tree grew at all. Next to the restaurant are tubes in the earth which produce instantaneous geysers, with an impressive whoosh of steam, when water is poured into them.

If you want to get a good look at the volcanoes you must take a special bus tour. The road runs close to the most awe-inspiring craters, through the immense sea of lava, 'which first advanced as fast as water, forming swirls, and then densely and heavily like honey, destroying villages on the way,' according to the priest of Yaiza who saw the eruption. The solidified rivers of lava, called *malpaíses* ('badlands' where nothing will grow), vary in colour and geological formation between black basalt, beige pumice and *amalgras* – burnt red-ochre earth. The commentary on the bus, interspersed with music and sound effects of bubbling, hissing and explosions, reveals that there are 36 volcanoes within a triangle of eight kilometres (five miles). After hanging over an abyss as we negiotiate some steep corners on the narrow track, we believe anything we are told.

One of the volcanoes is yellow, another red; the ground is black, ochre, or burnt sienna; the shadows in the deepest craters an intense dark purple. Not a green leaf is visible, just the grey-green of lichen on some northern slopes. The hot, dusty wind of the Sahara blows over this scene from Dante's *Inferno*: 'Abandon hope, all ye who enter here.' An earlier visitor described the volcanoes as 'a scenario by Jules Verne and settings by Noguchi for a film about the moon.'

On our safe return to the haven of the Isloto, opinion is divided between those who find the desolate landscape both frightening and disturbing, and those who think the grandeur elevating – like the Swiss tourist on her twelfth visit to the island who says with eyes shining: 'It's like a cathedral.'

To see a different view of the park, take a side-turning to the left off the Yaizo-Tinajo road, three kilometres (1¾ miles) beyond the entrance to the park. At present it is marked only by a sign warning 'Camino en mal estado' (track in bad condition), which indeed it is. As you walk or bump over the potholes by car, a view slowly unfolds of the wide spaces of the northern limit of the park, winding down to a small beach called Playa de la Madera. Looking back to the red volcano and striated cliffs, the silence is absolute, except for the splash of waves on the rocks, the colours shifting as the shadows lengthen and the constant wind lessen. A rabbit appears, the only sign of life; with nothing to eat but lichen, and no water, how can it survive?

BEFORE YOU GO
Maps: SGE 1:50,000 Nos. 1,082, 1,083, 1,084, 1,087, 1,088 and 1,089; and IGN 1:200,000 Mapa provincial of Las Palmas.
Guidebook: *Tenerife and its Six Satellites* by Olivia M. Stone (London, 1889).

GETTING THERE
By air: you can fly to the island from most major European airports, or by interchange at Gran Canaria, to the airport west of Arrecife.
By sea: there is a regular service between the main islands and Arrecife run by the Compañía Transmediterránea.
ON THE ISLAND
By car: cars can be hired at the airport or from Avis, Puerto del Carmen, Arrecife, T: (928) 82 52 54.
By bus: 3 bus routes serve the island – north, south and central.
   From Arrecife there are also frequent bus excursions to Timanfaya; also from the other resort towns of Puerto del Carmen, Playa Blanca, La Caleta.
By taxi: available around the larger hotels.

WHERE TO STAY
Arrecife, Puerto del Carmen and Playa Blanca all have a wide range of pensions and hotels, ranging from the simple to the 4-star; for instance, in Arrecife is the Miramar, T: (928) 81 04 38, and in Puerto del Carmen, Los Fariones, T: (928) 82 51 75. Yaiza, the nearest town to the *parque nacional*, has the attractive 1-star Hostal Yaiza. Puerto del Carmen and Playa Blanca are both within easy driving distance of the park.

ACTIVITIES
Parque Nacional de Timanfaya: the park entrance

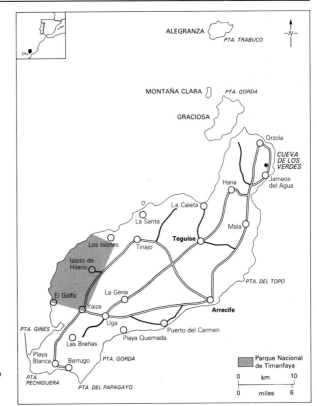

is 8km (5 miles) north of Yaiza. The most spectacular site is the Montañas de Fuego ('Fire Mountains'), at the Islote de Hilario, which are circled by the Ruta de los Volcanes ('route of the volcanoes').
   A bus tour from Islote de Hilario traverses the extensive lava fields and provides panoramic views of this extraordinary landscape; you are not allowed to visit this area independently. The route is 14km (8½ miles) long and the bus trip takes about 1hr.
North of Arrecife: you can visit the ancient capital of the island, Teguise, with its beautiful Palacio de Spinola, and just to the north, the Castillo de Guanapay, which is situated on the edge of the

Guanapay volcano and offers fantastic views across the island. Further on you pass through the highly cultivated Los Valles and into Haria, one of the most beautiful of the villages, set in a valley filled with hundreds of palm trees. At the northern tip of the island is the tiny village of Orzola from where you can catch a boat to Isla Graciosa and a good bathing beach.
South of Arrecife: La Geria is set in an extraordinary black desert-like landscape, from which is produced the famous Malvasia wines. Here the vines are grown in volcanic ash pits that protect them from the prevailing north-easterly winds.
   From Yaiza, take the road to El Golfo, in which is

193

situated a bright-emerald coloured *laguna* set between the sea and a steep black cliff: a good picnic and bathing spot. Just south is Los Hervideros, where you can watch the sea 'boil' in caverns formed by lava flow. Down the coast from here are the Janubio salt pans – a spectacular sight with brilliant white pyramidal sand-forms against the azure water. At the southern tip of the island is Papagayo Point with its splendid walks and relatively deserted beaches.

Camels: you can ride a camel from Yaiza and do some exploring up Timanfaya, but no self-drive is allowed; an experienced driver leads each caravan of 10 or more camels.

Caves: there are 2 caves famous for being the homes of the *Munidopsis polymorpha*, a 1-cm (½-in) long albino crab, which has not been discovered anywhere else in the world. Los Verdes cave, on the north-east of the island, has about a mile of illuminated galleries showing the shaped and coloured rock formations. One of these galleries has been turned into an auditorium; open 11am–6pm; guided tours are available.

Just east of here, on the coast, is Jameos del Agua – a seawater *laguna* in a cave in the lava rock, converted by the artist and town planner, Manrique, into a concert auditorium; it also houses a restaurant and nightclub.

Diving: the island offers some good diving and there is a professionally run diving school, Clubulanza in Puerto del Carmen, T: (922) 82 60 61, where tuition and equipment can be obtained.

Museums: in Arrecife, the Castillo de San Gabriel (built under Charles III), is now an archeological and anthropological museum and
194

stands on the isle of the same name, which is connected to Lanzarote by Puerto de Las Bolas. There is a small ethnographic museum in Mozaga, in the central area of the island. The Castillo de San José, which overlooks the main harbour of Arrecife, contains a modern art gallery.

FURTHER INFORMATION
Tourist information: T: (928) 81 18 60.
  There is an information centre in the Parque Nacional de Timanfaya, at Islotte de Hilario.

The Island of Fuerteventura

Rare species of fleabane and hare's-ear thrive on the island, along with many interesting birds

In outline, Fuerteventura resembles a northwards-facing tadpole: the 'tail' is the old volcanic ridge of Jandía, joined to the remainder of the island by a narrow sandy isthmus. The northern part of the island comprises deeply gullied hills and a central plain, with an extensive sand dune system along the coast. This is the closest of the Canaries to Africa.

From a botanical point of view, it is the dune area and the Jandía peninsula that are the most exciting. The dunes are alive with salt-tolerant species (halophytes), including the attractive *Androcymbium psammophilum*, for which this is the type locality. Other interesting plants, such as the shrubby, yellow-flowered legume *Lotus lancerottensis* and a creeping, silvery leaved member of the pink family,

Polycarpaea nivea, are typical species of the coastal dunes.

The island's most diverse flora grows on the Jandía peninsula, with its steeply sloping volcanic ridge that sweeps down to sandy beaches on either side. The highest point, Pico de la Zarra, is home to many rare plants, some of which can also be found on Lanzarote, at Famara. Of particular interest is the blue-flowered viper's bugloss, *Echium handiense*, which is not found elsewhere in the Canaries and is very rare, and a woody species of hare's-ear, *Bupleurum handiense*, both of which are named after the 'Handia' – or Jandía – locality. There are 2 extremely rare species growing on the coast in this southern part of Fuerteventura: a fleabane, *Pulicaria burchardii*, known to grow in only a few square metres, and a succulent spurge species, *Euphorbia handiensis*, resembling a red-flowered cactus of the spiny variety, which is now in grave danger of extinction.

Interesting birds also have their home here. Fuertenventura is the stronghold of the endemic Canary Island chat, a sort of 'washed-out' stonechat found nowhere else in the world. With a tiny population, this bird is in great danger of extinction, but may still be seen around the *barranco* near the airport. Another Canary Island endemic is Berthelot's pipit, which is relatively common in the same area. Although the Houbara buzzard is not an endemic, Fuerteventura is probably the

The menacing cone of a volcano rises above Timanfaya, on Lanzarote's west coast. Although the last eruption was in 1825, soil temperatures remain high

The viper's bugloss family features prominently in the Canaries' flora

best place to see this magnificent semi-desert bird that roams as far east as Pakistan.

Before you go *Maps:* SGE 1:50,000 Nos. 1,092, 1,096, 1,102 and 1,103.

Getting there *By air:* the island has a small airport. For details of flights, contact Iberia, T: (928) 85 12 50.

By sea: regular car and passenger ferries run from Playa Blanca (on Lanzarote) to Corralejo, the northern point of Fuerteventura. This route is also serviced by a hydrofoil Wed–Fri.

ON THE ISLAND

Cars can be hired from several firms in the capital of Puerto del Rosario; driving is the most reliable and convenient form of transport on the island.

Where to stay: the island's *parador nacional* is situated

196

near the airport at Playa Blanca, Puerto del Rosario, T: (928) 85 11 50. Other hotel accommodation can be found in Puerto del Rosario, Corralejo, Pájara, Tarajalejo, and Tuineje.

Activities *Diving:* underwater diving is particularly good off the coast here. For courses or organized dives contact Barakuda Club Corralejo, C. José Segura Torres 20, Corralejo, T: (928) 88 62 43.

Boats: can be hired in the small fishing village of Corralejo to Lobos Island where the underwater diving is excellent.

Fishing: deep-sea fishing for tuna, swordfish, etc. Ask at the airport information desk for details.

Further information *Tourist information:* T: (928) 85 12 62.

The Island of Gran Canaria

Island whose widely-ranging climate ensures great variety of plantlife

Probably the best-known of the Canary Islands – its capital, Las Palmas, is the destination of tourists by the million – Gran Canaria occupies a central position in the archipelago. Like Gomera, the island is almost circular, with a central plateau and large numbers of radial *barrancos* and subsidiary volcanic cones. Once out of Las Palmas, there are treasures aplenty waiting to be discovered in these volcanic hills.

The western side of the island is rich in endemics, in particular the rare and endangered *Dendriopoterium menendezii*, a tall, palm-like burnet and one of the few members of the rose family to

be found in the archipelago. It is confined to this area of Gran Canaria, growing with a tree-like knapweed, *Centaurea arbutifolia*.

The Barranco de Guayedra supports 3 rare composite species – *Tanacetum ferulaceum, Sonchus brachylobus* and *Argyranthemum frutescens* – but it is higher up on these cliff faces that one of the rarest plants in the whole of the Canary Islands is to be found. Although it is a member of the daisy family, the foliage of *Sventenia bupleuroides* resembles that of spurge-laurel, with leaves arranged in whorls; the yellowish flowers, however, indicate its true status, being similar to those of the closely related sow-thistles. Other plants of interest on Gran Canaria are: the very rare St John's wort, *Hypericum coadunatum*, which grows on wet cliffs in the area around one of the highest points of the island – Cruz de Tejeda (1,600m/5,250ft); *Orchis canariensis*, a pink-purple species, and 1 of only 5 orchid species that occur in the Canaries; and 2 of the multiple species of *Aeonium* that abound on the islands, both fleshy, yellow-flowered shrubs endemic to Gran Canaria – *A. undulatum* and *A. manriqueorum*. The rare composite *Tanacetum ptarmaciflorum* grows in the south of the island, around Paso de la Plata, and nearby you might see the equally scarce member of the potato family, *Solanum lidii*.

The rare and endemic plants that grow on Gran Canaria reflect the special location of this island, sited as it is midway between the hot, dry eastern elements and the oceanic, more humid western isles; it follows, then, that it combines features of the typical flora of both.

Before you go *Maps:* SGE 1:50,000 Nos. 1,100, 1,101, 1,108, 1,109, 1,113 and 1,114.
Getting there *By air:* a wide choice of international flights to the island. Iberia offers a number of daily flights from mainland Spain and between the Canary Islands. The airport is situated on the east coast, just south of Las Palmas.
By sea: a ferry service runs from Cádiz to Las Palmas (Muelle de Santa Catalina); it takes about 36hrs. There is also a jet-foil service between Las Palmas and Santa Cruz de Tenerife, and various other inter-island connections, all run by the Compañía Transmediterránea.
ON THE ISLAND
By car: the best way to see the island is by car, moped or bicycle. Cars can be hired at the airport and in Las Palmas; small cars are in demand and it is wise to book in peak season.
Mopeds/bicycles: these are a popular way of getting around, and are available for hire in Las Palmas at some of the bigger hotels.
By bus: a good local bus service covers the whole island; tourist offices will be able to provide you with up-to-date schedules (see below for addresses and telephone nos.).
Where to stay: there is a wide range of hotels, pensions and hostels in Las Palmas, Maspalomas, Mogán, Playa del Inglés and San Bartólome Tirajana. Accommodation is also available in Agaete, Arguineguín, Gáldar, Los Palmitos, Puerto de Mogán, San Augustín, Santa Brigida, Tafira Alta, Tafira Baja, Tejeda, Telde, Teror and Vecindario. Cruz de Tejeda has a Parador Hostería, Cruz

de Tejeda, T: (928) 65 80 50.
Outdoor living: there are no official camping grounds on this island.
Activities *Walking/climbing:* in the island's northern sector, at Arucas, you can follow a road up past the church and on to Montaña de Arucas, where there is a superb view of the town and the hinterland. The cliffs around Gáldar are honeycombed with caves. The well-known Cueva Pintada with its decorative wall paintings is here. Just north of the town is the Guanche Necropolis, and south, on the way to Agaete – a small, attractive and not over-touristed village, worth a visit in itself – are the Cuevas de las Cruces.

La Caldera de Bandama can be thoroughly explored from Bandama, as can the Pico de Bandama. It takes about ½hr to climb the peak of the volcano, and a further 1hr to make the strenuous descent into the crater. The actual walk around the perimeter of the crater itself takes about ¾hr.

Also in the north but in the interior is the town of Teror, 'town of balconies'. There are wonderful views from the road and it is an excellent starting point both for walking and for exploring parts of the interior. From here the road continues to twist its way to Artenara, the island's highest village. It is another extremely convenient base for good hikes.

The centre of the island: heading south from Tejeda on the C811, turn right on to the 17-3 to the small village of Cueva Grande. From here you can walk up the massive Cueva del Rey – a steep 10–15-min ascent which begins alongside the first house in the village. Another fine crater is the Caldera de los Marteles

situated off the 18-3. Both this and the luxuriant *barranco* valley right next to it are favourite hiking areas for locals and visitors alike.

For the more ambitious, the strenuous hike to the top of the Pico de las Nieves, (1,947m/6,386ft) should not be missed. This peak can be approached from Cruz Grande on the 815 and takes about 1½hrs to reach.

The Ojeda, Inagua and Pajonales nature reserves can be explored from the small town of El Juncal on the 17-2; take the road opposite the church which will take you right down to the floor of the valley.

South: Los Palmitos makes a good base for interesting walks in this area, including a 3-hr hike to the Guanche Necropolis, just south of Arteara.

The Barranco de Arguineguín between Cercado Espina and Soria provides a memorable setting for walks among palm trees.
Gardens: Aruca's municipal park has an interesting collection of native plants, and its Gothic church stands amid a variety of fruit trees. Tafira Alta, too, has an excellent botanical garden.
Museums: the Canarian Museum, on C. Dr. Verneau, Las Palmas, has an extensive collection of Guanche and other pre-Hispanic art as well as artifacts from the island.
Sailing/diving: the Sporting Centre of the Hotel Don Gregory, San Augustín, T: (928) 76 26 62, hires equipment and arranges tuition.
Further information *Tourist information:* Parque Santa Catalina, Las Palmas, T: (928) 27 07 90, 27 16 00 and 26 46 23. ICONA, Avda Marítima del Norte, T: (928) 24 87 35.

The Island of Tenerife

Largest of the Canary Islands with a diverse endemic flora
Includes the Parque Nacional de las Cañadas del Teide

The most spectacular feature of Tenerife is the peak of El Teide (3,710 metres/ 12,160ft), which is not only the highest of the Canary Islands, but also of the whole of Spain.

For centuries another notable feature of Tenerife was the legendary 6,000-year-old dragon tree (*Dracaena draco*) at Orotava on the north coast, which unfortunately perished in the hurricane of 1867, but was reputed to have been more ancient than the Pyramids. This veritable giant among trees measured some 24 metres (78 feet) in circumference just prior to its demise, and was later found to be more than 23 metres (75 feet) high. The dragon tree yields a red gum, known in some circles as 'dragon's blood', which was believed by the alchemists of the Middle Ages to carry both mystical and healing powers. Wild specimens today are very rare, although it is extensively cultivated in botanical gardens; it is one of the few woody members of the lily family in Europe. A less ancient but hardly less venerable dragon tree survived the hurricane and can still be seen in the north-east village of Icod.

Tenerife is a large, triangular island traversed from the centre to the northern end by a deeply serrated ridge. The northern coast is bordered by steep cliffs, but the southern part of the island slopes down to one of the few regions of level coastal plain in the volcanic archipelago.

The flora of Tenerife is almost as diverse and restricted in its distribution as that of Gran Canaria. Some outstanding botanical localities include that of El Fraile, on the northern cliffs, which harbours such rarities as *Lavatera phoenicea* and *Marcetella moquiniana*, members of the mallow and rose families, respectively. This area also boasts some 300 species of flowering plant in only a few hectares – one of the richest botanical assemblages in the islands. Other endemic species of the cliffs of El Fraile include *Centaurea canariensis*, *Vieraea laevigata*, *Tolpis crassiuscula* and the sea lavender *Limonium fruticans*, all in fairly stable populations.

In other localities on the island grow some interesting endemics: for instance, the white-flowered trailing vetch *Vicia scandens*, which grows on the caldera cliffs, and the xerophilic species on El Medano at the southern tip of the island, where plants have adapted to the almost Saharan conditions that prevail. Another special locality is the cliffs of the Ladera de Güimar, on the eastern coast of Tenerife, which harbour such rare endemics as *Monanthes adenosce-pes* and *Micromeria teneriffae* (a succulent of the stonecrop family and a labiate, respectively), as well as being the only known Tenerife locality for *Pterocephalus dumetorm*, a pink-flowered scabious (it also grows round Roque Nublo in Gran Canaria).

The islanders have recently become concerned about preserving the delicate equilibrium between people and nature, and have realized that the growth of tourism must be drastically curtailed in order to preserve their natural resources. There is an alarming prediction that if growth continues at the present rate, by the end of the century three-quarters of the island's population will be tourists or foreigners. It is now intended to re-evaluate and reduce planning permission for hotels and tourist developments.

The Parque Nacional de las Cañadas del Teide dominates the island, floating serene-ly in sunlight above a constant sea of clouds; when the weather is cloud-free it is clearly visible from the other islands of the group. The *parque nacional* encloses the extensive volcanic plateau around the mountain, within the steep, almost sheer, encircling walls of the crater.

Arriving at Tenerife by air, your first view is of the peak, suddenly lost to view as you dip through the cloud layer below, then out into the sunlight again on the harsh, arid south side of the island. Driving from the airport to the park takes more than an

The explosive history of the island is recorded in multi-coloured layers of lava deposits near El Teide on Tenerife

hour, winding slowly upwards through the small villages of Granadilla and Vilaflor, where vines are cultivated on terraces covered with pumice stones to retain the moisture; then it's upwards again through chestnuts and scattered pines until the pine forest becomes dense, the trees' spreading branches meeting overhead while the cloud layer closes down.

The last time I visited, children were collecting pine-needles in the forest, piling them into bundles; a woman was walking gracefully towards a little truck with an immense bundle balanced on her straw hat, looking in the misty light like a hallucinatory moving mushroom. Later, and further down the mountain in the vineyard area in Valle San Lorenzo, I saw the practical application of this mirage: the needles were being spread on the vine terraces to supply a slow-acting mulch on top of the thin layer of soil, then covered with pumice stones to retain the moisture.

The view from Teide's peak is breathtaking, with the islands of Gran Canaria, Gomera, El Hierro and La Palma spread across the sea, and the jagged peaks of the caldera rim all round below you. The varied colours of the many different types of volcanic rocks are seen most clearly from here: ochre and rust, black and beige. Bushy clumps of the Teide daisy shine on the highest slopes.

There is very little indigenous fauna in the park, but both the endemic Canary and the blue chaffinch are found here, the latter feeding around picnic sites just like their more widespread relations elsewhere. In May and June the spectacular tall red spikes of the Teide viper's bugloss (*Echium wildprettii*) bloom; the flowers grow to two metres (six feet), and the spikes remain standing after the flowers have died.

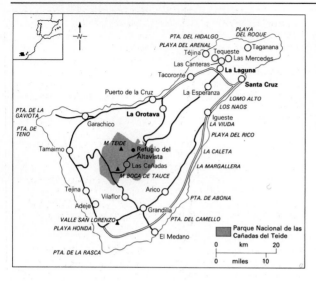

BEFORE YOU GO

Maps: SGE 1:50,000 Nos. 1,096, 1,097, 1,102, 1,103, 1,104, 1,105, 1,109, 1,110, 1,111, 1,118, 1,119 and 1,124; and IGN 1:200,000 Mapa provincial of Santa Cruz de Tenerife.

Guidebooks: *Landscapes of Tenerife* by Noel Rochford (London, 1984); *Parques Nacionales de Canarias* by Marisol García Sánchez and María José Medina Valbuena (Madrid, 1986); and *Tenerife and other Canary Islands* by Norah B. Spowart (Brentford, 1984).

GETTING THERE

By air: Tenerife has 2 airports. The newer one on the south-east corner of the island, Reina Sofía, is used for international flights; the old one in the mountains of the north, Los Rodeos, is vulnerable to poor weather conditions and now used only for inter-island and pleasure flying.

By sea: the Compañía Transmediterránea runs ferries from Cádiz, Valencia and Barcelona to Tenerife. There are also ferry connections to other islands in the archipelago.

ON THE ISLAND

There is a good local bus service and regular buses through the Parque Nacional de las Cañadas del Teide. Cars can be hired and taxis will take you to the park if you want a private tour.

WHERE TO STAY

The 2-star Parador Nacional de las Cañadas del Teide, T: (922) 33 23 04, is situated within the park, with a magnificent view of the mountain peak. Santa Cruz de Tenerife, La Orotava, Puerto de la Cruz and La Laguna all have a wide choice of accommodation to suit every taste and budget. Try the 2-star pension, Silene, T: (922) 33 01 99, in La Orotava, or the 3-star Los Príncipes, T: (922) 38 33 53, in Puerto de la Cruz.

Outdoor living: there are no campsites on the island. Camping or sleeping out in the park is strictly forbidden.

Refuges: there is a mountain refuge near the peak of Teide, the Refugio de Altavista at Rambleta; it has 40 beds, is open 1 Apr–14 Dec, and bookings can be made through the park information centre or from the tourist office in Santa Cruz (see below).

ACTIVITIES

Parque Nacional de las Cañadas del Teide: located in the centre of the island, the park can be approached from the north via the Orotava road; from the south via the Vilaflor road; from the east via the lateral road starting at La Laguna; and the west via the Chío–Boca de Tauce road.

There is a cable car less than 2km (1 mile) beyond the Parador Nacional de las Cañadas del Teide; it can carry you more than 1,000m (3,300ft) upward in about 15min to within a short walk of the summit. The walk is stiff and the wind chilly, even on a sunny day.

A good local bus service runs regularly from both Santa Cruz and Puerto de la Cruz (No. 348) through the park, with stops at the cable car and the Parador, both in easy walking distance of Monte Teide.

Within the park there are 2 forest access roads: the route of the Cañadas skirts the edge of the crater in parts; from the

The giant red flower spikes of *Echium wildprettii* provide welcome splashes of colour on Tenerife

200

Orotava–Vilaflor road there is a route up the side of Montaña Rajada as far as Montaña Blanca.

The park contains an extensive network of footpaths, and you are advised to pick up a local map of these from the information centre. Not all areas of the park are open to the public; you must follow the marked paths. Walking on solidified lava can be extremely difficult and somewhat treacherous – wear flat, comfortable shoes; the volcanic rock is very sharp, and small stones will fill loose sandals.

North: the Anaga region's rough landscape includes the famous *laurisilva* forest near La Laguna. The town of La Laguna is situated on the southern edge of the mountains in the north, on the fringe of the Laurisilva de las Mercedes. This is the last remaining place on the island where these ancient woods can now be seen. Here are found 2 of the Canary Islands'

7 endemic species of birds – Boll's pigeon and the white-tailed laurel pigeon. These dark forest birds have only recently been separated by ornithologists and are difficult to locate. Their future depends entirely on the survival of these forests. The trade winds blowing down from the north west produce clouds over the islands which are then prevented from rising and dispersing by the trade winds from the north east; the condensation is trapped by the foliage of the laurel forest and the pine woods, and serves as a vital source of freshwater, as the rainfall is very low.

Near the town of Tacoronte is a steep road leading down to the Playa de Las Gaviotas, a black sandy beach where nude bathing is permitted. **East:** the region of Teno also has rugged features, notably near the town of Adeje, the Barranco del Infierno ('hell's gorge'), renowned for its botanical and zoological variety. Its vertical walls are

perforated with burial caves and are largely overgrown. **Fishing:** contact the Club de Pesca Neptuno, C. de Pérez Galdós 19, Santa Cruz. **Museum:** the archeological museum is on Pl. de España, Santa Cruz. **Sailing:** for details, contact Real Club Náutico, Carretera de San Andrés, Santa Cruz; and Club La Galera, Candelaria. **Underwater diving:** Club de Pesca Neptuno, C. Pérez Galdós 19, Santa Cruz; and diving school, Fernández Herrero 11, Santa Cruz.

FURTHER INFORMATION

Tourist information: Pl. de España, Santa Cruz, T: (922) 24 22 27; and in Puerto de la Cruz, Pl. de la Iglesia 3, T: (922) 38 43 28. ICONA, Avda de los Reyes Católicos, Santa Cruz, T: (922) 28 35 58 or 28 35 66.

An information centre is located on the north-west of the Parque Nacional de las Cañadas del Teide.

The Island of Gomera

Tiny volcanic cone, tranquil and densely-forested
Including the Parque Nacional de Garajonay

The islanders of Gomera are justly proud of their history and traditions. Christopher Columbus set sail from here to look for the Tierra Incognita, which turned out to be the West Indies. When a passing peasant woman stopped to talk to me, and I said 'how beautiful your island is,' she replied with a little smile: '*Disfrutamos de la tranquilidad*' (we enjoy the tranquility). Do not, however, place too much confi-

dence in the islanders' ability to give directions: asking for the nearest road to the Parque Nacional de Garajonay, I was told to carry straight on. The narrow road turned into an unpaved track that clung to a steep mountain slope, then, rounding a sharp corner, it disappeared into the waters of a new dam. I was thankful that it was daylight. I retraced my route with difficulty and started again.

This tiny circular volcanic island rises to a central peak of almost 1,490 metres (4,888 feet), the cone scoured by radiating *barrancos* that terminate suddenly some way above sea level. The more barren parts of the island, often composed of raw basaltic rock, have their own characteristic flora, as do the steep-sided *barrancos* which shelter more sensitive species from the extremes of climate which are often experienced here. Particularly interesting species of Gomera

201

include the legume *Lotus emeroides*, which is endemic to the island, as are the blue-flowered *Echium acanthocarpum*, the shrubby crucifer *Crambe gomeraea*, a yellow-flowered composite *Argyranthemum callichrysum*, and two species of sow-thistle which occur only in the area around Agulo to the north-east of the island: *Sonchus gonzalez-padronii* and *S. regis-jubae*.

I drove down the luxuriantly cultivated slopes of Vallehermoso ('beautiful valley') to the town of the same name. At siesta time on a hot day it was as deserted as the Marie Celeste, though brilliant with geraniums and bougainvillea. Suddenly, rounding a corner, I caught sight of three huge figures seated round a table; two more figures were placed at either end of a bench, in what seemed to be a children's playground. The figures were more than three metres (ten feet) high, seated. I searched in vain for the name of the sculptor, or for an explanation. One had a stylized helmet, in Henry Moore mode, which made me wonder if they represented the Guanche ancestors in conference – then I found at each end of the bench the letters PAPA and MAMA. It would have been interesting to see the children at play among them, but the siesta hour was sacrosanct and the mystery unsolved.

It was a totally unexpected touch of fantasy in a practical agricultural community, busy producing tomatoes, maize and bananas – everywhere bananas. You drive back to the port of San Sebastián round the lower slopes of the mountain on the eastern side, through prickly pears, palm trees and an infinite variety of spurges. With El Teide a silent presence across the sea, like a Pillar of Hercules, the islands are truly the gardens of the Hesperides.

Driving into the forest of the Parque Nacional de Garajonay, the cloud cover became thicker, the road more winding, until I became slightly disoriented; no sun, no sound, no view further than six metres

Walking over the jagged volcanic rocks of Las Cañadas del Teide can be painful, and is never to be undertaken lightly

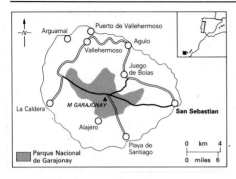

Asplenium onopteris, Athyrium umbrosum and Woodwardia radicans, as well as the yellow-flowered succulent Aichryson punctatum.

The contrast of vegetation between Tenerife and La Gomera is striking; the only point of Tenerife that comes close to the greenness of Garajonay is the relatively small area of mixed woodlands, or lauri-silva, near La Laguna on the north of the larger island.

The varied trees of the Gomera forest, so densely packed and often clinging to precipitous slopes, provide the 'green lung' for the whole island. The cistus and heather of the lower slopes, becoming denser and taller towards the heights, mixed with the shiny foliage of the laurels, the bright yellow of Canary broom and trailing lengths of lichen, create a living tapestry of plants that must be seen in order to imagine how the islands must have looked in the days of the Guanches, the aboriginals of the group.

From their early folklore comes the name of the park: Gara was a beautiful Gomeran girl who fell in love with a boy named Jonay from Tenerife, who would swim to visit her. Her relations were bitterly opposed to her union with an outsider, so the couple fled up into the heights of the mountain, where they died in each other's arms, pierced through by the thorn of a tree – hence Garajonay, to perpetuate the union.

The north-western tip of the park includes some rocky open terrain, towards the attractive hamlet of Arguamal. There the rocks by the road are studded with rosettes of succulents: Aeonium nobile, green with pink-tipped leaves and pink flowers; and many varieties of golden-flowering broom.

(20 feet) ahead, below or above. The cloud layer that rests almost permanently on the shoulders of Gomera streams downwards through the trees, catching and blowing free like fleece on bushes. Again I was completely lost, this time for more than an hour, and was eventually relieved to see an ordinary black chicken cross the rutted track.

Relating the story later to one of the park guardians, he said severely that no one should ever go into the forest alone or without a good map of all the tracks. He told me of two tourists who disappeared from their hotel, failed to return in the evening, and were eventually found 36 hours after they had set out, suffering from exposure and dehydration, after all the police and park wardens had been mobilized in the search.

Here, in this forest, Canary willow and holly (Salix canariensis and Ilex canariensis) grow together with Laurus azorica and the aromatic evergreen myrtle, Myrica faya, which also grows in sandy localities of southern Portugal. The woodland is of particular interest for its lush vegetation, due to the abundance of moisture. And the result is several fern species, including

---

BEFORE YOU GO
Maps: SGE 1:50,000 Nos. 1,108, 1,109, 1,116 and 1,117.

Do not place your trust entirely in the maps of the island: one of them already features an airport on a site where an airport is only proposed – however, there is a

strong Green lobby to help preserve Gomera's inaccessibility and it may be many years before the map is correct.
Guidebook: P. Romero, *Parque Nacional de Garajonay, Itinerarios Autoguiados* (Madrid, 1987).

GETTING THERE
By air: currently there is no airport (see above).
By sea: a ferry of the Fred Olsen Line leaves 3 times daily from Los Cristianos, on the south coast of Tenerife, taking 1½hrs to reach Gomera; there are 3 daily

departures, and 2 return sailings from Gomera. Summer and winter timetables are not identical.

Another ferry, operated by the Compañía Transmediterránea, runs from Santa Cruz de Tenerife to San Sebastián, but takes 23hrs to get there, stopping at La Palma and El Hierro on the way. If you enjoy cruises, you could see the Canaries from the sea, but otherwise this ferry seems to have little to recommend it.

ON THE ISLAND
For information about buses and taxis, T: (928) 80 54 80.

All petrol stations on the island, except one at Chipude, are closed on Sun and public holidays.

WHERE TO STAY
The Parador Conde de la Gomera is one of the most beautiful *paradors* in Spain, T: (928) 87 11 00. It is ideally situated above the port of San Sebastián to command a good view and benefit from a sea breeze. Accommodation is also available in San Sebastián, Playa de Santiago and La Calera.

Outdoor living: there is a camping ground within the park, Campamento Antiguo, and one just outside the park's boundary, at El Cedro.

ACTIVITIES
Parque Nacional de Garajonay: it takes nearly 1hr to get to the park from San Sebastián. The park is closed on Tue, Sat and Sun; this does not mean that you cannot gain access, only that the information centre will be closed. There are no refreshments available in the park: take iron rations, especially water or fruit, if you intend to walk in the forest for any length of time.

The tourist information

centre at San Sebastián (see below) will arrange visits to the park.

Valle Gran Rey makes a good day excursion. From San Sebastián, take the Playa de Santiago road, but instead of turning into the town go straight ahead towards the Valle Gran Rey. At Guadá you get fantastic views over the whole valley. Further north at Arure, in the Cueva de María, fine pieces of Gomera pottery are for sale and there is a magnificent view down to the little village of Taguluche, nestling by the coast.

Los Organos is a 100-m (330-ft) high cliff facing the Atlantic Ocean, with the appearance of a massive organ; there are many gorges worth exploring in the area, but they can only be seen from a boat.

Museum: the San Sebastián museum has a fascinating collection of historical items found on the island.
Sailing: contact Club Nautique, C. del Conde, T: (928) 87 10 53, in San Sebastián de la Gomera.

FURTHER INFORMATION
Tourist information: T: (928) 80 54 80.

There is a park information centre at Degollada Peraza, on the San Sebastián de la Gomera side of the park.

The Island of Hierro

Smallest island of the Canaries group, whose forests have to cling to near-vertical slopes

This roughly triangular island has the distinction of being both the southernmost and westernmost of the Canaries archipelago, and is reputed to

have been formed from the fragment of an ancient volcano – the evidence is a central semi-circular ridge oriented to the north west. Hierro is also the smallest of the 7 islands, but the high point exceeds 1,500m (4,900ft); the slopes down to sea level are thus almost vertical in places.

The crater area is known as El Golfo, and it is this semi-circular cliff and bay area that holds the most botanical interest. The steep backdrop to the bay supports dense pine and laurel forest, which seems to cling precariously to the cliffs. The ground flora includes such interesting species as the Canary cranesbill (*Geranium canariense*), and a pink-flowered forget-me-not, *Myosotis latifolia*. Other parts of the forest have a canopy dominated by the huge spurge *Euphoria regis-jubae*, known locally as *tabaiba*, and often growing with the mocan tree (*Visnea mocanera*). Other rarities of the El Golfo area include the pink-flowered *Echium hierrense*, the endemic sow-thistle *Sonchus gandogeri*, the knapweed *Centaurea durannii*, which is rare in the lower cliffs of this bay and found nowhere else, and the pink-flowered campion species *Silene sabinosae*.

Before you go *Maps:* SGE 1:50,000 Nos. 1,112 and 1,115.
Getting there *By air:* there is a small airport at Tamaduste, T: (922) 55 08 78, serviced by Iberia airlines.
By sea: a ferry runs to Puerto de la Estaca from Santa Cruz de la Palma, San Sebastián de la Gomera, Los Cristianos (Tenerife) and Santa Cruz de Tenerife.
Where to stay: the 3-star Parador Nacional de El Hierro, T: (922) 55 01 01, is located about 10km (6 miles)

from Valverde. There are also various hostels in both Frontera and Valverde; contact the tourist office for more information.

Activities *Walking:* along the rim of El Golfo from the Roques de Salmor to Sabinosa there are fine walks through laurels, giant briars and banana trees. In Sabinosa itself is a spa renowned for the medicinal qualities of its water. La Dehesa, too, offers some interesting walks. A large pine wood at El Pinar on the eastern side of the island is a beautiful place in which to stroll.

It takes about 15–20min to walk from Guarazoca up to the belvedere of El Hierro from where the whole crater can be viewed; west of San Andrés runs a track to the Mirador de Jinama; El Rincón is approached by a track across La Dehesa.

Diving: the island offers superb underwater diving off its rocky coast. La Restinga, to the south of the island, is probably the best region for diving and snorkeling.

FURTHER INFORMATION
Tourist information: T: (928) 80 54 80.

There is a park information centre at Degollada Peraza, on the San Sebastián de la Gomera side of the park.

The Island of La Palma

Including the Parque Nacional de la Caldera de Taburiente
Differs from the other islands in the group in the fertility of its cultivated areas

From sea level the island of La Palma rises steeply to wooded, rocky heights; only from the highest points can you see into the deepest crater in the world, La Caldera de Taburiente. The slopes of the *caldera* are forested with pine trees, in some places of massive girth (the most famous has a circumference of eight metres/ 26 feet). Beneath these grow thick bushes of broom with bright yellow flowers. Because of the numerous springs on the island, the cultivated areas are very fertile.

A great variety of tropical fruit is grown on the island: papayas, pomegranates, pineapples and avocado pears, oranges, loquats, bananas and small sweet mirabelle plums. There are woods of lime and laurel on the heights of Los Sauces, and an astonishing variety of wild flowers. Plant species which are endemic to La Palma include the forest-dwelling *Echium pininana*, which produces huge spikes, up to four metres (13 feet) of pale blue flowers, and of which only a few specimens remain; the bright yellow-flowered *Gonospermum canariense*, from the north-eastern forests, known locally as *faro* ('lighthouse') due to the beacon effect of its flowers; the composite *Argyranthemum webbii*; and the viper's bugloss named after the same botanist, *Echium webbii. Lactucosonshus webbii*, was recently rediscovered on the coast near Barlovento after an absence of more than a century.

Banana plantations cover the lower slopes of the mountains, protected from the winds by perforated walls. Above these are narrower terraces for tomatoes and cabbages, then vines where the slopes become so steep that only the most determined *campesinos* would plant anything. Nevertheless the ground is fertile enough to grow good grapes from which a delicious white wine is produced. The other Canary

Many introduced shrubs and cacti compete with the indigenous laurels on La Palma

Gomera flourishes in the humidity of its almost permanent cloud-cover, which has produced this dramatic aerial rainbow (left)

speciality, a banana liqueur, is an acquired taste which I have not acquired. Above the last terraces the chestnut trees start, then the bracken and broom between scattered pines, until at last you reach the *barranco* in full sunlight, looking down at the thin layer of clouds below.

It is well worth a visit to the southern tip of the island to see the black landscape produced by the most recent volcanic eruption on any of the islands: that of the Vulcán de Teneguía. Taking the road south from Santa Cruz through the little white villages of the lower slopes, such as Breña Baja, you come to a pottery in a windmill selling attractive black 'pinch' pots; they are made by hand, not thrown on a wheel, exactly as the Guanche ancestors of the islanders used to make them. Other island crafts are still thriving: lace-making, embroidery and beautiful baskets made of palm fronds, wicker and even of long, pliant brambles. Understandably, the last is now a dying art, since the young no longer have the patience to learn such a prickly *metier*.

Near the town of Fuencaliente ('hot spring'), the earth turns black, and looking south you can see two volcanic cones, those of San Antonio and Teneguía. When Teneguía spouted fire, rocks and lava in 1971, during a short-lived but violent eruption, showers of lapilli rained down on the surrounding countryside. The first wild plants have just gained a tentative roothold, and already vines have been planted, brilliantly green against the black background. In fact, the Roque de Teneguía is the only known locality of the shrubby, mauve-flowered knapweed *Centaurea junoniana*; many typical Canarian species also favour this area but grow in stunted dwarf varieties, such as the composite *Phagnalon umbelliforme*.

Back again to Santa Cruz via the coast road, to walk along the sea front and enjoy the evening breeze blowing in from the Atlantic. Glancing up a side turning, a wooden ship rides a concrete wave, bow pointed out to sea; a monument to the courage and imagination of Christopher Columbus in setting off on his great voyage in such a cockleshell of a craft. To the east

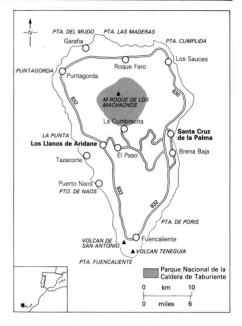

lies Africa and the other Canary Islands; to the west, the wide Atlantic and the continent which brave Colombus stumbled upon in his search for the Indies.

La Palma's Parque Nacional de la Caldera de Taburiente is a fascinating place. Unlike the bleak, apocalyptic landscape of Lanzarote, the Taburiente crater is lined with pine woods, and near the base there are deciduous woods with streams flowing along the floor of the crater. The 770-metre (2,525-foot) walls are vertiginous from above and impressive from below; the filtered sunlight through the branches of the huge Canary pines makes it seem almost as if the vegetation had tamed and softened the harsh volcanic rocks.

The differential between summer and winter temperatures is not great – only 6°C (12°F); nevertheless, the greater humidity of winter makes walking in the caldera much safer. That doesn't mean it is easy in the summer. You soon become aware of the precarious balance between the trees which stabilize the slopes of the volcano with their roots, and the natural process of erosion which is very gradually breaking down the mountain and causes long screes to form. A track from the entry point at La Cumbrecita to the Lomo de las Chozas was blocked to cars after a rockfall, but some people were walking across the fall on foot. As I started across, the heap of loose rock and small pebbles began to bounce down; I beat a hasty retreat. In a flash, the pebbles became bigger stones, like an avalanche of dust, sliding down the mountain. The brave walkers who had already crossed found it considerably more difficult on their return. Because of this tendency for the rocks to crack in the summer heat rockfalls are a dangerous possibility, and few guided walks are arranged at this time of year.

The best viewpoint on the island is the Roque de los Muchachos, on the northern tip of the crater at 2,423 metres (7,950 feet) from which you can look south into the abyss, or north to the sea. You will also find a well-developed sub-alpine flora, containing a number of species confined to these La Palma mountains, including the violet *Viola palmensis*, the very rare viper's bugloss *Echium gentianoides*, the highly attractive deep magenta flowers of the scabious-like *Pterocephalus porphyranthus*, also very rare, and the composite *Tolpis calderae*.

BEFORE YOU GO
Maps: SGE 1:50,000 Nos. 1,085, 1,090 and 1,084; and Clyde Ltd 1:150,000 (and other scales) Leisure map of the Canary Islands.

GETTING THERE
By air: there is an airport at Santa Cruz de la Palma, T: (922) 41 15 40.
By sea: there are regular ferries calling at the other islands. The Cádiz ferry also calls here. All services are run by the Compañía Transmediterránea, T: (922) 28 78 50.

WHERE TO STAY
Santa Cruz on the east coast, Puertos Naos on the west, and Tazacorte, 12km (7½ miles) north of Puerto Naos, have good selections of hotels and pensions of all categories. The 3-star Parador de Santa Cruz de la Palma, T: (922) 41 23 40, is situated on the sea front at Santa Cruz in an attractive old balconied building.

ACTIVITIES
Parque Nacional de Taburiente: to reach the park, tourist bus, taxi or hired car are the only means of transport; there is no regular bus service. Water flows in abundance through this volcanic landscape; as you walk in the crater you will see 'fountains', springs and waterfalls. At the falls of Desfondada a small stream drops 150m (500ft); the cascade is a 1-hr walk away from Taburiente. The cave at Tanausú, situated halfway between Tenerra and the few houses of Taburiente, is also worth a visit.

From El Paso, there is a 9-km (5½-mile) route up to the Mirador of La Cumbrecita where from the lookouts Las Chozas and Roques you will get splendid views of the park from a vantage point on the very edge of the crater. From Los Llanos de Aridane, take the rough road to Lomo de los Caballos, then to the 'cliff of anguish' and up to La Farola; the bridle path begins from here, taking you into the caldera. From Mirca, continue to Los Andenes (33km/20 miles) and on to Roque de los Muchachos (36km/22 miles) where you can walk to the highest *mirador* (viewpoint) on the island.
Other interesting places: the Teneguía volcano is still active (it last erupted in 1971). It is near Fuencaliente, the most southern town of the island. When heading north to the *parque nacional*, driving from Santa Cruz to Los Sauces, you pass many caves, most of which are abandoned and overgrown, and an abundance of terraced banana plantations.
Beaches: Las Cançajos, near Santa Cruz at Breña Baja; Tazacorte and Puerto Naos are the main bathing beaches.
Caves: the Guanche caves of Hoya Grande and Fuente de la Zanza have prehistoric inscriptions decorating their walls, as does the cave of Belmaco in Mazo. Cuera Bonita is notable for its dramatic, completely natural, light show.

FURTHER INFORMATION
Tourist information: Palacio Salazar, Avda O'Daly, Santa Cruz; all trips to the caldera must be arranged first at this office.

A sub-tropical sunset (overleaf) may be brief, but over cloud-capped La Palma it is an unforgettable sight

USEFUL ADDRESSES

The following organizations provide useful information and assistance for those interested in exploring Wild Spain and in learning about its flora and fauna. Several of them are mentioned throughout this book, often in abbreviated form.

Asociación Asturiana de Amigos de la Naturaleza (ANA), C/ Uria 16–2°; Oviedo, Asturias

Asociación para la Defensa y Estudio del Medio, Los Pedroches, Guadamatilla, C3 Jose Estevez 5, 14400 Pozoblanco, Córdoba

Asociación de Estudios y Protección de la Naturaleza (AEPDEN), Esparteros 11–4°; 1–C, 28012 Madrid

Asociación para la Defensa de la Naturaleza (ADENA), C/ Santa Engracia 6–2° izda, 28010 Madrid

Asociación para la Defensa de los Recursos Naturales de Cantabria (ARCA), Apartado 421, Santander, Cantabria

Colectivo Montañero por la Defensa de los Picos de Europa, Viaducto Ingeniero Marquina 4, Semisótano Izquierda, 33004 Oviedo, Asturias

Direccion General del Medio Ambiente, Paseo de la Castellana 67, 28046/28071 Madrid

Federacíon d'Entitas Excursionistas de Catalunya, Rambla 61, 08002 Barcelona

Federacíon Española de Montañismo, Alberto Aguilera 3, 4 Izquierda, Madrid 15

Fondo Asturiano para la Proteccion de los Animales Salvages (FAPAS), Apartado 106, Llanes, Asturias

Grupe Asturiano para el Estudio y Conservacion de los Murcielagos, Avda Aureliano San Roman 12, 2–A, 33011 Oviedo, Asturias

Instituto Cartografico de Catalunya, Balmes 209, 08006 Barcelona

Instituto Geográfico Nacional, Calle General Ibanez de Ibero 3, Madrid 3

Libreria Quera, Petrixtol 2, Barcelona 2 (*the best bookshop in Spain for the walker, climber and naturalist*)

National Institute for the Conservation of Nature (ICONA), Gran Vía de San Francisco 35, 28079 Madrid

Sociedad Española de Ornithologia, Faculdad de Biologia Planta 9, Cuidad Universitaria, 28040 Madrid

FURTHER READING

A. Allee, *Andalusia – Two Steps from Paradise* (Nelson 1974).

A. Chapman and W. J. Buck, *Wild Spain* (London 1893).

A. Chapman and W. J. Buck, *Unexplored Spain* (London 1910).

E. Duffey, *National Parks and Nature Reserves of Europe* (Macdonald & Co 1982).

J. A. Fernandez, *Doñana: Spain's Wildlife Wilderness* (Collins 1975).

C. Grey-Wilson and M. Blamey, *The Alpine Flowers of Britain & Europe* (Collins 1979).

L. Jonsson, *Birds of the Mediterranean and the Alps* (Croome Helm 1982).

R. Macaulay, *Fabled Shore* (London 1949).

W.B.L. Manley and H.G. Allcard, *A Field Guide to the Butterflies and Burnets of Spain* (Classey 1970).

J.A. Michener, *Iberia – Spanish Travels & Reflections* (2 vols, Corgi 1968).

H. Myhill, *The Spanish Pyrenees* (Faber & Faber 1966).

G. Mountfort, *Portrait of a Wilderness: the story of the Coto Doñana* (Expeditiona 1968).

A. Paterson, *Birdwatching in Southern Spain* (Golf-Area S.A., Costa del Sol 1987).

O. Polunin and M. Walters, *A Guide to the Vegetation of Britain & Europe* (OUP 1985).

D. Poore and P. Gryn-Ambroes *Nature Conservation in Northern and Western Europe* (UNEP/IUCN/WWF 1980).

R.F. Porter et al, *Flight Guide to the Identification of European Raptors* (Poyser 1981).

A.W. Taylor, *Wild Flowers of Spain and Portugal* (Chatto & Windus 1972).

A.W. Taylor, *Wild Flowers of the Pyrenees* (Chatto & Windus 1972).

H. Vedel, *Trees and Shrubs of the Mediterranean* (Penguin 1978).

W. Verner, *My Life among the Wild Birds of Spain* (J. Bales & Sons 1909).

K. Whinnom, *A Glossary of Spanish Bird Names* (Tamesif Books 1966).

INDEX

Species are indexed only where information is provided in addition to general description and location, and where they are illustrated; page references in *italics* refer to illustrations.

PICTURE CREDITS

Jacket Front Cover – Gunter Ziesler/Bruce Coleman Ltd. 10/11, 14 – Richard Kemp/Remote Source. 19 – A.G.E. FotoStock. 22 – David Simson. 23 – Tony Stone Worldwide. 26/27 – Fred Grunfeld. 30 – David Simson. 31 – Fred Grunfeld. 34/35 – Teresa Farino. 43 – M. Chinery/Natural Science Photos. 46, 47, 51 – Teresa Farino. 54/55 – Firo-Foto. 58, 59 – Paul Sterry/Nature Photographers Ltd. 62 – Fred Grunfeld. 66 – A.G.E. FotoStock. 67 – Natural Science Photos. 70/71 – Paul Sterry/Nature Photographers Ltd. 75, 78, 79 – A.G.E. FotoStock. 82/83 – Kevin Carlson. 87, 90, 91, 94, 95 – Fred Grunfeld. 98 – J.L.G. Grande/Bruce Coleman Ltd. 102 – Kevin Carlson. 103, 106/107 – A.G.E. FotoStock. 114/115 – David Simson. 118, 119, 123, 126 – A.G.E. FotoStock. 127 – Kevin Carlson. 130/131 Robert Harding Picture Library. 135 – Christopher Grey-Wilson/Nature Photographers Ltd. 138, 143, 147, 151 – A.G.E. FotoStock. 155 – Brian Hawkes. 158 – Fred Grunfeld. 159 – R & J Kemp/Remote Source. 163 – Charles Henneghien/Bruce Coleman Ltd. 166/167 – Archie Miles. 170, 174 – Prisma/Planet Earth Pictures. 175, 178/179 – Fred Grunfeld. 182 – Robert Harding Picture Library Ltd. 183 – Agencia Zardoya. 186/187 – George Wright. 191 – David George/Planet Earth Pictures. 195 – Firo-Foto. 199 – Ernest Newal/Planet Earth Pictures. 202 – Alex Williams/Planet Earth Pictures. 206 – Prisma/Planet Earth Pictures. 207, 210/211 – George Wright.

ACKNOWLEDGEMENTS

The editors wish to extend special thanks to Dr Iain Bishop, Martin Gardiner and Tony Hare for their assistance; and also to Anthony Bonner, Valerie Chandler, Franky Eynon, Antonio Lardiez, Irene Martin, Timothy Osborne, Maria Teresa Palau, Mike Rosenberg, Charlie Spring-Rice, Mercedes Sus, Teresa Tinsley and Brigitte Vienneaux.